HE
Y

taphysics

CAMBRIDGE TEXTS IN THE HISTORY OF PHILOSOPHY

Series editors

KARL AMERIKS

Professor of Philosophy at the University of Notre Dame

DESMOND M. CLARKE

Professor of Philosophy at University College Cork

The main objective of Cambridge Texts in the History of Philosophy is to expand the range, variety and quality of texts in the history of philosophy which are available in English. The series includes texts by familiar names (such as Descartes and Kant) and also by less well-known authors. Wherever possible, texts are published in complete and unabridged form, and translations are specially commissioned for the series. Each volume contains a critical introduction together with a guide to further reading and any necessary glossaries and textual apparatus. The volumes are designed for student use at undergraduate and postgraduate level and will be of interest not only to students of philosophy, but also to a wider audience of readers in the history of science, the history of theology and the history of ideas.

For a list of titles published in the series, please see end of book.

IMMANUEL KANT

Prolegomena to Any Future Metaphysics

That Will Be Able to Come Forward as Science

with Selections from the *Critique of Pure Reason*

TRANSLATED AND EDITED BY

GARY HATFIELD

University of Pennsylvania

CAMBRIDGE
UNIVERSITY PRESS

PUBLISHED BY THE PRESS SYNDICATE OF THE UNIVERSITY OF CAMBRIDGE
The Pitt Building, Trumpington Street, Cambridge, United Kingdom

CAMBRIDGE UNIVERSITY PRESS
The Edinburgh Building, Cambridge CB2 2RU, UK
40 West 20th Street, New York, NY 10011–4211, USA
10 Stamford Road, Oakleigh, VIC 3166, Australia
Ruiz de Alarcón 13, 28014 Madrid, Spain
Dock House, The Waterfront, Cape Town 8001, South Africa

http://www.cambridge.org

First published 1997
Reprinted 1999, 2001

Printed in the United Kingdom at the University Press, Cambridge

A catalogue record for this book is available from the British Library

Library of Congress Cataloguing in Publication data
Immanuel Kant: Prolegomena to any future metaphysics that will be able to come forward
as science / translated and edited, with an introduction, and selections from the
Critique of pure reason, by Gary Hatfield.
p. cm. – (Cambridge texts in the history of philosophy)
Includes bibliographical references and index.
1. Kant, Immanuel, 1724–1804. Prolegomena.
2. Kant, Immanuel, 1724–1804. Kritik der reinen Vernunft.
3. Knowledge, Theory of. 4. Metaphysics.
1. Hatfield, Gary C. (Gary Carl) II. Kant, Immanuel, 1724–1804. Prolegomena. English.
III. Kant, Immanuel, 1724–1804. Kritik der reinen Vernunft. English. IV. Series.
B2787.Z71483 1996
110–dc20   96–29100 CIP

ISBN 0 521 57345 9 hardback
ISBN 0 521 57542 7 paperback

CE

Contents

Contents

Acknowledgments

This work of translation has benefited from the advice of colleagues, students, and friends. Rolf Peter Horstmann read and commented on an early draft, raising many interesting points for discussion. Henry Allison, Peter Heath, and Karl Ameriks each provided timely and helpful comments and suggestions on a later version. During the academic year 1995–6 I met with a group of students and recent Ph.D's at the University of Pennsylvania to discuss translating and to go over the translation; I am especially indebted to Lanier Anderson, Curtis Bowman, Cynthia Schossberger, and Lisa Shabel for their contributions to these discussions. Bowman and Michelle Casino later served as my research assistants in preparing the typescript of the *Prolegomena* and selections from the *Critique of Pure Reason* for publication. Lindeth Vasey at Cambridge prepared the typescript for printing with care and thoughtfulness. Finally, Holly Pittman read the typescript with an eye for intelligibility to a new reader of Kant. Her advice and suggestions helped greatly.

Introduction

It was characteristic of the great modern philosophers to attempt, each in his own way, to rebuild philosophy from the ground up. Kant embraced this goal more fully than any other classical modern philosopher. And his work did in fact change philosophy permanently, though not always as he had intended. He wanted to show that philosophers and natural scientists were not able, and would never be able, to give final answers to questions about the nature of the physical world and of the human mind or soul, and about the existence and attributes of a supreme being. While he did not accomplish precisely that, his work changed philosophy's conception of what can be known, and how it can be known. Kant also wanted to set forth new and permanent doctrines in metaphysics and morals. Though his exact teachings have not gained general acceptance, they continue to inspire new positions in philosophical discussion today.

Kant stands at the center of modern philosophy. His criticism of previous work in metaphysics and the theory of knowledge, propounded in the *Critique of Pure Reason* and summarized in the *Prolegomena*, provided a comprehensive response to early modern philosophy and a starting point for subsequent work. He rejected previous philosophical explanations of philosophical cognition itself. His primary target was the rationalist use of reason or "pure intellect" – advanced by Descartes and Leibniz – as a basis for making claims about God and the essences of mind and matter. Kant argued that these philosophers could not possibly know what they claimed to know about such things, because direct knowledge of a mind-independent reality exceeds the capacity of the human intellect. He thus had some sympathy with the conclusions of empiricist philosophers, such as Locke and Hume, who prescribed limits to human understanding. But, he contended, because these philosophers also did not analyze human cognition properly, they lacked knowledge of the principles by which the boundaries of human knowledge might be charted, and they did not understand the foundation of the legitimate metaphysics falling within those boundaries. Kant maintained that even the empiricist attitude to knowledge, if unchecked by an account of reason's boundaries, would inevitably extend beyond its own domain in the world of nature, and would lead to unjustified assertions about such topics as the free will of human beings and the existence of God, assertions that he feared would conflict with a proper theory of morals.

Kant explained his own revolutionary insight by analogy with the Copernican revolution in astronomy. As Kant observed, Copernicus was better able to account for the phenomena of astronomy by assuming that the motion attributed to the stars actually results from the motion of the observer as stationed on the earth.[1] The sixteenth-century astronomer attributed a daily rotation to the earth, rather than to the planets and stars themselves, and he accounted for yearly cycles in the motions of the sun and planets by attributing a yearly revolution to the earth. Kant held that he could account for the human ability to know the basic properties of objects only on the assumption that the knower him- or herself contributes certain features to those objects as known. He thus held that the fundamental characteristics of objects as experienced – characteristics described by mathematics (especially geometry) and also by metaphysical concepts such as cause and substance – result from something that the knowing subject brings to the experience of those objects. At the same time, he did not deny that objects taken as things in themselves play a role in producing perceptual experience – though this aspect of his position has proven difficult to interpret. The questions that he raised about the relation of the knower to the known, and the perspective he provided concerning the contribution of the knower to the representation or cognition of the

---

[1] Kant, *Critique of Pure Reason*, Bxvi; the relevant passage may be found in the selections from the *Critique* included in this volume. The use of "A" and "B" to cite the first and second editions of the *Critique* is explained in the Note on texts and translation; other abbreviations used in citing Kant's works are explained in the section on Further reading, which also provides publication details for other works cited. Page and section numbers appearing in the text of this Introduction are to the *Prolegomena* and selections as translated herein.

world as it is known, produced a revolution that continues to influence philosophy today. Philosophers as diverse as G. W. Hegel, Rudolph Carnap, C. I. Lewis, and Hilary Putnam have positioned themselves in relation to Kant.

Kant was deeply engaged with the intellectual issues of his time and culture. In what he termed "theoretical philosophy" (now called "metaphysics and epistemology"), he not only directly engaged the current philosophical theories of cognition, but he tested their ability to account for paradigmatic instances of knowledge, in the mathematics and natural science of his day. He was intent that theoretical philosophy explain the doctrines, nature, and cognitive basis of both of these "sciences" (as he called any systematic body of knowledge). Kant was especially interested in the philosophical implications of Newton's physics in relation to both metaphysics and morals, for he was concerned that the deterministic picture of the world in physics posed a threat to the idea of moral freedom. At the same time, he hoped to help advance natural science in its own right, by fully analyzing its cognitive foundation and fundamental concepts.

From the time Kant's writings appeared, they have been the object of philosophical discussion and debate. Many interpretations have been offered, which differ both on large questions, including interpreting the fundamental message of Kant's philosophy, and in the more detailed assessment of his particular arguments and doctrines. Such interpretive disagreement is normal in the case of writings that are both difficult and important. Further, part of the value of philosophical writing lies in the effort that each reader must make to understand its arguments and its conclusions, its assumptions and its overall vision, for him- or herself. The primary aim of this Introduction, then, is neither to characterize the results of two centuries of interpretive responses to Kant, nor to describe the present state of debate. Rather, it is to provide a context within which readers can approach Kant's texts for themselves.

Life and writings

Immanuel Kant was born in Königsberg on 22 April 1724. Königsberg (now Kaliningrad), located near the southeastern shore of the Baltic Sea, was an important regional port, alive with English, Dutch, Polish, and Russian traders. It was the capital of East Prussia, which had become a "kingdom" in 1701 when Frederick I crowned himself in Königsberg. In the year of Kant's birth, the "old city" of Königsberg was joined with two neighboring towns to become a city of 50,000, which was larger than Berlin, where the Prussian rulers resided. It had a castle and a garrison, was a regional center of the arts, and had its own university, founded as the Collegium Albertinus in 1544 and known in Kant's time as the Albertus University in Königsberg.

Kant was the fourth born of many children, of whom five lived to adulthood. His parents were pietist Lutherans of modest means, his father a master harness maker. After a few years of grammar school Kant's talent was recognized by a family friend, the Lutheran pietist preacher Franz Albert Schultz, who had studied with the foremost philosopher in Germany Christian Wolff. Schultz recommended to Kant's mother that the boy (then eight) should attend the Lutheran Collegium Fridericianum. It was primarily a Latin school, strict and pedantic, where Kant studied the classics, largely by rote; the enforced outward piety experienced in this school was an impetus to his lifelong endeavor to separate the social practices of religion from its intellectual and moral substance. Kant's mother, whom he greatly respected and admired, died in 1737. He went on to study at the University in Königsberg from 1740 to 1746, supporting himself with the help of his uncle, by tutoring, and through his skill at billiards and card games. He was especially drawn to mathematics, natural science, and philosophy, which he studied under the Professor of Logic and Metaphysics, Martin Knutzen, a student of Wolff's. It was in this period that Kant came to admire the work of Isaac Newton as a paradigmatic achievement in natural science, and in 1746 he wrote a paper on the *True Estimation of Living Forces*,[2] attempting to settle a dispute in mechanics that had arisen from G. W. Leibniz's criticism of Descartes' mechanics during the 1690s.

Kant finished his doctoral dissertation in 1755 and received his Habilitation that same year, which meant that he could serve as a private lecturer licensed by the University (but paid directly by the students). He was a popular lecturer and covered a broad curriculum, which included logic, mathematics, morals, physics, metaphysics, and physical geography. During this time he was a productive writer, publishing

---

[2] Full English titles to Kant's major works are listed in the Chronology.

several works in natural science, including his contribution to the Kant–Laplace nebular hypothesis in 1755 and the *Physical Monadology*, which posits repulsive forces to explain the space-filling character of matter, in 1756. In the *New Elucidation*, also from 1755, he first addressed the theme of metaphysical cognition, which was to occupy him all his life. His *Only Possible Argument* of 1763 was an extended reflection on unity, harmony, and order in nature as an argument for the existence of God. In the *Distinctness of the Principles of Natural Theology and Morality*, Kant analyzed metaphysical cognition in relation to mathematical cognition, emphasizing their dissimilarity. His *Dreams of a Spirit-Seer* of 1766 described metaphysics as investigating "the boundaries of human reason."[3] During the 1760s Kant became an admirer of the writings of Jean-Jacques Rousseau on education and moral philosophy.

As his reputation grew Kant turned down opportunities for appointment elsewhere, having his heart set on a professorship in Königsberg. In March 1770, at the age of 45, he finally received his appointment at the Albertus University, as Professor of Logic and Metaphysics. He continued to lecture on the topics already mentioned, and during the 1770s added anthropology, education, natural theology, and natural law to his repertoire. His "Inaugural Dissertation" for the new appointment was *On the Form and Principles of the Sensible and the Intelligible World*,[4] where he distinguished sensible and intelligible "worlds," the first being known via sensory cognition of things as they appear (i.e., phenomena), the second via intellectual cognition of things as they are in themselves (i.e., noumena). He regarded space and time as phenomena determined *a priori* (i.e., independently of experience) by the "forms" or laws of human sensibility. By contrast, intellectual cognition of things via the intellect alone (in its "real," as opposed to "logical," use) proceeds apart from the senses and from the forms of space and time, and grasps the intelligible world of substance through the "form" of its causal relations.

After the publication of the Inaugural Dissertation, Kant entered his "silent decade," which produced no major publications and which ended in 1781 with his most significant work of all, the *Critique of Pure Reason*. In September 1770, just after the Inaugural Dissertation had appeared, Kant wrote to the philosopher J. H. Lambert that he intended

---

[3] Ak 2:368.
[4] *De mundi sensibilis atque intelligibilis forma et principiis* (Königsberg, Royal Court and University Printing Works, 1770); English translation in *Theoretical Philosophy, 1755–1770*.

to put forth a more extended treatment of both metaphysics and morals; he also spoke of a discipline that must "precede" metaphysics, called "general phenomenology," in which "the principles of sensibility, their validity and limitations, would be determined, so that these principles do not confound our judgments concerning objects of pure reason."[5] In 1772 he conveyed his current thoughts on these projects to his friend and student Marcus Herz. He predicted that the first part of his new investigation, concerning "the sources of metaphysics, its methods and limits," would be completed about three months hence; he called the entire investigation of theoretical and practical cognition from the intellect alone a "critique of pure reason." He reported that, having reflected on previous efforts in theoretical philosophy (including his own), he saw the need to pose a new question, which contained the "key" to metaphysics: "I asked myself: What is the ground of the relation to the object of that in us which is called representation?"[6] This question was one spark leading to Kant's "critical philosophy"; later he also credited the stimulus of the "antinomies" of pure reason – reason's conflicts with itself on basic metaphysical questions – as something that drove him to investigate the cognitive basis of metaphysics,[7] as well as a nudge from Hume awakening him from his "dogmatic slumber" (p. 10), a nudge that presumably arose from Hume's questioning the rational justification of the law of causation (that every event has a cause).

Kant's *Critique of Pure Reason* appeared not three months, but nine years after his letter to Herz. It was followed by another major work about every two years until 1790; these included the *Prolegomena*, the *Metaphysics of Morals*, the *Metaphysical Foundations of Natural Science*, and the second and third of his major "critical" works, the *Critique of Practical Reason* and the *Critique of Judgment*.[8] When the 1781 edition of the first *Critique* appeared, Kant did not yet foresee the second and third *Critiques*, which respectively explained the possibility of moral

---

[5] Kant to Lambert, 2 September 1770, Ak 10:98 (2d edn.); translation modified from *PC*, p. 59.
[6] Kant to Herz, 21 February 1772, Ak 10:132, 130; translation modified from *PC*, pp. 73, 71.
[7] Kant to Christian Garve, 21 September 1798, Ak 12:257–58; *PC*, p. 99; see also Kant to J. Bernoulli, 16 November 1781, in which Kant recalls having realized, by 1770, that metaphysics was in need of a "touchstone," since equally persuasive metaphysical propositions could lead to contradictory conclusions (Ak 10:277; *PC*, p. 97).
[8] The word "critique" translates the German *Kritik* (*Critick*, or *Critik* in Kant's day), which could also be translated as "criticism." But "critique" is used in English to denote Kant's special project of criticism, and the adjective "critical" is used as a label for his philosophy as expressed in the three *Critiques* and related writings.

judgment and examined the conditions for judgments of beauty and of natural purpose (teleology). They continued Kant's exploration of the function of reason itself, as a faculty that seeks unity between the understanding's cognition of nature and natural laws, and its own grasp of the moral law and of the harmony, systematicity, beauty, and organization of nature. The vision of reason as seeking unity between the natural and moral worlds was an inspiration to many of Kant's philosophical descendants, including the German Idealists (J. G. Fichte, F. W. Schelling, and Hegel) and the influential Neo-Kantians (Heinrich Rickert, Wilhelm Dilthey, and Ernst Cassirer). It remains of interest today, as philosophers reflect on the natural scientific picture of the world and seek to determine the relation between that picture and the moral, political, historical, legal, and aesthetic visions inherent in the social and cultural world of humankind.

Kant continued to work throughout the 1790s. His *Religion within the Bounds of Reason Alone* (1793) examined the limits to any attempt to base religion on natural speculative reason, and endorsed a compatibility between religion and practical or moral reason. After his retirement from teaching in 1796 he revised and published his lecture notes on anthropology (1798). Others subsequently published his lecture notes in other subjects, including logic (1800), physical geography (1802), and pedagogy (1803), and after his death the notes of students who attended his courses were published in various collections and editions.

He was struggling with another major work intended to "complete" the critical system when his health failed him at the age of 79. By December 1803, he could no longer write his name, and by the following 3 February he was speaking in broken phrases. Yet when his physician, who was also Rector of the University, called upon him, he insisted on standing until his guest was seated, putting enough words together to explain his act of politeness by saying, "The sense of humanity has not yet abandoned me."[9] From that day he faded quickly, eating almost nothing, and he died on 12 February 1804. Kant's body lay in state until 28 February when a long procession, led by a group of university students carrying the body, brought it to the cathedral for interment in the "professors' vault." The complete text of his last, unfinished work was only published more than a century later (in

---

[9] Cassirer, *Kant's Life and Thought*, pp. 412–13.

1936–8), under the title *Opus postumum*. On the hundredth anniversary of Kant's death a monument was erected in Königsberg, containing a famous line from the concluding section of the *Critique of Practical Reason*: "Two things fill the mind with always fresh and growing wonder and veneration, the more often and the more continuously they are reflected upon: the starry heaven above me, and the moral law within me."[10]

Kant's project to reform metaphysics

When Kant conceived the first *Critique* and the *Prolegomena*, metaphysics was a much-discussed field of philosophy with a long history, and it was a regular part of the university curriculum. Alexander Baumgarten's *Metaphysics*, a popular textbook, which Kant used in his courses, defined metaphysics as "the science of the first principles in human cognition."[11] Baumgarten followed Wolff's division of metaphysics into ontology, cosmology, psychology, and natural theology. He defined ontology as the science of the "predicates of being," i.e., of general predicates for describing what does or might have being, or exist. (Examples of such predicates include "possible" and "true," "substance" and "accident," and "cause" and "effect.") Cosmological topics included the world as a whole, its order and causal structure, the substances composing it, and the relation of natural and supernatural. Psychology considered the existence and properties of the soul or mind, the various "mental faculties," such as sense, imagination, and intellect, the freedom of the will, and the immortality of the human soul. Natural theology sought to determine the existence and the attributes of God or a supreme being without appeal to faith, i.e., by appealing only to facts as evaluated by natural human reason.

At the time Kant was lecturing on Baumgarten, Aristotle's *Metaphysics*, in which the Greek philosopher discussed both "being" and a "first being," had been an object of philosophical discussion for more than

---

[10] Ak 5:161.

[11] Alexander Gottlieb Baumgarten, *Metaphysica*, 7th edn. (Halle, 1779), §1. The 4th edn. is reprinted in Ak 15:5–53, 17:5–226, along with Kant's annotations. His most direct discussions of Baumgarten's metaphysics are found in his *Lectures on Metaphysics*, ed. and trans. by K. Ameriks and S. Naragon (Cambridge, Cambridge University Press, 1996); the lecture set closest in time and content to the *Prolegomena* is the Metaphysics Mrongovius, dating from 1782–3.

2,000 years.[12] Modern metaphysicians developed alternatives to Aristotelianism. In the *Meditations on First Philosophy* (1641), Descartes argued for a dualistic metaphysics in which mind and body are distinct substances.[13] Wolff's important metaphysical system, partly inspired by that of Leibniz, helped to make Leibniz's own metaphysics of simple substances or "monads" better known. Although there was no universally accepted definition of metaphysics, most agreed that it was concerned with the basic structure of reality. There was disagreement over its method. Descartes wanted to base his metaphysics on the pure intellect alone, independent of sensory experience. Wolff and Baumgarten, by contrast, admitted empirical propositions into metaphysics.[14] Kant rejected this view, contending that metaphysical propositions must possess absolute certainty of a kind that could not be attained from sensory experience, but could be achieved only by the pure understanding. But although Kant had written metaphysical works based on the presumed "real use" of the intellect, from 1772 on he was deeply skeptical of metaphysical claims put forward on this basis when they concerned objects (including God and the soul) that could not be objects of sensory perception. And yet he also (at least eventually) held that it is inevitable that human reason be drawn toward making such claims – for he considered the impulse toward metaphysics to be as "natural" to human beings as the impulse toward breathing (p. 121).[15]

---

[12] According to an oft-repeated story, which apparently first arose in the sixteenth century, Andronicus of Rhodes, who edited Aristotle's works in the first century BC, coined the term "metaphysics" to describe his placement of Aristotle's work on first philosophy "after the physics" ("meta" being one sense of "after"). In his lectures Kant questioned the plausibility that the name "metaphysics" arose in this manner, arguing that the term fits the subject matter too well, for one sense of "meta" is "beyond," and the subject matter of metaphysics includes what is "beyond the physical" (Ak 28.1:174). Takatura Ando, *Metaphysics: A Critical Survey of Its Meaning*, 2nd edn. (The Hague, Nijhoff, 1974), pp. 3–6, summarizes a more recent argument against the Andronicus story.

[13] The standard edition, containing all of Descartes' works cited herein, is *The Philosophical Writings of Descartes*, ed. by John Cottingham, Robert Stoothoff, and Dugald Murdoch, 2 vols. (Cambridge, Cambridge University Press, 1984–5).

[14] Christian Wolff, *Philosophia rationalis, sive logica* (Frankfurt and Leipzig, 1740), preliminary discourse, §§10, 34, 55–9, 99–101; Baumgarten, *Metaphysica*, §§351, 503. On Wolff's philosophy, and his relation to Leibniz, see Beck, *Early German Philosophy*, ch. 11 (on Leibniz himself, see ch. 10).

[15] Consider the first sentence of the "A" Preface to the first *Critique of Pure Reason* (A vii), where Kant says, concerning metaphysics: "Human reason has the peculiar fate in one genus of its cognition: that it is troubled by questions that it cannot refuse; for these questions are put to it by the nature of reason itself, which cannot answer them, for they surpass all power of human reason."

Kant was not the first to call metaphysics into question. John Locke, in his *Essay Concerning Human Understanding* (1690), had questioned the possibility of knowledge of the "real essences" of substances, including mind and body. David Hume raised serious objections against the possibility of metaphysical knowledge, including knowledge of the soul as a substance, and knowledge of the existence and attributes of God. Though Hume's three-volume *Treatise of Human Nature* (1739–40) was not translated into German until 1790–1, his *Inquiry Concerning Human Understanding* appeared in translation in 1755. Hume elaborated his arguments against natural theology in the *Dialogues Concerning Natural Religion* (1779); Kant presumably cites the German translation of 1781 below (§58), since he did not read English.

During his "silent decade" Kant had undertaken to evaluate the very possibility of metaphysical cognition. This led him to investigate the "origin" of that cognition in the faculties of the human mind. He came to see metaphysical cognition, as well as the fundamental propositions of mathematics and natural science, as having a peculiar, and hitherto unrecognized, cognitive status, which he described as "synthetic *a priori.*" Kant divided all judgments, and the propositions expressing those judgments, into "analytic" and "synthetic." He held that an analytic judgment can be known to be true solely on the basis of the concepts used in the judgment, because the predicate term is already "contained in" the concept of the subject. Thus, the judgment "ontology is the science of being" could be known to be true solely by reflection on the concept of ontology, for this concept includes the meaning "science of being." In synthetic judgments, by contrast, the predicate term adds something new to the concept of the subject. "Metaphysics is in trouble" is a synthetic judgment Kant would have accepted – but on any reasonable definition, "being in trouble" was not part of the very concept of metaphysics. Kant also divided propositions into *a posteriori*, i.e., "based on sensory experience," and *a priori*, i.e., "known independently of sensory experience." Neither of these divisions was wholly new with Kant; what was new was his suggestion that metaphysical cognition is characterized by synthetic *a priori* propositions, that is, by propositions in which a new predicate is conjoined to the subject term, and in which the basis for this connection is known *a priori*, independently of sensory experience.

Although other modern philosophers before Kant, including

Descartes,[16] Locke, and Hume, had conceived of the project of examining the knower and the knower's cognitive capacities, Kant's investigation stands apart because he provided a novel and an especially thorough examination of the powers and capacities, or "faculties," of the human mind, which he explicitly linked to determining the very possibility of metaphysics. Moreover, Kant's conclusions differed significantly from those of his predecessors. His so-called "deduction" of metaphysical concepts claims to justify the use of such concepts, but it justifies them differently than would either a rationalist or an empiricist. This deduction also put limits on the use of these concepts, of a kind that would undercut rationalist metaphysics. Like Descartes, Kant thought that metaphysics could provide a systematic body of theoretical first principles, but he denied that it provides knowledge of substances as they are in themselves. And like Locke and Hume, he held that human speculative cognition must be limited to the domain of human sensory experience, but he did not agree that all knowledge comes from sensory experience – some knowledge is based in the synthetic *a priori* propositions of mathematics, natural science, and metaphysics.

Significantly, Kant did not hold that the knowledge conveyed by these synthetic *a priori* propositions exhausts what can be discussed in metaphysics. For he affirmed that transcendental philosophy, in determining the boundaries of metaphysical cognition, makes room for the (perhaps "problematic") concept of "intelligible beings," beings existing apart from sensory experience (though in some cases underlying sensory experience). He restricted metaphysical *knowledge* to propositions that can be justified by appeal to the conditions of possible experience, but he allowed metaphysical *thinking* to cover a broader range. In his view, a proper science of metaphysics must set out the legitimate propositions of metaphysics, while also determining the boundaries of their application. The latter task included assuring that the objects of experience are not taken to exhaust the entire domain of being.

---

[16] Descartes, *Rules for the Direction of the Mind*, rules 8, 12, proclaims the need to examine the "knowing subject" in order to determine what can be known. On theories of cognition more generally prior to Kant, see Gary Hatfield, "The Cognitive Faculties," in *Cambridge History of Seventeenth Century Philosophy*, ed. Michael Ayers and Daniel Garber (Cambridge, Cambridge University Press, forthcoming).

Origin and purpose of the *Prolegomena*

Kant had several aims in the *Prolegomena*. He wanted to offer "preparatory exercises" to the *Critique of Pure Reason* (pp. 11, 25). He wanted to give an overview of that work, in which the plan of the whole could be more readily discerned (p. 13). He wanted to restate its main arguments and conclusions following the "analytic" method of exposition (as opposed to the "synthetic" method of the *Critique*), a method that starts from some given proposition or body of cognition and seeks principles from which it might be derived, as opposed to a method that first seeks to prove the principles and then to derive other propositions from them (pp. 13, 25–6).[17] He considered the analytic mode of exposition to be more suited to clarity and to "popular" consumption (to the extent that that could be achieved).[18] Finally, Kant wanted to clarify some points of the exposition (pp. 135–6), not being satisfied with the corresponding chapters of the *Critique* (including the "deduction" of the categories and the "paralogisms" of pure reason). The new work was motivated both by a desire to redress the disappointing reception of the *Critique* by publishing a more approachable work, and by a desire to improve the exposition of crucial points.

Kant was correct to think that an overview would be of great value. The *Critique of Pure Reason* is an imposing book. In 1781, even sympathetic readers found it difficult to comprehend. Kant soon wrote to Herz expressing his discomfort in learning that the eminent philosopher Moses Mendelssohn had "laid my book aside," since he felt that Mendelssohn was "the most important of all the people who could explain this theory to the world."[19] Mendelssohn later wrote to Elise Reimarus confessing that he did not understand the work, and professing pleasure at learning that, in the opinion of her brother, he would not be "missing much" if he continued not to understand it.[20] Kant's friend and former student J. G. Hamann wrote to Kant's publisher in November, 1781, confessing that he had read the book three or four

---

[17] The distinction between analytic and synthetic *methods* is entirely separate from the distinction between analytic and synthetic *judgments*, as is explained subsequently in this Introduction.

[18] *Logik: Ein Handbuch zu Vorlesungen*, ed. G. B. Jäsche (Königsberg, 1800).

[19] Kant to Herz, after 11 May 1781, Ak 10:270; *PC*, p. 96.

[20] Mendelssohn to Elise Reimarus, 5 January 1784, in his *Gesammelte Schriften* (Stuttgart, Frommann, 1971–), vol. 3, p. 169; her brother was Johann, and their father was the noted natural theologian Hermann Samuel Reimarus.

times, and that now his best hope was the projected "abstract" or "textbook" version (the *Prolegomena*).[21] Kant's colleague in Königsberg, Johann Schultz, in the preface to his 1784 *Exposition of Kant's Critique of Pure Reason*, mentioned the "nearly universal complaint about the unconquerable obscurity and unintelligibility" of the work, saying that for the largest part of the learned public it was "as if it consisted in nothing but hieroglyphics."[22]

That the *Critique of Pure Reason* should have seemed imposing to Kant's contemporaries is not surprising. After all, the work constituted an avowed attempt to introduce a new question into metaphysics – that of the possibility of metaphysics itself – and to answer this question within a framework set by Kant's new thesis that metaphysics rests on synthetic *a priori* cognition. Kant's denial of a "real use" of the intellect (such as would provide "intellectual intuition" of the natures of things) would have puzzled rationalists, just as his argument that laws of nature can be derived from the conditions on any possible experience of objects would have been difficult for empiricists to understand. In any case, based on his new framework, Kant wove a set of difficult arguments, with whose exposition he was in several cases displeased, and which filled 856 pages in the first edition. As Kant expressed it in the *Prolegomena*, he had reason to fear that his work would "not be understood ... because people will be inclined just to skim through the book, but not to think through it; and they will not want to expend this effort on it, because the work is dry, because it is obscure, because it opposes all familiar concepts and is long-winded as well" (p. 11). Such an investigation, he said at the time, must "always remain difficult, for it involves the *metaphysics of metaphysics*."[23]

Kant was at work on the *Prolegomena* by August 1781, he finished writing in Fall 1782, and it had appeared by mid-April of 1783.[24] While he was working on it the first two reviews of the *Critique* appeared, and

---

[21] Hamann to Hartknoch, November 1781, *Hamanns Leben und Schriften*, ed. by C. H. Gildemeister, 6 vols. (Gotha, 1875), vol. 2, p. 370.
[22] *Erläuterungen über des Herr Professor Kant, Critik der reinen Vernunft* (Königsberg, 1784), pp. 5, 7.
[23] Kant to Herz, after 11 May 1781, Ak 10:269; *PC*, p. 95.
[24] This chronology is based on the following: Hamann to Hartknoch, 11 August 1781, in *Hamanns Schriften*, ed. by Friedrich Roth, 8 vols. (Berlin, 1821–5), vol. 6, p. 206; Hamann to Hartknoch, September 1782, *Hamanns Leben*, vol. 2, p. 409; Plessing to Kant, 15 April 1783, Ak 10:311.

he responded directly to both of them in the Appendix of the *Prolegomena*. The first, written by Christian Garve and heavily edited by J. G. Feder, came out anonymously in January 1782. Kant was greatly displeased at what he considered to be the unfair treatment he had received by a reviewer who did not understand the aim and method of his work. As he observes, the reviewer failed even to mention his important claim that metaphysical cognition is synthetic *a priori*, choosing instead to focus on the "transcendental idealism" that formed part of Kant's answer to the question of how synthetic *a priori* cognition can be achieved in metaphysics. Kant was especially sensitive to the charge that his position amounted to Berkeleyan idealism, that is, to a denial of the reality of anything except immaterial minds and their ideas and representations. The second and third Notes at the end of the First Part of the *Prolegomena* most likely were added in response to this charge. The second review appeared in August 1782, when Kant was nearly finished writing. He was pleased with this one, and offered it as a model for how the critical philosophy should be judged: carefully, suspending judgment at first, and working through it bit by bit (pp. 134–5).

To aid this process, Kant offered the *Prolegomena* "as a general synopsis, with which the work itself might occasionally be compared" (p. 135). The *Prolegomena* are to be taken as a plan, synopsis, and guide for the *Critique of Pure Reason*. They were not meant to replace the *Critique*, but as "preparatory exercises" they were intended to be read prior to the longer work. Yet to do so can pose a problem, since in the *Critique* Kant had introduced his own special terminology (discussed below), which he often used in the *Prolegomena* without explaining it. (Though in some cases, such as the distinction between analytic and synthetic judgements, he explained his terminology more fully in the later work, and he used the new material in the second edition of the *Critique*.) Partly in order to make up for this practice, this volume includes some selections from the *Critique* in which Kant explains his terminology. In addition, some of the appended selections provide further statements of Kant's conception of the critical philosophy, including his famous comparison of his new theory of the relation of cognition to its objects with the Copernican revolution in astronomy. And some of the selections supplement the discussion in the *Prolegomena* with key portions of the *Critique*, including the "Metaphysical

Exposition of the Concept of Space" from the "Transcendental Aesthetic"; Kant's introduction of the notion of a deduction from the "Analytic"; and a sample of the original statement of one of the antinomies from the "Dialectic."

Notes on terminology

Kant's elaborate terminology can seem imposing. But it must be mastered, because his philosophy cannot be understood without a good grasp of the vocabulary in which he expressed it. Problems arise for the present-day reader not only because Kant used special terminology, but also because since the time he wrote the meanings of words have changed (in both English and German).

Consider the word "science." English speakers are familiar with "science" as having the connotation "natural science," and hence as denoting physics, chemistry, biology, and (sometimes) psychology. In the eighteenth century the German word *Wissenschaft*, as well as the French, Latin, Italian, and English cognates for "science," were understood to mean any systematic body of knowledge, usually with the implication that it would be organized around first principles from which the rest of the body of knowledge might be derived (more or less rigorously). Mathematics, and especially Euclid's geometry, was a model for how "scientific" expositions of knowledge should be organized. Disciplines as diverse as mathematics, metaphysics, and theology were all called "sciences." Hence, it was entirely normal for Kant to speak of metaphysics as a science.

For his analysis of the faculties of cognition, Kant largely drew on an existing technical vocabulary for discussing the processes and objects of human cognition, adapting it to his own ends. Included here are terms for various mental "representations," including "intuitions" and "concepts," and for various cognitive acts, such as "judgment" and "synthesis." "Intuition" translates the German term *Anschauung*; both have the etymological sense of "looking at" or "looking upon." In this context the word "intuition" does not have the connotation of "following a feeling," as when we speak in English of "deciding by intuition." Rather, it describes a mental representation that is particular (not abstract), and that presents objects concretely (as an image does). Kant contrasts intuitions with concepts, which he considered to be abstract and general representations, potentially relating to many objects at once (pp. 164–5, 168–9).

Kant's important distinction between analytic and synthetic judgments has been discussed above. We have also seen that he used the terms "analytic" and "synthetic" in another context, separate from this distinction, when he distinguished the "synthetic" method of the *Critique* from the "analytic" method of the *Prolegomena*. Here, "method" refers to both method of exposition and method of arguing; whereas the analytic method starts from a given body of cognition and seeks the principles from which it might be derived (in the present case, by analyzing the cognitive powers and capacities of the knower), the synthetic method seeks to establish those principles directly, only then using them to establish other propositions. Kant also contrasts the "analytic" part of what he calls "transcendental logic" with the "dialectic" part. Here, "analytic" means analysis of the procedures of understanding and reason into their "elements," and discovery of the principles for the critique of such knowledge, especially those principles that set the conditions for the very thought of an object.

In Kant's usage, "logic" meant not only general logic, which in his time was syllogistic logic, but also what he called "transcendental logic," in which the cognitive conditions on "thinking" objects are determined. The term "to think an object" is a characteristically Kantian form of expression. Kant used the German *denken* (English "to think") as a transitive verb taking a direct object. This gives the connotation not merely of "thinking of an object," as when we picture an object, such as a favorite chair, to ourselves, but it expresses a conception of this process as an active forming of a mental representation of the chair.

Special attention should be given to Kant's use of the words "subject" and "object" (which are direct translations of the German *Subjekt* and *Objekt*). Except in the compound phrase "subject matter," the word "subject" in what follows always means the thinking subject, that is, the one who is having the thoughts or doing the cognizing. "Object" can mean physical objects located in space, or it can mean the object of thought, that is, the object currently represented in thought, or toward which one's thought is currently directed (as in "the object of my desire").

Kant used many other words in semi-technical ways, sometimes drawing on established patterns of usage in the eighteenth century, and sometimes initiating new usage. The reader is advised to pay close attention to how words are used in varying contexts, and to consult a good English dictionary to gain familiarity with the interpretive possibilities for terms whose meaning seems difficult to grasp. One especially noteworthy case is the term "deduction," which Kant used to name an important part of the critical philosophy; this term does not denote *logical* deduction, but, as he explained in the *Critique* (p. 171), it is a legal term for a response to a demand for justification. Other cases requiring special attention include "condition" and "conditioned"; something is "conditioned" by antecedent states of affairs that set the "conditions" for its occurrence, as the heat of the fire is a "condition" that determines the temperature of the soup, the heated soup then being a state of affairs that is "conditioned." Another problematic word is "determine," which translates the German *bestimmen*. It has various meanings that shade into one another. It can mean "to ascertain," as when a botanist "determines" the species of a plant; it can mean "to render definite or specific," as when, with several options open, an outcome is determined or "made determinate"; it can mean "produced according to a strict rule or law," as when an action follows "deterministically," or is "determined according to natural law." Finally, the word "merely" is used frequently to translate Kant's word *bloss*, which can mean "just" and "only"; it need not, and usually does not, have a derogatory connotation, but, as in the case of "mere understanding," is used to indicate that the discussion pertains to the understanding by itself, alone, or independent of the other faculties.

Yet other terms might be discussed, such as "aesthetic," which names a division of critical philosophy, or "transcendental philosophy" and "critical philosophy" themselves, as well as technical terms such as "construction in intuition" or "philosophical analysis of concepts." These are explicitly discussed by Kant in various places; their interpretation, which requires seeing the role they play in Kant's philosophy, is left to the reader. Some further questions about terminology, including the use of the English term "cognition" to translate *Erkenntnis*, the use of the English term "principle" to translate several German terms, and some issues concerning Kant's long sentences and his use of punctuation (especially the colon), are addressed in the Note on texts and translation.

Structure of the work

The *Prolegomena* sets a problem and offers a solution based on extended argument. This section lays out the main features of this structure, indicating, but not fully summarizing, key points of the argument.

Preface (pp. 5–14). Kant describes the need for his critique of metaphysics, the relation of his project to previous philosophy, and the relation of the *Prolegomena* to the *Critique*. His program begins by asking the novel question: "Whether such a thing as metaphysics is even possible at all?" Hume challenged metaphysics with his doubt that reason perceives a necessary connection between cause and effect; Hume did not question whether the concept of cause "is right, useful, and, with respect to all cognition of nature, indispensable," but whether the causal connection "is thought through reason *a priori*," and thus "has an inner truth independent of all experience" that allows it "a much more widely extended use which is not limited merely to objects of experience." Hume's question "awakened" Kant from his "dogmatic slumber"; he realized that valid metaphysical cognition must be based on *a priori* concepts of the understanding. The "deduction" of the (pure) concepts of the understanding resulted, leading to the discovery of principles that determine the boundaries of metaphysical knowledge, and establishing the basic content of any possible metaphysics. Because the *Critique* is long and difficult, Kant is abridging its contents in these *Prolegomena*, following the "analytic" as opposed to the "synthetic" method.

Preamble (§§1–3). Kant presents criteria by which metaphysical cognition can be distinguished from that of other sciences. §1. By its very nature, metaphysical cognition has an *a priori* source (from pure reason); it is philosophical, as opposed to mathematical. §2. Analytic and synthetic judgments are distinguished. 2a. The predicate in analytic judgments is already "thought" in the concept of the subject. 2b. Analytic judgments are based on the principle of contradiction: any denial of their truth leads to a contradiction. Kant holds "gold is yellow" to be analytic, its truth following from the fact that (as he thinks) "gold is not yellow" is self-contradictory. Synthetic judgments cannot be based on this principle.[25] Such judgments can be either *a*

---

[25] Kant does not provide an example at this point; presumably, the judgment "this gold is mine" is not analytic but synthetic because its opposite, "this gold is not mine," can be thought without contradiction.

posteriori, that is, founded on experience, or *a priori*, arising from the pure understanding. 2b.1. Judgments of experience are always synthetic; an analytic judgment would not need to be based on experience. 2b.2. Mathematical judgments are synthetic *a priori*; they rely on the *construction of concepts* in intuition, not on the mere analysis of concepts. 2b.3. Properly metaphysical propositions, such as the judgment that substance persists, are synthetic and *a priori*, and the aim of metaphysics is to generate such propositions. §3. Previous metaphysicians, including Wolff and Baumgarten, did not realize that metaphysical judgments are synthetic, and so tried to derive them from the principle of contradiction; Locke dimly understood the distinction between analytic and synthetic judgments, but Hume did not.

General Question (§4). Because no undisputed body of metaphysical knowledge exists, the General Question of the *Prolegomena* arises: "Is metaphysics possible at all?" Following the analytic method, Kant will first determine how synthetic *a priori* cognition is possible in pure mathematics and pure natural science; he will then "derive, from the principle of the possibility of the given cognition, the possibility of all other synthetic cognition *a priori*."

General Question (§5). Kant restates the question as: "How are synthetic propositions *a priori* possible?" The existence of metaphysics as science depends on a successful answer to this difficult question, which belongs to "transcendental philosophy," a science that precedes metaphysics and determines its possibility. The "main transcendental question" is further divided into four questions: the first two respectively ask about the possibility of pure mathematics and pure natural science, the third asks about the possibility of metaphysics in general, and the fourth asks about the possibility of metaphysics as science.

First Part (§§6–13, Notes). Kant asks how mathematical cognition, which is apodictic (i.e. absolutely certain) and hence *a priori*, is possible (§6); he answers that such cognition, being intuitive rather than discursive, must be based, *a priori*, on construction in intuition (§7). He then asks how an intuition could be *a priori* (§8), and answers that, since intuition of things "as they are in themselves" would have to be based on experience, intuition can be *a priori* only if it contains the mere form of sensibility, which precedes all actual sensory impressions and determines the form in which objects can be intuited; hence, propositions that are *a priori* valid of the objects of the senses can relate only to the form of intuition, and *a priori* intuitions cannot relate to objects other than those of the senses (§9). Space and time are the forms of sensory intuition, upon which the propositions of geometry, arithmetic, and pure mechanics are based; they make possible *a priori* cognitions of objects only as they *appear* to us (§10); pure mathematics is therefore possible only because it relates merely to objects of the senses, and then only to the form of sensibility, which provides the basis for pure *a priori* intuition (§11). In geometry, proofs of the equality of two figures depend on judgments of congruence, based upon "immediate intuition"; if such intuition were empirical, it could not support the apodictically certain propositions of geometry; Kant mentions other geometrical proofs to show that they cannot be based on concepts but require intuition. Hence pure mathematics is based on pure *a priori* intuitions (§12). The consideration of incongruent counterparts shows that spatial objects cannot be adequately cognized by concepts alone, but require intuitions; this observation will free the reader of the conception that space and time are qualities of things in themselves (§13).[26] Note I. The applicability of geometry to objects in physical space can be guaranteed only if those objects are regarded as appearances and space as the *a priori* form of sensibility. Note II. Kant's position is not (genuine) idealism, which holds that there are only thinking beings, for he affirms the existence of objects considered as things in themselves, while limiting our knowledge of such objects to their appearances; he maintains what are called the primary qualities – extension, place, space, and all that depends on it – pertain only to appearance, just as Locke had earlier asserted of warmth, color, and taste that they pertain to appearances, not to things in themselves. Note III. Kant's position does not turn bodies into illusion, but it explains how pure mathematics can apply to bodies (and so, how geometry can be taken as describing the properties of bodies in space), and it prevents transcendental illusion as found in the antinomies; hence, his transcendental or critical idealism is to be distinguished from the empirical or dreaming idealism of Descartes and the mystical or fanatical idealism of Berkeley.

---

[26] Presumably Kant is here arguing against a position according to which knowledge of the intelligible world could not come via the forms of sensibility, but would result from the "real use" of the intellect, hence would be mediated by intellectual representations alone, i.e., by concepts. For further discussion, see Jill Vance Buroker, *Space and Incongruence: The Origin of Kant's Idealism* (Boston, Kluwer, 1981).

Second Part (§§14–39). §§14–17. Kant asks how pure natural scientific cognition, i.e., cognition of the laws of universal natural science, is possible. Such laws include: "*that substance remains* and persists," and "that *everything that happens is* always previously *determined by a cause* according to constant laws" (§15). Such laws could never be known to apply to things in themselves, but only to nature as an object of experience, or as the sum total of objects of experience; truly universal laws, however, cannot be based on experience, but must be *a priori* (§§14, 16). Kant then asks (§17): "How is it possible to cognize *a priori* the necessary conformity to law *of experience* itself with regard to all of its objects in general?" He introduces a distinction between "judgments of experience" and "judgments of perception."[27] The latter concern only the subjective states of individual perceivers; the former are valid for other perceivers and at other times (§18). Genuine experience of nature (expressing universally valid laws) must be judgments of experience (§19). Kant finds that judgments of experience are possible only through the *a priori* application of pure concepts of the understanding, elsewhere called the categories (§20). He discusses the derivation of these concepts from the logical table of judgments (§21), and the need for them in all judgments of experience (§22). Such judgments provide rules or principles for the possibility of experience, and these rules are laws of nature; therefore the problem of *a priori* cognition of the laws of nature has been solved (§23). After some cryptic remarks on the Pure physiological table (§§24–5), Kant sums up by observing that the ground for explaining (and proving) the possibility of *a priori* cognition of nature at the same time limits such cognition to objects of experience as opposed to things in themselves (§26).

Kant then sets about to dispel Hume's doubt about causality, also extended to the concepts of substance and their causal interaction (§27). The law of cause (and principles concerning the persistence of substances, and their interaction) can be sustained only when limited to the domain of possible experience (§§28–31). Similarly (§32), the pure concepts of the understanding and the principles based upon them are valid only for appearances (phenomena), not for things in themselves (noumena). Though pure concepts can seem to have a transcendent use,

---

[27] Although this precise distinction is not found in the *Critique*, it captures aspects of the Deduction. A similar contrast between "perception" and "experience" occurs in the "B" Deduction, §26 (B 159–61).

beyond all possible experience, this appearance is illusory; the senses do not permit us to cognize the objects of pure concepts concretely, but only in relation to schema, and the pure concepts themselves have no meaning outside experience (§§33–4). Only a "scientific" self-knowledge of reason can prevent the understanding from being deceived into thinking it can apply its principles outside experience (§35). Further discussion (§§36–8) of the idea that human understanding can supply laws to nature (e.g., the inverse square law) precedes an Appendix on the usefulness of the tables of judgments, categories, and principles (§39).

Third Part (§§40–60). Kant cannot point to an actual science of metaphysics and ask how it is possible; his investigation is needed because metaphysics as science is not actual. Pure mathematics and pure natural science had no need of demonstration of their possibility; such a demonstration was undertaken in the service of metaphysics. The impulse in human beings toward metaphysics is actual; Kant will both explain how that impulse is possible and assess the boundary of metaphysical cognition. §40. Metaphysics is concerned with the concepts whose objects are never given in experience, and also with the absolute totality of all possible experience itself; both are *ideas* of reason that transcend any possible experience. These ideas produce an illusion that reason can cognize objects through them. §§41–5. Kant emphasizes the importance of the distinction between *ideas* of reason and *categories* or pure concepts of the understanding. The transcendental ideas are obtained by reflecting on the three forms of the syllogism (categorical, hypothetical, disjunctive). The function of the ideas is to drive the understanding toward completeness in its cognition; the search for completeness leads the understanding to want to cognize *noumena*, which it cannot do. I. Psychological ideas (§§46–9). The concept of the self, as subject of all thinking, leads us to posit the self as a simple, immaterial substance. But such a posited self transcends possible experience, hence cannot be cognized, and cannot serve to support claims of the persistence of the soul after death. Cartesian idealism (doubt about the existence of bodies) can be removed by noting that bodies are equally well known as the *I*, both being appearances. II. Cosmological ideas (§§50–4). Reason's drive for completion of the series of conditions leads it to pose questions such as whether the world is infinite or finite in time and space, and whether freedom is a cause in the domain of appearances, or is excluded by natural necessity. Equally plausible proofs can be given for apparently contradictory answers to each of four antinomies. In the first two (or "mathematical") antinomies, both thesis and antithesis are false, because both confuse appearances with things in themselves, and thus expect appearances to exhibit properties that they cannot, as appearances, possess. In the third and fourth antinomies, both thesis and antithesis can be true, but only when referred to things taken in different respects, in one case as appearance, in the other as things in themselves. III. Theological idea (§55). Kant refers the reader to the first *Critique*. General note (§56). The transcendental ideas express the natural vocation of reason to seek systematic unity in the use of the understanding; this unity is regulative, not constitutive. (In the *Critique* Kant explains this distinction thus: a regulative use of ideas guides the search for completeness in cognition; a constitutive use attempts to think objects determinately, and so as constitutive of concrete objects of cognition or laws of nature, A 179–80/B 222–3, A 647/B 675.) Conclusion (§§57–60). The possibility of metaphysics in general has been explained insofar as metaphysics is a natural disposition of human reason to seek completeness. We cannot cognize things in themselves, but we should not deny their existence, either; that would be to mistake limits on the use of our reason for limits on the possibility of things in themselves. Reason finds its use bounded, but these boundaries presuppose a "space" on the other side. Reason takes us up to the boundary, and we are permitted, by means of pure concepts unrelated to intuition or to possible experience, to *think* the relation between appearances and things in themselves. We are thus permitted to think the theistic concept, as if the world were created by an all-wise being. The *ideas* of reason are useful to us in determining the boundary of reason. Thus both the possibility and the usefulness of the transcendental ideas in metaphysics have been explained.

Solution to the General Question: "How is metaphysics possible as science?" (pp. 119–25). Kant asserts that it is possible only through a critique of pure reason, which must set out and analyze the entire stock of *a priori* concepts; which must refer such concepts to the various sources for their cognition (sensibility, understanding, reason); which must "deduce" the possibility of synthetic *a priori* cognition; and which must determine the principles of and the boundaries for the use of all *a priori* concepts. Kant hopes that the *Prolegomena* will excite investigation in this field, because metaphysics will not go away, given reason's natural impulse toward metaphysical speculation.

Appendix (pp. 126–37). Kant proposes that the best route to rendering metaphysics as science actual would be a full examination of the *Critique of Pure Reason*. He defends the *Critique* against the Garve–Feder review and its charge of Berkeleyan idealism, and he proposes that the *Critique* and these *Prolegomena* be made the basis for working out a new metaphysics, limited to the principles for possible experience.

Evaluating the critical philosophy

As evaluated against the standard of historical influence and significance, Kant's philosophy possesses tremendous importance. For present-day philosophers, and for individual readers of Kant, another kind of evaluation is germane: that of the success of his arguments, and the truth or insight of his doctrines. There are various perspectives from which such assessments might be carried out. One could seek to determine how successful Kant's arguments are in terms of their logical coherence and internal consistency, or when viewed as a response to the philosophical context of his time, or from the perspective of what insight they hold for us now. The first sort of assessment is basic to reading any philosophical text; in the case of a past text such as Kant's, the assessment of consistency requires being able to understand the words he has written on the page (or their translation), which means learning about eighteenth-century philosophical terminology and philosophical assumptions. This takes us to the second perspective, that of assessing Kant's arguments in their historical context. The material included in this Introduction and in the explanatory footnotes is some aid in this task, though of course a more general knowledge of the history of modern philosophy is also needed. Any attempt to carry out the third sort of assessment depends to some extent on the first two, since one will need to have read and understood Kant's arguments before attempting to assay their present usefulness.

Soon after the appearance of the *Prolegomena*, Kant provided his own list of the factors he considered relevant to evaluating the critical philosophy.[28] There were three stages: first, a decision about whether

---

[28] Kant to Mendelssohn, 16 August 1783, Ak 10:344–5; *PC*, pp. 324–5.

the problem of the existence of metaphysics is correctly stated as the need for a deduction of the possibility of synthetic *a priori* judgments; second, whether his own deduction and its implication concerning the bounds of human cognition are correct; and finally, whether his transcendental idealism, which limits metaphysical cognition to appearances as opposed to things in themselves, is correct, and whether it is also correct that his position implies the existence of things in themselves as that which must underlie these appearances. As it actually happens, the place of the "thing in itself" in Kant's philosophical system has long been a matter of contention; many have found his talk of a "thing in itself" to be both contradictory and unnecessary, while others believe it is essential to his position. More generally, in the two centuries since Kant wrote, everything from his specific conclusions to his general framework has been called into question. Hegel challenged the distinction between appearances and things in themselves. After the discovery of non-Euclidean geometry, Kant's claims for the synthetic *a priori* status of Euclid's geometry as a description of physical space came into question. Neo-Kantians such as Cassirer questioned whether the categories of human understanding are truly fixed, as Kant had suggested, or change throughout the history of human thought. Others have sought to determine what might be lasting in his analysis of the structure of human cognition, and in the question of the relation of our modes of representation to the reality they are purported to represent. Is it proper to expect a theory of the processes of human cognition to answer questions about the justification of knowledge?[29] Even if one were to agree that the contribution of the knower (or "cognizer") must be factored into any philosophical analysis of human knowledge, does this require accepting Kant's transcendental idealism, according to which primary features of objects as experienced are contributed by the knowing mind? Or is transcendental idealism not essential to Kant's insight?

There is ongoing debate on these and other questions. In framing his or her own understanding and evaluation of Kant's philosophy, the reader is advised to consult some of the literature in the Further

---

[29] Some philosophers, perhaps influenced by Kant himself, describe the attempt to theorize about the justification of knowledge using natural scientific psychology the "fallacy" of psychologism; see Nicola Abbagnano, "Psychologism," *Encyclopedia of Philosophy*, ed. by Paul Edwards, 8 vols. (New York, Macmillan, 1967), vol. 7, pp. 520–1.

reading, and also to return frequently to Kant's own work. Like all philosophy, Kant's texts can best be understood through repeated rereading. And, like all good philosophy, they will repay rereading with insight and understanding.

Chronology

1756	April, disputation held on the Latin treatise *Physical Monadology*
1757	Locke's *An Essay Concerning Human Understanding* (1690) published in German translation
1758–62	Russian occupation of Königsberg
1762–4	Johann Gottfried Herder attends Kant's lectures
1762	*The False Subtlety of the Four Syllogistic Figures*
1763	*The Only Possible Argument in Support of a Demonstration of the Existence of God* (actually appeared at the end of 1762)
1764	Declines appointment as Professor of Poetry and Oratory in Königsberg
	Inquiry Concerning the Distinctness of the Principles of Natural Theology and Morality, finished in December 1762, submitted to the competition of the Berlin Academy for 1763, won second prize (published along with the winning essay by Moses Mendelssohn)
	Attempt to Introduce the Concept of Negative Magnitudes into Philosophy (written in Summer 1763)
1765	Leibniz's *Nouveaux essais sur l'entendement humain* published
1766	Appointed assistant librarian, Royal Library in Königsberg
	Dreams of a Spirit-seer Elucidated by Dreams of Metaphysics
1768	*Concerning the Ultimate Foundations of the Differentiation of Regions in Space*
1769–70	Turns down appointment as Professor of Logic and Metaphysics in Erlangen, and appointment as Professor in philosophy at Jena
1770	March, appointed Professor of Logic and Metaphysics at the Albertus University in Königsberg; Inaugural Dissertation: *On the Form and Principles of the Sensible and Intelligible World*, in Latin; public disputation, 21 August, with four students in opposition and Marcus Herz responding
1772	21 February, Kant's letter to Herz stating his plan to write a critique of pure reason
1781	May, *Critique of Pure Reason*, first edition (A)
	Kant begins speaking of a more popular treatment of the subject matter of the *Critique*
	Hume's *Dialogues Concerning Natural Religion* (1779) published in German translation

1782	January, Garve–Feder review of *Critique*
1783	*Prolegomena to Any Future Metaphysics*
1784	*Ideas toward a Universal History from a Cosmopolitan Point of View*
	An Answer to the Question: What Is Enlightenment?
1785	*Groundwork of the Metaphysics of Morals*
1786	*Metaphysical Foundations of Natural Science*
	Elected to the Academy of Sciences, Berlin; Summer Semester, Rector at Albertus University
	Frederick the Great dies; his nephew, Frederick William II, crowned and reverses his predecessor's policy of religious toleration
1787	*Critique of Pure Reason*, second edition (B)
1788	*Critique of Practical Reason*
	Concerning the Use of Teleological Principles in Philosophy
	Summer Semester, Rector at Albertus University
1790	*Critique of Judgment*, first edition
1793	*Critique of Judgment*, second edition
	Religion within the Limits of Reason Alone
1794	Censured by the Prussian Minister of Culture, agrees not to write about religion again (while the present King lives); elected to the Academy of Sciences, St. Petersburg
1796	July, Kant's last lecture
1797	*Metaphysics of Morals*
	Frederick William II dies; succeeded by Frederick William III
1798	Envisions a new book to fill a "gap" in the critical philosophy involving the transition from metaphysical foundations to physics itself; the unfinished work was published as the *Opus postumum* in 1936–8
	The Conflict of the Faculties
	Anthropology from a Pragmatic Point of View
1800	*Immanuel Kant's Logic, A Manual for Lectures*, edited by Gottlob Benjamin Jäsche
1803	Kant falls ill
1804	12 February, Kant dies; 28 February, interred

Further reading

Introductory overviews of Kant's philosophy in general may be found in John Kemp, *Philosophy of Kant* (Oxford, Oxford University Press, 1968) and Otfried Höffe, *Immanuel Kant*, trans. by Marshall Farrier (Albany, State University of New York Press, 1994). Greater detail is provided by the *Cambridge Companion to Kant*, ed. by Paul Guyer (Cambridge, Cambridge University Press, 1992), which includes separate essays on the major aspects of Kant's work and intellectual development, each of which supplies further references. A more advanced introduction, mainly focusing on the material of the first *Critique*, but also taking in the topics associated with the other two, is Ralph C. S. Walker, *Kant: The Arguments of the Philosophers* (London, Routledge, 1978).

Good introductory discussions of Kant's critical philosophy as expressed in the first *Critique* and the *Prolegomena* include W. H. Walsh, *Kant's Criticism of Metaphysics* (Edinburgh, Edinburgh University Press, 1975), and A. C. Ewing's older but still useful *Short Commentary on Kant's Critique of Pure Reason* (Chicago, University of Chicago Press, 1938). More advanced studies abound in many languages, and include the two currently prominent readings of the first *Critique*: Henry Allison, *Kant's Transcendental Idealism: An Interpretation and Defense* (New Haven, Yale University Press, 1983), and Paul Guyer, *Kant and the Claims of Knowledge* (Cambridge, Cambridge University Press, 1987). Norman Kemp Smith's *Commentary on the Critique of Pure Reason*, 2nd edn., revised and enlarged (Atlantic Highlands, NJ, Humanities Press, 1992; originally published in 1923), is the standard full commentary written in English. *Kant's Transcendental Deductions: The Three Critiques and the Opus postumum*, ed. Eckart Förster (Stanford,

Stanford University Press, 1989), collects a number of important articles; Lewis White Beck, *Essays on Kant and Hume* (New Haven, Yale University Press, 1978) contains much of use in interpreting the content and development of Kant's critical philosophy. But the reader is especially encouraged to continue on to the entire *Critique of Pure Reason*, and to other of Kant's works in theoretical philosophy, including the Inaugural Dissertation and the *Metaphysical Foundations of Natural Science*, respectively in *Theoretical Philosophy, 1755–1770*, trans. and ed. by D. Walford and R. Meerbote (Cambridge, Cambridge University Press, 1992), and *Theoretical Philosophy After 1781*, ed. by H. Allison and P. Heath (Cambridge, Cambridge University Press, forthcoming). The standard German edition of Kant's works is the Academy Edition of *Kants gesammelte Schriften* (1900–), referred to herein as "Ak" (plus volume and page numbers). All of his published writings, and many originally unpublished items found in Ak, are being newly translated in the Cambridge Edition of the Works of Immanuel Kant, under the general editorship of Paul Guyer and Allen Wood.

Material devoted directly to the introductory study of the *Prolegomena* itself is more sparse. The only commentaries devoted exclusively to it are older works in German, including Max Apel, *Kommentar zu Kants Prolegomena*, 2nd edn. (Leipzig, Felix Meiner, 1923) and Benno Erdmann, *Historische Studien über Kants Prolegomena* (Halle, Niemeyer, 1904). A sense of the reaction to the first *Critique* can be gained from Johann Schultz's *Exposition of Kant's Critique of Pure Reason*, trans. by James C. Morrison (Ottawa, University of Ottawa Press, 1996), which also translates the Garve–Feder review. Additional context for the origin of the critical philosophy is provided by letters to and from Kant in the years 1770 to 1783, in *Philosophical Correspondence* ed. and trans. by Arnulf Zweig (Chicago, University of Chicago Press, 1967), referred to as "*PC*"; the original letters are contained in vol. 10 of Ak.

A sense of the intellectual context in which Kant wrote, and an overview of Kant's life and work, are offered in L. W. Beck's monumental *Early German Philosophy: Kant and His Predecessors* (Cambridge, MA, Harvard University Press, 1969). The standard biographies of Kant remain Karl Vorländer, *Immanuel Kant: Der Mann und das Werk*, 2 vols. (Leipzig, Felix Meiner, 1924) and Ernst Cassirer, *Kant's Life and Thought*, trans. by James Haden (New Haven, Yale University Press, 1981).

Note on texts and translation

The translation has been made using a reprint of the original edition of the *Prolegomena zu einer jeden künftigen Metaphysik die als Wissenschaft wird auftreten können* (Riga, Hartknoch, 1783; reprint, Erlangen, Harald Fischer Verlag, 1988), and Karl Vorländer's edition, as revised (Hamburg, Felix Meiner Verlag, 1976); on occasion, Benno Erdmann's edition in Ak, vol. 4, has been consulted. As is customary, the page numbers of Ak are shown in the margins of the present translation. Vorländer's edition, completed after Ak, collects significant textual variants from many previous editions; both editions contain much useful information on texts and printings. (Neither, however, record their emendations to the punctuation, which are many in Vorländer, fewer in Ak.) Vorländer's edition incorporates a major reorganization of the Preamble and first General Question in accordance with Hans Vaihinger's "galley switching" thesis.[1] Vaihinger convincingly argued, on internal textual grounds and by comparison with corresponding sections of the "B" edition of the *Critique*, that a galley of 100 lines was transposed during the printing of the Preamble. The emended text is not without minor problems (for the correction of which a paragraph break has been added), but it is much improved over editions that do not accept the reorganization.

The present translation varies slightly from my contribution to the Cambridge Edition of the Works of Immanuel Kant, *Theoretical Philosophy After 1781*. That publication contains more extensive critical apparatus than would be useful here, where the original German is

---

[1] "Eine Blattversetzung in Kants *Prolegomena*," *Philosophische Monatshefte*, 15 (1879), 321–32, 513–32; Vorländer summarizes the evidence in his edition, pp. xxxvii–xl.

given only occasionally, to permit a general understanding of Kant's terminology. (When German words are given, modern orthography is used, and declination is shown.) Similarly, the factual notes provided herein are sometimes less extensive, though in other cases new notes have been provided for the non-specialist reader.

The *Prolegomena* has been translated into English several times before, including those by John P. Mahaffy and John H. Bernard, 2nd edn. (London, 1889); Ernest Belfort Bax, 2nd edn. (London, 1891); Paul Carus, 3rd edn. (Chicago, 1912); and Peter G. Lucas (Manchester, 1953); and also revisions of Carus by Lewis White Beck (Indianapolis, 1950) and by James W. Ellington (Indianapolis, 1977). I have made a new translation. On occasion, however, I have consulted the earlier works, especially Lucas and Beck.

Every translator must interpret. In doing so, one can seek greater or lesser adherence to standards of literalness. This translation adopts the principles of the Cambridge Edition: seek terminological consistency, avoid sacrificing literalness for ostensible ease in reading, preserve Kant's own sentence and paragraph breaks, keep emendations and interpolations to a minimum, and strictly separate *Kant's own footnotes* (marked with an asterisk, [*]), from both the translator's *textual notes* (marked with superscript letters), which pertain to the German text and its translation, and *factual notes* (marked with superscript numerals), in which historical figures are more fully identified, certain points are explained, and Latin, Greek, and French phrases are translated. Though Kant's long sentences are challenging, his thought is more clearly presented by leaving them intact than by breaking them up, thereby compromising their internal logical and grammatical relations. Differences in German and English syntax have sometimes caused me to alter the internal punctuation of Kant's sentences. I have tried to avoid introducing ambiguities into the English that would result from the fact that German pronouns carry gender in relation to all nouns, and are more fully declined than English pronouns; hence, on many occasions I have replaced pronominal expressions with their antecedents. I have sought to avoid the gender bias that arises from the fact that the German *man*, which is gender-neutral in meaning, is declined as masculine. In other cases, as when Kant used *er* (English "he") to refer to unnamed philosophers, I have let the masculine stand as a reflection of his time. In interpreting Kant's German, which can be archaic even for its day, a variety of dictionaries and reference works have been of use; because language changes, works near Kant's time have proven especially valuable.[2]

The translator of Kant is faced with many choices, especially regarding the rendering of Kant's technical vocabulary into English. I have followed the standard practice of rendering *Anschauung* as "intuition," *Begriff* as "concept," and *Vorstellung* as "representation." I have departed from some translators in rendering *sinnliche Anschauung* as "sensory intuition," rather than "sensible intuition." This choice accords with Kant's own advice about the related terms *intelligibel* and *intellektuel* (below, §34n), the first of which he restricted to "intelligible" objects (those able to be cognized by the intellect), as opposed to "intellectual" cognitions (cognitions belonging to the intellect as a faculty). Although "sensual intuition" would be the most literal translation for *sinnliche Anschauung*, it brings its own ambiguities, so I have opted for "sensory" in cases when the adjective *sinnlich* is used to indicate the kind of cognition, rather than to describe an object as being capable of being sensed (i.e., as being "sensible"). I have been careful to translate *Erfahrungserkenntnis* with such phrases as "cognition of experience" or "cognition in experience," rather than as "empirical cognition," because Kant often uses it in proximity to *Erfahrungsurteil* ("judgment of experience"), which he explicitly distinguishes from *empirisches Urteil* ("empirical judgment").

I have chosen to follow the recent tendency of translating *Erkenntnis* as "cognition" rather than as "knowledge." "Cognition" accords better with the fact that Kant is most often discussing *Erkenntnis* as a process or as a cognitive achievement of a mind. The word "knowledge" is more appropriate when speaking of the end product of cognition, the organized bodies of knowledge preserved in books, and I have sometimes used it in such contexts, though I have also been willing to speak of "bodies of cognition" to characterize whole fields of knowledge.

In some cases, subsequent philosophical developments, sometimes

---

[2] Joachim Heinrich Campe, *Wörterbuch der deutschen Sprache*, 6 vols. (Braunschweig, 1807–13; reprint, Hildesheim, Olms, 1969–70); Nathan Bailey, *Englisch-deutsches und deutsches-englisches Wörterbuch*, 2 vols. (Leipzig and Jena, 1810); Johann August Eberhard, Johann Gebhard Ehrenreich Maass, and Johann Gottfried Gruber, *Deutsche Synonymik*, 4th edn., 2 vols. (Leipzig, 1852–3; reprint, Hildesheim, Olms, 1971); and U. U. W. Meissner, *Vollständiges englisch-deutsches und deutsch-englisches Wörterbuch*, 2 vols. (Leipzig, 1847).

inspired by Kant's own writings, have rendered certain English terms into technical philosophical terms, while their German counterparts were no such thing in his day. Thus, Kant often uses the expression *zum Grunde liegen*, one translation of which is "to lie at the foundation of," or even "to be the foundation of." But the English word "foundation," because of more recent philosophical discussions, can call to mind the notion of epistemological foundations, or foundationalism. Thus, I have tended to use other English words, such as "to be the basis for," or, changing voice, "to be based on," to translate this and related German phrases. In other cases, when Kant is playing on the etymological meaning of a given word, as he does with *Vernunftschluss*, which means "syllogism," but literally is "inference of reason," I have expanded the single German word by giving one English variant as a gloss of the other. This has been useful to do for other terms, as when Kant discusses *Grundsätze* as a subclass of *Prinzipien*; both words might be translated as "principles," which would be awkward in this case, so I have occasionally shown other variants of the first term, including "fundamental propositions" and "basic principles." ("Principles" is used again to translate *Satz des Widerspruchs* as "principle of contradiction"; and *Satz* is elsewhere rendered as "proposition," or even "thesis.") A similar device is used in translating *gesunder Menschenverstand* and related terms; they are now and were in the Kant's time understood as equivalent to the English "common sense," though he sometimes plays on the fact that they include the German root *Verstand* ("understanding").

I have followed as much as possible Kant's original punctuation for mentioning propositions or for marking off foreign words. Kant tended to set off propositions with colons, as in, "the proposition: that substance remains and persists, ..."; in such cases, the mentioned proposition usually ends at the first comma, semicolon, or period. On rare occasions Kant uses quotations to set off a proposition, and in those cases I have followed suit; other than §56 (Kant's note), only in the Appendix, where he quotes the Garve–Feder review, have I found these to be word-for-word quotations from another source. In the first edition of the *Prolegomena* Latin and French words were set in roman type, by contrast with the gothic of the original German; I have used italics for Latin, French, and Greek words, by contrast with the roman font of the main text. I have also used italics to show Kant's indications of emphasis. For book titles, the italics have been added in all but a few cases; Kant rarely marked book titles typographically, and he played on the fact that the German counterparts to "critique of pure reason" and "prolegomena" can be used both as ordinary nouns for a type of critical activity or for a kind of written work, and as titles for his own writings. Other emphasis follows the first edition, with minor modifications. Vorländer and Ak, following now-standard conventions of German typography, emphasize all proper names of persons; the first edition did not, and it has been followed without further note.

The selections from the *Critique of Pure Reason* are translated from a reprint of the second edition (B) of the *Kritik der reinen Vernunft* (Riga, Hartknoch, 1787; reprint, London, Routledge/Thoemmes Press, 1994), silently taking into account emendations proposed in the editions of Erich Adickes (Berlin, 1889) and Benno Erdmann (Ak, vol. 3); a reprint of the first edition (A) was consulted as needed (Riga, Hartknoch, 1781; reprint, London, Routledge/Thoemmes Press, 1994). Of course, Kant's own references in the *Prolegomena* are to the "A" edition, the only one extant when he wrote. In the selections for which there is a significant difference between the two editions (the Introduction and Transcendental Aesthetic), I have followed the "B" edition because it was emended in ways I found useful, especially for avoiding overlap with the *Prolegomena*. In any case, where corresponding pages from "A" exist, the numbers have been given. In the sections with both "A" and "B" pages, only the larger deviations of "B" from "A "have been marked; those interested in an exact accounting of the differences should consult a critical edition or a full translation. In a few places in which Kant discusses key concepts, I have, for the sake of clarity, silently italicized key words or adopted emphasis found in "A" but not "B."

Prolegomena to Any Future Metaphysics

That Will Be Able to Come Forward as Science

Contents^a

---

^a This table of contents has been constructed from the section titles. The original editions did not
contain a table of contents.

Preface

These prolegomena are not for the use of apprentices, but of future teachers, and indeed are not to help them to organize the presentation of an already existing science, but to discover this science itself for the first time.

There are scholars for whom the history of philosophy (ancient as well as modern) is itself their philosophy; the present prolegomena have not been written for them. They must wait until those who endeavor to draw from the wellsprings of reason itself have finished their business, and then it will be their turn to bring news of these events to the world. Failing that, in their opinion nothing can be said that has not already been said before; and in fact this opinion can stand for all time as an infallible prediction, for since the human understanding has wandered over countless subjects in various ways through many centuries, it can hardly fail that for anything new something old should be found that has some similarity with it.

My intention is to convince all of those who find it worthwhile to occupy themselves with metaphysics that it is unavoidably necessary to suspend their work for the present, to consider all that has happened until now as if it had not happened, and before all else to pose the question: "whether such a thing as metaphysics is even possible at all."

If metaphysics is a science, why is it that it cannot, as other sciences, attain universal and lasting acclaim? If it is not, how does it happen that, under the pretense of a science it incessantly shows off, and strings along the human understanding with hopes that never dim but are never fulfilled? Whether, therefore, we demonstrate our knowledge or our ignorance, for once we must arrive at something certain concerning the nature of this self-proclaimed science; for things cannot possibly remain on their present footing. It seems almost laughable that, while every other science makes continuous progress, metaphysics, which desires to be wisdom itself, and which everyone consults as an oracle, perpetually turns round on the same spot without coming a step further. Furthermore, it has lost a great many of its adherents, and one does not find that those who feel strong enough to shine in other sciences wish to risk their reputations in this one, where anyone, usually ignorant in all other things, lays claim to a decisive opinion, since in this region there are in fact still no reliable weights and measures with which to distinguish profundity from shallow babble.

It is, after all, not completely unheard of, after long cultivation of a science, that in considering with wonder how much progress has been made someone should finally allow the question to arise: whether and how such a science is possible at all. For human reason is so keen on building that more than once it has erected a tower, and has afterwards torn it down again in order to see how well constituted its foundation may have been. It is never too late to grow reasonable and wise; but if the insight comes late, it is always harder to bring it into play.

To ask whether a science might in fact be possible assumes a doubt about its actuality.[a] Such a doubt, though, offends everyone whose entire belongings may perhaps consist in this supposed jewel; hence he who allows this doubt to develop had better prepare for opposition from all sides. Some, with their metaphysical compendia in hand, will look down on him with scorn, in proud consciousness of their ancient, and hence ostensibly legitimate, possession; others, who nowhere see anything that is not similar to something they have seen somewhere else before, will not understand him; and for a time everything will remain as if nothing at all had happened that might yield fear or hope of an impending change.

Nevertheless I venture to predict that the reader of these prolegomena who thinks for himself will not only come to doubt his previous science, [4:257] but subsequently will be fully convinced that there can be no such science unless the requirements expressed here, on which its possibility rests, are met, and, as this has never yet been done, that there is as yet no metaphysics at all. Since, however, the demand for it can never be

---

[a] *Wirklichkeit*

6

exhausted,* because the interest of human reason in general is much too intimately interwoven with it, the reader will admit that a complete reform or rather a rebirth of metaphysics, according to a plan completely unknown before now, is inevitably approaching, however much it may be resisted in the meantime.

Since the Essays of *Locke* and *Leibniz*,[2] or rather since the rise of metaphysics as far as the history of it reaches, no event has occurred that could have been more decisive with respect to the fate of this science than the attack made upon it by *David Hume*.[3] He brought no light to this kind of knowledge,[b] but he certainly struck a spark from which a light could well have been kindled, if it had hit some welcoming tinder whose glow was carefully kept going and made to grow.

Hume started mainly from a single but important concept in metaphysics, namely, that of the *connection of cause and effect* (and of course also its derivative concepts, of force and action, etc.), and called upon reason, which pretends to have generated this concept in her womb, to give him an account of by what right she thinks: that something could be so constituted that, if it is posited, something else necessarily must thereby be posited as well; for that is what the concept of cause says. He indisputably proved that it is wholly impossible for reason to think such a connection *a priori* and from concepts, because this connection contains necessity; and it is simply not to be seen how it could be, that because something is, something else necessarily must also be, and therefore how the concept of such a connection could be introduced *a priori*. From this he concluded that reason completely and fully deceives herself with this concept, falsely taking it for her own child, when it is really nothing but a bastard of the imagination, which, impregnated by [4:258] experience, and having brought certain representations under the

---

*
  Rusticus exspectat, dum defluat amnis, at ille
  Labitur et labetur in omne volubilis aevum. Horace.[1]

[b] *Erkenntnis*; in most instances, this word has been translated as "cognition."

[1] "A rustic waits for the river to flow away, but it flows on, and will so flow for all eternity." Horace *Epistles*, I. ii. 42–3.

[2] John Locke (1632–1704), *An Essay Concerning Human Understanding*. Gottfried Wilhelm Leibniz (1646–1716), *Nouveaux essais sur l'entendement humain*, in his *Œuvres philosophiques* (Amsterdam and Leipzig, 1765); German translation, 1778–80, though Kant read the French edition soon after its appearance; English translation, *New Essays on Human Understanding*, trans. by P. Remnant and J. Bennett (Cambridge, Cambridge University Press, 1981).

[3] David Hume (1711–76). On Kant's relation to the relevant works by Hume, see the Introduction.

law of association, passes off the resulting subjective necessity (i.e., habit) for an objective necessity (from insight). From which he concluded that reason has no power at all to think such connections, not even merely in general, because its concepts would then be bare fictions, and all of its cognitions allegedly established *a priori* would be nothing but falsely marked ordinary experiences; which is so much as to say that there is no metaphysics at all, and cannot be any.*

As premature and erroneous as his conclusion was, nevertheless it was at least founded on inquiry, and this inquiry was of sufficient value, that the best minds of his time might have come together to solve (more happily if possible) the problem in the sense in which he presented it, from which a complete reform of the science must soon have arisen.

But fate, ever ill-disposed toward metaphysics, would have it that *Hume* was understood by no one. One cannot, without feeling a certain pain, behold how utterly and completely his opponents, *Reid, Oswald, Beattie*, and finally *Priestley*,[6] missed the point of his problem, and misjudged his hints for improvement – constantly taking for granted just what he doubted, and, conversely, proving with vehemence and, more often than not, with great insolence exactly what it had never

---

* All the same, *Hume* named this destructive philosophy itself metaphysics and placed great value on it. "Metaphysics and morals," he said (*Essays*, 4th pt., p. 214, German translation), "are the most important branches of science; mathematics and natural science are not worth half so much."[4] The acute man was, however, looking only to the negative benefit that curbing the excessive claims of speculative reason would have, in completely abolishing so many endless and continual conflicts that perplex the human species; he meanwhile lost sight of the positive harm that results if reason is deprived of the most important vistas, from which alone it can stake out for the will the highest goal of all the will's endeavors.[5]

[4] This quotation in Kant's text contains an ellipsis that somewhat distorts Hume's statement, which reads in full: "Monarchies, receiving their chief Stability from a superstitious Reverence to Priests and Princes, have abridged the Liberty of Reasoning, with Regard to Religion and Politics, and consequently Metaphysics and Morals. All these form the most considerable Branches of Science. Mathematics and natural Philosophy, which are the only ones that remain, are not half so valuable" (Essay 5, "Of the Rise and Progress of the Arts and Sciences," *Essays, Moral and Political*, 2 vols. [Edinburgh, 1741–2], vol. 2, p. 79).

[5] Kant considered the overextension of empirical concepts to be a threat to the idea of freedom and hence to morality; see Selections, pp. 152–4.

[6] Thomas Reid (1710–96), *An Inquiry into the Human Mind, on the Principles of Common Sense* (Dublin and Edinburgh, 1764), French translation, 1768, German, 1782; James Oswald (d. 1793), *An Appeal to Common Sense in Behalf of Religion* (Edinburgh, 1766), German translation, 1774; James Beattie (1735–1803), *An Essay on the Nature and Immutability of Truth, in Opposition to Sophistry and Scepticism* (Edinburgh, 1770), German translation, 1772; Joseph Priestley (1733–1804), *An Examination of Dr. Reid's Inquiry into the Human Mind, on the Principles of Common Sense, Dr. Beattie's Essay on the Nature and Immutability of Truth, and Dr. Oswald's Appeal to Common Sense in Behalf of Religion* (London, 1774).

entered his mind to doubt – so that everything remained in its old condition, as if nothing had happened. The question was not, whether the concept of cause is right, useful, and, with respect to all cognition of nature, indispensable, for this Hume had never put in doubt; it was rather whether it is thought through reason *a priori*, and in this way has [4:259] an inner truth independent of all experience, and therefore also a much more widely extended use which is not limited merely to objects of experience: regarding this *Hume* awaited enlightenment. The discussion was only about the origin of this concept, not about its indispensability in use; if the former were only discovered, the conditions of its use and the sphere in which it can be valid would already be given.

In order to do justice to the problem, however, the opponents of this celebrated man would have had to penetrate very deeply into the nature of reason so far as it is occupied solely with pure thought, something that did not suit them. They therefore found a more expedient means to be obstinate without any insight, namely, the appeal to **ordinary common sense**.[7] It is in fact a great gift from heaven to possess right (or, as it has recently been called, plain) common sense. But it must be proven through deeds, by the considered and reasonable things one thinks and says, and not by appealing to it as an oracle when one knows of nothing clever to advance in one's defense. To appeal to ordinary common sense when insight and science[c] run short, and not before, is one of the subtle discoveries of recent times, whereby the dullest windbag can confidently take on the most profound thinker and hold his own with him. So long as a small residue of insight remains, however, one would do well to avoid resorting to this emergency help. And seen in the light of day, this appeal is nothing other than a call to the judgment of the multitude; applause at which the philosopher blushes, but at which the popular wag becomes triumphant and defiant. I should think, however, that *Hume* could lay just as much claim to sound common sense as *Beattie*, and on top of this to something that the latter certainly did not possess, namely, a critical reason, which keeps ordinary common sense in check, so that it doesn't lose itself in speculations, or, if these are the sole topic of discussion, doesn't want to decide anything, since it doesn't understand the justification for its own principles; for

---

[c] *Wissenschaft*

[7] The words translated as "common sense" include the German root *Verstand*, or "understanding."

only so will it remain sound common sense. Hammer and chisel are perfectly fine for working raw lumber, but for copperplate one must use an etching needle. Likewise, sound common sense and speculative [4:260] understanding are both useful, but each in its own way; the one, when it is a matter of judgments that find their immediate application in experience, the other, however, when judgments are to be made in a universal mode, out of mere concepts, as in metaphysics, where what calls itself (but often *per antiphrasin*)[8] sound common sense has no judgment whatsoever.

I freely admit that the remembrance of *David Hume* was the very thing that many years ago first interrupted my dogmatic slumber and gave a completely different direction to my researches in the field of speculative philosophy. I was very far from listening to him with respect to his conclusions, which arose solely because he did not completely set out his problem, but only touched on a part of it, which, without the whole being taken into account, can provide no enlightenment. If we begin from a well-grounded though undeveloped thought that another bequeaths us, then we can well hope, by continued reflection, to take it further than could the sagacious man whom one has to thank for the first spark of this light.

So I tried first whether *Hume's* objection might not be presented in a general manner, and I soon found that the concept of the connection of cause and effect is far from being the only concept through which the understanding thinks connections of things *a priori*; rather, metaphysics consists wholly of such concepts. I sought to ascertain their number, and as I had successfully attained this in the way I wished, namely from a single principle, I proceeded to the deduction of these concepts,[9] from which I henceforth became assured that they were not, as *Hume* had feared, derived from experience, but had arisen from the pure under-standing. This deduction, which appeared impossible to my sagacious predecessor, and which had never even occurred to anyone but him, even though everyone confidently made use of these concepts without asking what their objective validity is based on – this deduction, I say, was the most difficult thing that could ever be undertaken on behalf of metaphysics; and the worst thing about it is that metaphysics, as much of it as might be present anywhere at all, could not give me the slightest

---

[8] "by way of expression through the opposite"
[9] On the idea of a "deduction," see Selections, pp. 171–3.

help with this, because this very deduction must first settle the possibility of a metaphysics. As I had now succeeded in the solution of the Humean problem not only in a single case but with respect to the entire faculty of pure reason, I could therefore take sure, if still always [4:261] slow, steps toward finally determining, completely and according to universal principles, the entire extent of pure reason with regard to its boundaries as well as its content, which was indeed the very thing that metaphysics requires in order to build its system according to a sure plan.

But I fear that the *elaboration* of the Humean problem in its greatest possible amplification (namely, the *Critique of Pure Reason*) may well fare just as the *problem* itself fared when it was first posed. It will be judged incorrectly, because it is not understood; it will not be understood, because people will be inclined just to skim through the book, but not to think through it; and they will not want to expend this effort on it, because the work is dry, because it is obscure, because it opposes all familiar concepts and is long-winded as well. Now I admit that I do not expect to hear complaints from a philosopher regarding lack of popularity, entertainment, and ease, when the matter concerns the existence of highly prized knowledge that is indispensable to humanity, knowledge that cannot be constituted except according to the strictest rules of scholarly exactitude, and to which popularity may indeed come with time but can never be there at the start. But with regard to a certain obscurity – arising in part from the expansiveness of the plan, which makes it difficult to survey the main points upon which the investigation depends – in this respect the complaint is just; and I will redress it through the present *Prolegomena*.

The previous work, which presents the faculty of pure reason in its entire extent and boundaries, thereby always remains the foundation to which the *Prolegomena* refer only as preparatory exercises; for this *Critique* must stand forth as science, systematic and complete to its smallest parts, before one can think of permitting metaphysics to come forward, or even of forming only a distant hope for metaphysics.

We have long been accustomed to seeing old, threadbare cognitions newly trimmed by being taken from their previous connections and fitted out by someone in a systematic garb of his own preferred cut, but under new titles; and most readers will beforehand expect nothing else from the *Critique*. Yet these *Prolegomena* will bring them to understand

[4:262] that there exists a completely new science, of which no one had previously formed merely the thought, of which even the bare idea was unknown, and for which nothing from all that has been provided before now could be used except the hint that *Hume's* doubts had been able to give; Hume also foresaw nothing of any such possible formal science, but deposited his ship on the beach (of skepticism) for safekeeping, where it could then lie and rot, whereas it is important to me to give it a pilot, who, provided with complete sea-charts and a compass, might safely navigate the ship wherever seems good to him, following sound principles of the helmsman's art drawn from a knowledge of the globe.

To approach a new science – one that is entirely isolated and is the only one of its kind – with the prejudice that it can be judged by means of one's putative cognitions already otherwise obtained, even though it is precisely the reality of those that must first be completely called into question, results only in believing that one sees everywhere something that was already otherwise known, because the expressions perhaps sound similar; except that everything must seem to be extremely deformed, contradictory, and nonsensical, because one does not thereby make the author's thoughts fundamental, but always simply one's own, made natural through long habit. Yet the copiousness of the work, insofar as it is rooted in the science itself and not in the presentation, and the inevitable dryness and scholastic exactitude that result, are qualities that indeed may be extremely advantageous to the subject matter itself, but must of course be detrimental to the book itself.

It is not given to everyone to write so subtly and yet also so alluringly as *David Hume*, or so profoundly and at the same time so elegantly as *Moses Mendelssohn*;[10] but I could well have given my presentation popularity (as I flatter myself) if all I had wanted to do was to sketch a plan and to commend its execution to others, and had I not taken to heart the well-being of the science that kept me occupied for so long; for after all it requires great perseverance and also indeed not a little self-denial to set aside the enticement of an earlier, favorable reception for the expectation of an admittedly later, but lasting approval.

To make plans is most often a presumptuous, boastful mental

---

[10] Moses Mendelssohn (1729–86) was an acclaimed and prolific writer. His *Abhandlung über die Evidenz in metaphysischen Wissenschaften* (Berlin, 1764) won the prize competition set by the Royal Academy of Sciences in Berlin for 1763 (Kant took second place).

preoccupation, through which one presents the appearance of creative genius, in that one requires what one cannot himself provide, censures [4:263] what one cannot do better, and proposes what one does not know how to attain oneself – though merely for a sound plan for a general critique of reason, somewhat more than might be expected would already have been required if it were not, as is usual, to be merely a recitation of pious wishes. But pure reason is such an isolated domain, within itself so thoroughly connected, that no part of it can be encroached upon without disturbing all the rest, nor adjusted without having previously determined for each part its place and its influence on the others; for, since there is nothing outside of it that could correct our judgment within it, the validity and use of each part depends on the relation in which it stands to the others within reason itself, and, as with the structure of an organized body, the purpose of any member can be derived only from the complete concept of the whole. That is why it can be said of such a critique, that it is never trustworthy unless it is *entirely complete* down to the least elements of pure reason, and that in the domain of this faculty one must determine and settle either *all* or *nothing*.

But although a mere plan that might precede the *Critique of Pure Reason* would be unintelligible, undependable, and useless, it is by contrast all the more useful if it comes after. For one will thereby be put in the position to survey the whole, to test one by one the main points at issue in this science, and to arrange many things in the exposition better than could be done in the first execution of the work.

Here then is such a *plan* subsequent to the completed work, which now can be laid out according to the *analytic method*, whereas the *work* itself absolutely had to be composed according to the *synthetic method*, so that the science might present all of its articulations, as the structural organization of a quite peculiar faculty of cognition, in their natural connection. Whosoever finds this plan itself, which I send ahead as prolegomena for any future metaphysics, still obscure, may consider that it simply is not necessary for everyone to study metaphysics, that there are some talents that proceed perfectly well in fundamental and even deep sciences that are closer to intuition, but that will not succeed in the investigation of purely abstract concepts, and that in such a case [4:264] one should apply one's mental gifts to another object; that, however, whosoever undertakes to judge or indeed to construct a metaphysics, must thoroughly satisfy the challenge made here, whether it happens that they accept my solution, or fundamentally reject it and replace it with another – for they cannot dismiss it; and finally, that the much decried obscurity (a familiar cloaking for one's own indolence or dim-sightedness) has its use as well, since everybody, who with respect to all other sciences observes a wary silence, speaks masterfully, and boldly passes judgment in questions of metaphysics, because here to be sure their ignorance does not stand out clearly in relation to the science of others, but in relation to genuine critical principles, which therefore can be praised:

Ignavum, fucos, pecus a praesepibus arcent.

Virg.[11]

[11] "They protect the hives from the drones, an idle bunch." Virgil, *Georgica*, IV. 168.

Preamble on the Distinguishing Feature [4:265]
of All Metaphysical Cognition

§ 1

On the sources of metaphysics

If one wishes to present a body of cognition as *science*,[a] then one must first be able to determine precisely the differentia it has in common with no other science, and which is therefore its *distinguishing feature*; otherwise the boundaries of all the sciences run together, and none of them can be dealt with thoroughly according to its own nature.

Whether this distinguishing feature consists in a difference of the *object* or the *source of cognition*, or even of the *type of cognition*, or several if not all of these things together, the idea of the possible science and its territory depends first of all upon it.

First, concerning the *sources* of metaphysical cognition, it already lies in the concept of metaphysics that they cannot be empirical. The principles[b] of such cognition (which include not only its fundamental propositions[c] or basic principles, but also its fundamental concepts) must therefore never be taken from experience; for the cognition is supposed to be not physical but metaphysical, i.e., lying beyond experience. Therefore it will be based upon neither outer experience, which constitutes the source of physics proper, nor inner, which provides the foundation of empirical psychology.[d] It is therefore [4:266] cognition *a priori*, or from pure understanding and pure reason.

---

[a] *eine Erkenntnis als Wissenschaft*   [b] *Prinzipien*
[c] *Grundsätze*; the next three words are added by the translator as a gloss.
[d] *empirischen Psychologie*

15

In this, however, there would be nothing to differentiate it from pure mathematics; it must therefore be denominated *pure philosophical cognition*; but concerning the meaning of this expression I refer to the *Critique of Pure Reason*, pp. 712 f.,[1] where the distinction between these two types of use of reason has been presented clearly and sufficiently.— So much on the sources of metaphysical cognition.

§2

On the type of cognition, that alone can be called metaphysical

(a) On the distinction between synthetic and analytic judgments in general

Metaphysical cognition must contain nothing but judgments *a priori*, as required by the distinguishing feature of its sources. But judgments may have any origin whatsoever, or be constituted in whatever manner according to their logical form, and yet there is nonetheless a distinction between them according to their content, by dint of which they are either merely *explicative* and add nothing to the content of the cognition, or *ampliative* and augment the given cognition; the first may be called *analytic* judgments, the second *synthetic*.

Analytic judgments say nothing in the predicate except what was actually thought already in the concept of the subject, though not so clearly nor with the same consciousness. If I say: All bodies are extended, then I have not in the least amplified my concept of body, but have merely resolved it, since extension, although not explicitly said of the former concept prior to the judgment, nevertheless was actually thought of it; the judgment is therefore analytic. By contrast, the proposition: Some bodies are heavy, contains something in the predicate that is not actually thought in the general concept of body; it therefore [4:267] augments my cognition, since it adds something to my concept, and must therefore be called a synthetic judgment.

(b) The common principle of all analytic judgments is the principle of contradiction

All analytic judgments rest entirely on the principle of contradiction and are by their nature *a priori* cognitions, whether the concepts that serve

---

[1] See pp. 178–80.

for their material be empirical or not. For since the predicate of an affirmative analytic judgment is already thought beforehand in the concept of the subject, it cannot be denied of that subject without contradiction; exactly so is its opposite necessarily denied of the subject in an analytic, but negative, judgment, and indeed also according to the principle of contradiction. So it stands with the propositions: Every body is extended, and: No body is unextended (simple).

For that reason all analytic propositions are still *a priori* judgments even if their concepts are empirical, as in: Gold is a yellow metal; for in order to know this, I need no further experience outside my concept of gold, which included that this body is yellow and a metal; for this constituted my very concept, and I did not have to do anything except analyze it, without looking beyond it to something else.

(c) Synthetic judgments require a principle other than the principle of contradiction

There are synthetic judgments *a posteriori* whose origin is empirical; but there are also synthetic judgments that are *a priori* certain and that arise from pure understanding and reason. Both however agree in this, that they can by no means arise solely from the principle^e of analysis, namely the principle of contradiction; they demand yet a completely different principle,^f though they always must be derived from some fundamental proposition,^g whichever it may be, *in accordance with the principle of contradiction*; for nothing can run counter to this fundamental principle, even though everything cannot be derived from it. I shall first classify the synthetic judgments.

1. *Judgments of experience* are always synthetic. For it would be [4:268] absurd to base an analytic judgment on experience, since I do not at all need to go beyond my concept in order to formulate the judgment and therefore have no need for any testimony from experience. That a body is extended, is a proposition that stands certain *a priori*, and not a judgment of experience. For before I go to experience, I have all the conditions for my judgment already in the concept, from which I merely draw out the predicate in accordance with the principle of contradiction, and by this means can simultaneously become conscious

---

^e *Grundsatze*　　^f *Prinzip*　　^g *Grundsatze*

of the *necessity* of the judgment, which experience could never teach me.

2. *Mathematical judgments* are one and all synthetic. This proposition appears to have completely escaped the observations of analysts of human reason up to the present, and indeed to be directly opposed to all of their conjectures, although it is incontrovertibly certain and very important in its consequences. Because they found that the inferences of the mathematicians all proceed in accordance with the principle of contradiction (which, by nature, is required of any apodictic certainty), they were persuaded that even the fundamental propositions were known through the principle of contradiction, in which they were very mistaken; for a synthetic proposition can of course be discerned in accordance with the principle of contradiction, but only insofar as another synthetic proposition is presupposed from which the first can be deduced, never however in itself.

First of all it must be observed: that properly mathematical propositions are always *a priori* and not empirical judgments, because they carry necessity with them, which cannot be taken from experience. But if this will not be granted me, very well, I will restrict my proposition to *pure mathematics*, the concept of which already conveys that it contains not empirical but only pure cognition *a priori*.

One might well at first think: that the proposition $7 + 5 = 12$ is a purely analytic proposition that follows from the concept of a sum of seven and five according to the principle of contradiction. However, upon closer inspection, one finds that the concept of the sum of 7 and 5 contains nothing further than the unification of the two numbers into one, through which by no means is thought what this single number may be that combines the two. The concept of twelve is in no way already thought because I merely think to myself this unification of seven and five, and I may analyze my concept of such a possible sum for [4:269] as long as may be, still I will not meet with twelve therein. One must go beyond these concepts, in making use of the intuition that corresponds to one of the two, such as one's five fingers, or (like *Segner* in his arithmetic)[2] five points, and in that manner adding the units of the five given in intuition step by step to the concept of seven. One therefore truly amplifies one's concept through this proposition $7+5=12$ and adds to the first concept a new one that was not thought in it; that is, an

---

[2] Johann Andreas Segner (1704–77), *Anfangsgründe der Mathematik*, 2nd edn. (Halle, 1773).

arithmetical proposition is always synthetic, which can be seen all the more plainly in the case of somewhat larger numbers, for it is then clearly evident that, though we may turn and twist our concept as we like, we could never find the sum through the mere analysis of our concepts, without making use of intuition.

Nor is any fundamental proposition of pure geometry analytic. That the straight line between two points is the shortest is a synthetic proposition. For my concept of the straight contains nothing of magnitude,[h] but only a quality. The concept of the shortest is therefore wholly an addition and cannot be extracted by any analysis from the concept of the straight line. Intuition must therefore be made use of here, by means of which alone the synthesis is possible.

Some other fundamental propositions that geometers presuppose are indeed actually analytic and rest on the principle of contradiction; however, they serve only, like identical propositions, as links in the chain of method and not as principles: e.g., a = a, the whole is equal to itself, or (a + b) > a, i.e., the whole is greater than its part. And indeed even these, although they are valid from concepts alone, are admitted into mathematics only because they can be exhibited in intuition.

It[i] is merely ambiguity of expression which makes us commonly believe here that the predicate of such apodictic judgments already lies in our concept and that the judgment is therefore analytic. Namely, we *are required*[j] to add in thought a particular predicate to a given concept, and this necessity is already attached to the concepts. But the question is not, what we *are required to add in thought* to a given concept, but what we *actually think* in it, even if only obscurely, and then it becomes evident that the predicate attaches to such concepts indeed necessarily, though not immediately, but rather through an intuition that has to be added.[k]

The essential feature of pure *mathematical* cognition, differentiating it [4:272] from all other *a priori* cognition, is that it must throughout proceed *not from concepts*, but always and only through the construction of concepts

---

[h] *Grösse*
[i] Paragraph break added to reflect continuity with the three paragraphs prior to the preceding two sentences.
[j] *sollen*
[k] The following five paragraphs are taken from §4 in accordance with Vaihinger's galley-switching thesis (see Note on texts and translation).

(*Critique*, p. 713).[3] Because pure mathematical cognition, in its propositions, must therefore go beyond the concept to that which is contained in the intuition corresponding to it, its propositions can and must never arise through the analysis of concepts, i.e., analytically, and so are one and all synthetic.

I cannot, however, refrain from noting the damage that neglect of this otherwise seemingly insignificant and unimportant observation has brought upon philosophy. *Hume*, when he felt the call, worthy of a philosopher, to cast his gaze over the entire field of pure *a priori* cognition, in which the human understanding claims such vast holdings, inadvertently lopped off a whole (and indeed the most considerable) province of the same, namely pure mathematics, by imagining that the nature and so to speak the legal constitution of this province rested on completely different principles, namely solely on the principle of contradiction; and although he had by no means made a classification of propositions as formally and generally, or with the nomenclature, as I have here, it was nonetheless just as if he had said: Pure mathematics contains only *analytic* propositions, but metaphysics contains synthetic propositions *a priori*. Now he erred severely in this, and this error had decisively damaging consequences for his entire conception. For had he not done this, he would have expanded his question about the origin of our synthetic judgments far beyond his metaphysical concept of causality and extended it also to the possibility of *a priori* mathematics; [4:273] for he would have had to accept mathematics as synthetic as well. But then he would by no means have been able to found his metaphysical propositions on mere experience, for otherwise he would have had to subject the axioms of pure mathematics to experience as well, which he was much too reasonable to do.[4] The good company in which metaphysics would then have come to be situated would have secured it against the danger of scornful mistreatment; for the blows that were intended for the latter would have had to strike the former as well,

---

[3] See pp. 178–9.

[4] In fact, in the *Treatise* Hume had raised objections to the notions of equality and congruence (among others) in geometry, which objections appealed to experience (*Treatise*, I.ii.4, pp. 42–53), thereby subjecting mathematics to experience, and he also rejected the conception that mathematics considers its objects independently of their existence in nature; in the *Inquiry* he ascribed the basis of mathematics to judgments of relations of ideas, that is, to propositions which "are discoverable by the mere operation of thought, without dependence on what is any where existent in the universe" (sec. 4, pt. 1). (In 1783 Kant would not have been directly acquainted with the *Treatise*.)

which was not his intention, and could not have been; and so the acute man would have been drawn into reflections which must have been similar to those with which we are now occupied, but which would have gained infinitely from his inimitably fine presentation.[5]

3.[1] *Properly metaphysical* judgments are one and all synthetic. Judgments *belonging to metaphysics* must be distinguished from *properly metaphysical* judgments. Very many among the former are analytic, but they merely provide the means to metaphysical judgments, toward which the aim of the science is completely directed, and which are always synthetic. For if concepts belong to metaphysics, e.g., that of substance, then necessarily the judgments arising from their mere analysis belong to metaphysics as well, e.g., substance is that which exists only as subject, etc., and through several such analytic judgments we try to approach the definition of those concepts. Since, however, the analysis of a pure concept of the understanding (such as metaphysics contains) does not proceed in a different manner from the analysis of any other, even empirical, concept which does not belong to metaphysics (e.g., air is an elastic fluid, the elasticity of which is not lost with any known degree of cold), therefore the concept may indeed be properly metaphysical, but not the analytic judgment; for this science possesses something special and proper to it in the generation of its *a priori* cognitions, which generation must therefore be distinguished from what this science has in common with all other cognitions of the understanding; thus, e.g., the proposition: All that is substance in things persists, is a synthetic and properly metaphysical proposition.

If one has previously assembled, according to fixed principles, the *a priori* concepts that constitute the material of metaphysics and make up its building blocks, then the analysis of these concepts is of great value; it can even be presented separately from all the synthetic propositions that [4:274] constitute metaphysics itself, as a special part (as it were as *philosophia definitiva*)[6] containing nothing but analytic propositions belonging to metaphysics. For in fact such analyses do not have much use anywhere

---

[1] The numeral three is added in accordance with Vaihinger's thesis.

[5] In the corresponding section of the *Critique of Pure Reason* (B 17–18), a paragraph on natural science occurs here, with the heading: "Natural science (*physica*) contains within itself synthetic judgments *a priori*"; as examples of such judgments, it gives the conservation of the quantity of matter in the world, and the equality of action and reaction.

[6] Compare Friedrich Christian Baumeister (1709–85), *Philosophia definitiva*, new edn. (Vienna, 1775; first published in Wittenberg, 1733).

except in metaphysics, i.e., with a view toward the synthetic propositions that are to be generated from such previously analyzed concepts.

The conclusion of this section is therefore: that metaphysics properly
has to do with synthetic propositions *a priori*, and these alone constitute
its aim, for which it indeed requires many analyses of its concepts
(therefore many analytic judgments), in which analyses, though, the
procedure is no different from that in any other type of cognition when
one seeks simply to make its concepts clear through analysis. But the
generation of cognition *a priori*, in accordance with both intuition and
concepts, ultimately of synthetic propositions *a priori* as well, and
specifically in philosophical cognition, forms the essential content of
metaphysics.

[4:270]

§3

Note on the general division of judgments into analytic and synthetic

This division is indispensable with regard to the critique of human
understanding, and therefore deserves to be *classical* in it; other than
that I don't know that it has much utility anywhere else. And in this I
find the reason why dogmatic philosophers (who always sought the
sources of metaphysical judgments only in metaphysics itself, and not
outside it in the pure laws of reason in general) neglected this division,
which appears to come forward of itself, and, like the famous *Wolff*, or
the acute *Baumgarten* following in his footsteps,[7] could try to find the
proof of the principle of sufficient reason, which obviously is synthetic,
in the principle of contradiction.[8] By contrast I find a hint of this
division already in *Locke's* essays on human understanding. For in Book
4, chapter 3, §9 f., after he had already discussed the various connections
of representations[9] in judgments and the sources of the connections, of
which he located the one in identity or contradiction (analytic judgments) but the other in the existence of representations in a subject

---

[7] Christian Wolff (1679–1754) was the most important German philosopher of the mid-eighteenth
century; Alexander Gottlieb Baumgarten (1714–62) was an important follower.

[8] Baumgarten, *Metaphysica*, 7th edn. (Halle, 1779), §§10, 20–22. (On this work and Kant's
familiarity with it, see the Introduction.)

[9] In his description of Locke's work, Kant uses the term *Vorstellungen* for what Locke called
"ideas"; Kant's term is here translated as "representation," as in the rest of this volume.

(synthetic judgments), he then acknowledges in §10 that our cognition (*a priori*) of these last is very constricted and almost nothing at all. But there is so little that is definite and reduced to rules in what he says about this type of cognition, that it is no wonder if no one, and in particular not even *Hume*, was prompted by it to contemplate propositions of this type. For such general yet nonetheless definite principles are not easily learned from others who have only had them floating obscurely before them. One must first have come to them oneself through one's own reflection, after which one also finds them elsewhere, where one certainly would not have found them before, because the authors did not even know themselves that their own remarks were grounded on such an idea. Those who never think for themselves in this way nevertheless possess the quick-sightedness to spy everything, after it has been shown to them, in what has already been said elsewhere, where no one at all could see it before.

General Question of the Prolegomena
Is metaphysics possible at all?

§4

If a metaphysics that could assert itself as science were actual, if one could say: here is metaphysics, you need only to learn it, and it will convince you of its truth irresistibly and immutably, then this question would be unnecessary, and there would remain only that question which would pertain more to a test of our acuteness than to a proof of the existence of the subject matter itself, namely: *how it is possible*, and how reason should set about attaining it. Now it has not gone so well for human reason in this case. One can point to no single book, as for instance one presents a *Euclid*, and say: this is metaphysics, here you will find the highest aim of this science, knowledge[a] of a supreme being and a future life, proven from principles of pure reason. For one can indeed show us many propositions that are apodictically certain and have never been disputed; but these are collectively analytic and pertain more to the materials and building blocks of metaphysics than to the expansion of knowledge, which after all ought to be our real aim for it (§2c). But although you present synthetic propositions as well (e.g., the principle of sufficient reason), which you have never proven from bare reason and consequently *a priori*, as was indeed your obligation, and which are gladly ceded to you all the same: then if you want to use them toward your main goal, you still fall into assertions so illicit and precarious that one metaphysics has always contradicted the other,

---

[a] *Erkenntnis*

24

either in regard to the assertions themselves or their proofs, and thereby metaphysics has itself destroyed its claim to lasting approbation. The very attempts to bring such a science into existence were without doubt the original cause of the skepticism that arose so early, a mode of thinking in which reason moves against itself with such violence that it never could have arisen except in complete despair as regards satisfaction of reason's most important aims. For long before we began to question nature methodically, we questioned just our isolated reason, [4:272] which already was practiced to a certain extent through common experience: for reason surely is present to us always, but laws of nature must normally be sought out painstakingly; and so metaphysics was floating at the top like foam, though in such a way that as soon as what had been drawn off had dissolved, more showed itself on the surface, which some always gathered up eagerly, while others, instead of seeking the cause of this phenomenon in the depths, thought themselves wise in mocking the fruitless toil of the former.[b]

Weary therefore of dogmatism, which teaches us nothing, and also of [4:274] skepticism, which promises us absolutely nothing at all, not even the tranquility of a permitted ignorance; summoned by the importance of the knowledge[c] that we need, and made mistrustful, through long experience, with respect to any knowledge that we believe we possess or that offers itself to us under the title of pure reason, there remains left for us but one critical question, the answer to which can regulate our future conduct: *Is metaphysics possible at all?* But this question must not be answered by skeptical objections to particular assertions of an actual metaphysics (for at present we still allow none to be valid), but out of the still *problematic* concept of such a science.

In the *Critique of Pure Reason* I worked on this question *synthetically,* namely by inquiring within pure reason itself, and seeking to determine within this source both the elements and the laws of its pure use, according to principles. This work is difficult and requires a resolute reader to think himself little by little into a system that takes no foundation as given except reason itself, and that therefore tries to develop cognition out of its original seeds without relying on any fact whatever. *Prolegomena* should by contrast be preparatory exercises; they ought more to indicate what needs to be done in order to bring a science

[b] Here followed the five paragraphs that have been placed in §2 (pp. 19–22).
[c] *Erkenntnis*

[4:275] into existence if possible, than to present the science itself. They must therefore rely on something already known to be dependable, from which we can go forward with confidence and ascend to the sources, which are not yet known, and whose discovery not only will explain what is known already, but will also exhibit an area with many cognitions that all arise from these same sources. The methodological procedure of prolegomena, and especially of those that are to prepare for a future metaphysics, will therefore be *analytic*.

Fortunately, it happens that, even though we cannot assume that metaphysics as science is *actual*, we can confidently say that some pure synthetic cognition *a priori* is actual and given, namely, *pure mathematics* and *pure natural science*; for both contain propositions that are fully acknowledged, some as apodictically certain through bare reason, some from universal agreement with experience (though these are still recognized as independent of experience). We have therefore some at least *uncontested* synthetic cognition *a priori*, and we do not need to ask whether it is possible (for it is actual), but only: *how it is possible*, in order to be able to derive, from the principle of the possibility of the given cognition, the possibility of all other synthetic cognition *a priori*.

Prolegomena
General Question
How is cognition from pure reason possible?

§5

We have seen above the vast difference between analytic and synthetic judgments. The possibility of analytic propositions could be comprehended very easily; for it is founded solely upon the principle of contradiction. The possibility of synthetic propositions *a posteriori*, i.e., of such as are drawn from experience, also requires no special explanation; for experience itself is nothing other than a continual conjoining (synthesis) of perceptions. There remain for us therefore only synthetic propositions *a priori*, whose possibility must be sought or investigated, since it must rest on principles other than the principle of contradiction.

Here, however, we do not need first to seek the *possibility* of such [4:276] propositions, i.e., to ask whether they are possible. For there are plenty of them actually given, and indeed with indisputable certainty, and since the method we are now following is to be analytic, we will consequently start from the position: that such synthetic but pure rational cognition is actual; but we must nonetheless next *investigate* the ground of this possibility, and ask: *how* this cognition is possible, so that we put ourselves in a position to determine, from the principles of its possibility, the conditions of its use and the extent and boundaries of the same. Expressed with scholastic precision, the exact problem on which everything hinges is therefore:

How are synthetic propositions a priori *possible?*

For the sake of popularity I have expressed this problem somewhat differently above, namely as a question about cognition from pure reason, which I could well have done on this occasion without disadvantage for the desired insight; for, since we assuredly have to do here only with metaphysics and its sources, it will, I hope, always be kept in mind, following the earlier reminders, that when we here speak of cognition from pure reason, the discussion is never about analytic cognition, but only synthetic.*

[4:277]   Whether metaphysics is to stand or fall, and hence its existence, now depends entirely on the solving of this problem. Anyone may present his contentions on the matter with ever so great a likelihood, piling conclusion on conclusion to the point of suffocation; if he has not been able beforehand to answer this question satisfactorily then I have the right to say: it is all empty, baseless philosophy and false wisdom. You speak through pure reason and pretend as it were to create *a priori* cognitions, not only by analyzing given concepts, but by alleging new connections that are not based on the principle of contradiction and that you nonetheless presume to understand completely independently of all experience; now how do you come to this, and how will you justify such pretenses? You cannot be allowed to call on the concurrence of general common sense; for that is a witness whose standing is based solely on public rumor.

Quodcunque ostendis mihi sic, incredulus odi.

Horat.[1]

---

* When knowledge^a moves forward little by little, it cannot be helped that certain expressions which already have become classical, having been present from the very infancy of science, subsequently should be found insufficient and badly suited, and that a certain, newer and more apt usage should fall into danger of being confused with the old one. The analytic method, insofar as it is opposed to the synthetic, is something completely different from a collection of analytic propositions; it signifies only that one proceeds from that which is sought as if it were given, and ascends to the conditions under which alone it is possible. In this method one often uses nothing but synthetic propositions, as mathematical analysis exemplifies, and it might better be called the *regressive* method to distinguish it from the synthetic or *progressive* method. Again the name analytic is also found as a principal division of logic, and there it is the logic of truth and is opposed to dialectic, without actually looking to see whether the cognitions belonging to that logic are analytic or synthetic.

^a *Erkenntnis*
[1] "Whatsoever you show me thusly, unbelieving, I hate it." Horace, *Epistles*, II. iii.188.

As indispensable as it is, however, to answer this question, at the same time it is just as difficult; and although the principal reason why the answer has not long since been sought rests in the fact that it had occurred to no one that such a thing could be asked, nonetheless a second reason is that a satisfactory answer to this one question requires more assiduous, deeper, and more painstaking reflection than the most prolix work of metaphysics ever did, which promised its author immortality on its first appearance. Also, every perceptive reader, if he carefully ponders what this problem demands, being frightened at first by its difficulty, is bound to consider it insoluble and, if such pure synthetic cognitions *a priori* were not actual, altogether impossible; which is what actually befell *David Hume*, although he was far from conceiving the question in such universality as it is here, and as it must be if the reply is to be decisive for all metaphysics. For how is it possible, asked the acute man, that when I am given one concept I can go beyond it and connect another one to it that is not contained in it, and can indeed do so, as though the latter *necessarily* belonged to the former? Only experience can provide us with such connections (so he concluded from this difficulty, which he took for an impossibility), and all of this supposed necessity – or, what is the same – this cognition taken for *a priori*, is nothing but a long-standing habit of finding something to be true and consequently of taking subjective necessity to be objective.

If the reader complains about the toil and trouble that I will give him with the solution to this problem, he need only make the attempt to [4:278] solve it more easily himself. Perhaps he will then feel himself obliged to the one who has taken on a task of such profound inquiry for him, and will rather allow himself to express some amazement over the ease with which the solution could still be given, considering the nature of the matter; for indeed it cost years of toil to solve this problem in its full universality[b] (as this word is understood by the mathematicians, namely, as sufficient for all cases), and also ultimately to be able to present it in analytic form, as the reader will find it here.

All metaphysicians are therefore solemnly and lawfully suspended from their occupations until such a time as they will have satisfactorily answered the question: *How are synthetic cognitions* a priori *possible?* For

[b] *Allgemeinheit*

in this answer alone consists the credential which they must present if they have something to advance to us in the name of pure reason; in default of which, however, they can expect only that reasonable persons, who have been deceived so often already, will reject their offerings without any further investigation.

If, on the contrary, they want to put forth their occupation not as *science*, but as an *art* of beneficial persuasions accommodated to general common sense, then they cannot justly be barred from this trade. They will then use the modest language of reasonable belief, they will acknowledge that it is not allowed them even once *to guess*, let alone to *know*,ᶜsomething about that which lies beyond the boundaries of all possible experience, but only *to assume* something about it (not for speculative use, for they must renounce that, but solely for practical use), as is possible and even indispensable for the guidance of the understanding and will in life. Only thus will they be able to call themselves useful and wise men, the more so, the more they renounce the name of metaphysicians; for metaphysicians want to be speculative philosophers, and since one cannot aim for vapid probabilities when judgments *a priori* are at stake (for what is alleged to be cognized *a priori* is thereby announced as necessary), it cannot be permitted them to play

[4:279] with guesses, but rather their assertions must be science or they are nothing at all.

It can be said that the whole of transcendental philosophy, which necessarily precedes all of metaphysics, is itself nothing other than simply the complete solution of the question presented here, but in systematic order and detail, and that until now there has therefore been no transcendental philosophy; for what goes under this name is really a part of metaphysics, but this science is to settle the possibility of metaphysics in the first place, and therefore must precede all metaphysics. Hence there need be no surprise because a science is needed that is utterly deprived of assistance from other sciences and hence is in itself completely new, in order just to answer a single question adequately, when the solution to it is conjoined with trouble and difficulty and even with some obscurity.

In now setting to work on this solution – and indeed following the analytic method, in which we presuppose that such cognitions from

ᶜ *wissen*

30

pure reason are actual – we can appeal to only two *sciences* of theoretical knowledge (which alone is being discussed here), namely, *pure mathematics* and *pure natural science*; for only these can present objects to us in intuition, and consequently, if they happen to contain an *a priori* cognition, can show its truth or correspondence with the object *in concreto*, i.e., *its actuality*, from which one could then proceed along the analytic path to the ground of its possibility. This greatly facilitates the work, in which general considerations are not only applied to facts, but even start from them, instead of, as in the synthetic procedure, having to be derived wholly *in abstracto* from concepts.

But in order to ascend from these pure *a priori* cognitions (which are not only actual but also well-founded) to a possible cognition that we seek – namely, a metaphysics as science – we need to comprehend under our main question that which gives rise to metaphysics and which underlies its purely naturally given (though not above suspicion as regards truth) cognition *a priori* (which cognition, when pursued without any critical investigation of its possibility, is normally called metaphysics already) – in a word, the natural disposition to such a science; and so the main transcendental question, divided into four [4:280] other questions, will be answered step by step:

1. How is pure mathematics possible?
2. How is pure natural science possible?
3. How is metaphysics in general possible?
4. How is metaphysics as science possible?

It can be seen that even if the solution to these problems is intended principally to present the essential content of the *Critique*, still it also possesses something distinctive that is worthy of attention in its own right, namely, the search for the sources of given sciences in reason itself, in order to investigate and to measure out for reason, by way of the deed itself, its power to cognize something *a priori*; whereby these sciences themselves then benefit, if not with respect to their content, nonetheless as regards their proper practice, and, while bringing light to a higher question regarding their common origin, they simultaneously provide occasion for a better explanation of their own nature.

The Main Transcendental Question
First Part
How is pure mathematics possible?

§6

Here now is a great and proven body of cognition,[a] which is already of admirable extent and promises unlimited expansion in the future, which carries with it thoroughly apodictic certainty (i.e., absolute necessity), hence rests on no grounds of experience, and so is a pure product of reason, but beyond this is thoroughly synthetic. "How is it possible then for human reason to achieve such cognition wholly *a priori*?" Does not this capacity, since it is not, and cannot be, based on experience, presuppose some *a priori* basis for cognition, which lies deeply hidden, but which might reveal itself through these its effects, if their first beginnings were only diligently tracked down?

[4:281]

§7

We find, however, that all mathematical cognition has this distinguishing feature, that it must present its concept beforehand *in intuition* and indeed *a priori*, consequently in an intuition that is not empirical but pure, without which means it cannot take a single step; therefore its judgments are always *intuitive*,[b] in the place of which philosophy can content itself with *discursive*[c] judgments *from mere concepts*, and can indeed exemplify its apodictic teachings through intuition[d] but can

---

[a] *eine grosse und bewährte Erkenntnis*   [b] *intuitiv*   [c] *diskursiven*   [d] *Anschauung*

never derive them from it. This observation with respect to the nature of mathematics already guides us toward the first and highest condition of its possibility; namely, it must be grounded in some *pure intuition* or other, in which it can present, or, as one calls it, *construct* all of its concepts *in concreto* yet *a priori.** If we could discover this pure intuition and its possibility, then from there it could easily be explained how synthetic *a priori* propositions are possible in pure mathematics, and consequently also how this science itself is possible; for just as empirical intuition makes it possible for us, without difficulty, to amplify (synthetically in experience) the concept we form of an object of intuition through new predicates that are presented by intuition itself, so too will pure intuition do the same, only with this difference: that in the latter case the synthetic judgment will be *a priori* certain and apodictic, but in the former only *a posteriori* and empirically certain, because the former only contains what is met with in contingent empirical intuition, while the latter contains what necessarily must be met with in pure intuition, since it is, as intuition *a priori*, inseparably bound with the concept *before all experience* or individual perception.

§8

But with this step the difficulty seems to grow rather than diminish. For now the question runs: *How is it possible to intuit something* a priori? An intuition is a representation of the sort which would depend immediately on the presence of an object. It therefore seems impossible [4:282] *originally* to intuit *a priori*, since then the intuition would have to occur without an object being present, either previously or now, to which it could refer, and so it could not be an intuition. Concepts are indeed of the kind that we can quite well form some of them for ourselves *a priori* (namely, those that contain only the thinking of an object in general) without our being in an immediate relation to an object, e.g., the concept of quantity, of cause, etc.; but even these still require, in order to provide them with meaning and sense, a certain use *in concreto*, i.e., application to some intuition or other, by which an

---

* See *Critique* p. 713.[1]

[1] See pp. 178–9.

object for them is given to us. But how can the *intuition* of an object precede the object itself?

<h2 style="text-align:center">§9</h2>

If our intuition had to be of the kind that represented things *as they are in themselves*, then absolutely no intuition *a priori* would take place, but it would always be empirical. For I can only know what may be contained in the object in itself if the object is present and given to me. Of course, even then it is incomprehensible how the intuition of a thing that is present should allow me to cognize it the way it is in itself, since its properties cannot migrate over into my power of representation; but even granting such a possibility, the intuition still would not take place *a priori*, i.e., before the object were presented to me, for without that no basis for the relation of my representation to the object can be conceived; so it would have to be based on inspiration. There is therefore only one way possible for my intuition to precede the actuality of the object and occur as an *a priori* cognition, *namely if it contains nothing else except the form of sensibility, which in me as subject precedes all actual impressions through which I am affected by objects.* For I can know *a priori* that the objects of the senses can be intuited only in accordance with this form of sensibility. From this it follows: that propositions which relate only to this form of sensory intuition will be possible and valid for objects of the senses; also, conversely, that intuitions which are possible *a priori* can never relate to things other than objects of our senses.

[4:283]

<h2 style="text-align:center">§10</h2>

Therefore it is only by means of the form of sensory intuition that we can intuit things *a priori*, though by this means we can cognize objects only as they *appear* to us (to our senses), not as they may be in themselves; and this supposition is utterly necessary, if synthetic propositions *a priori* are to be granted as possible, or, in case they are actually encountered, if their possibility is to be conceived and determined in advance.

Now space and time are the intuitions upon which pure mathematics bases all its cognitions and judgments, which come forward as at once apodictic and necessary; for mathematics must first exhibit all of its concepts in intuition – and pure mathematics in pure intuition – i.e., it must first construct them, failing which (since mathematics cannot proceed analytically, namely, through the analysis of concepts, but only synthetically) it is impossible for it to advance a step, that is, as long as it lacks pure intuition, in which alone the material^e for synthetic judgments *a priori* can be given. Geometry bases itself on the pure intuition of space. Even arithmetic forms its concepts of numbers through successive addition of units in time, but above all pure mechanics can form its concepts of motion only by means of the representation of time.[2] Both representations are, however, merely intuitions; for, if one eliminates from the empirical intuitions of bodies and their alterations (motion) everything empirical, that is, that which belongs to sensation, then space and time still remain, which are therefore pure intuitions that underlie *a priori* the empirical intuitions, and for that reason can never themselves be eliminated; but, by the very fact that they are pure intuitions *a priori*, they prove that they are mere forms of our sensibility that must precede all empirical intuition (i.e., the perception of actual objects), and in accordance with which objects can be cognized *a priori*, though of course only as they appear to us.

§11

The problem of the present section is therefore solved. Pure mathematics, as synthetic cognition *a priori*, is possible only because it refers to no other objects than mere objects of the senses, the empirical intuition of which is based on a pure and indeed *a priori* intuition (of [4:284] space and time), and can be so based because this pure intuition is nothing but the mere form of sensibility, which precedes the actual appearance of objects, since it in fact first makes this appearance possible. This faculty of intuiting *a priori* does not, however, concern the matter of appearance – i.e., that which is sensation in the appearance, for that constitutes the empirical – but only the form of appearance, space and time. If anyone wishes to doubt in the slightest that the two are not determinations inhering in things in themselves but

---

^e *Stoff*

[2] Kant developed his analysis of motion and time in the *Metaphysical Foundations of Natural Science*.

only mere determinations inhering in the relation of those things to sensibility, I would very much like to know how he can find it possible to know, *a priori* and therefore before all acquaintance with things, how their intuition must be constituted – which certainly is the case here with space and time. But this is completely comprehensible as soon as the two are taken for nothing more than formal conditions of our sensibility, and objects are taken merely for appearances; for then the form of appearance, i.e., the pure intuition, certainly can be represented from ourselves, i.e., *a priori*.

§*12*

In order to add something by way of illustration and confirmation, we need only to consider the usual and unavoidably necessary procedure of the geometers. All proofs of the thoroughgoing equality of two given figures (that one can in all parts be put in the place of the other) ultimately come down to this: that they are congruent with one another; which plainly is nothing other than a synthetic proposition based upon immediate intuition; and this intuition must be given pure and *a priori*, for otherwise that proposition could not be granted as apodictically certain but would have only empirical certainty. It would only mean: we observe it always to be so and the proposition holds only as far as our perception has reached until now. That full-standing space (a space that is itself not the boundary of another space)[3] has three dimensions, and that space in general cannot have more, is built upon the proposition that not more than three lines can cut each other at right angles in one point; this proposition can, however, by no means be proven from [4:285] concepts, but rests immediately upon intuition, and indeed on pure *a priori* intuition, because it is apodictically certain; indeed, that we can require that a line should be drawn to infinity (*in indefinitum*), or that a series of changes (e.g., spaces traversed through motion) should be continued to infinity, presupposes a representation of space and of time that can only inhere in intuition, that is, insofar as the latter is not in itself bounded by anything;[4] for this could never be concluded from concepts. Therefore pure intuitions *a priori* indeed actually do underlie

---

[3] In Euclid's *Elements* points are said to be the extremities or boundaries of lines and lines of planes (Bk. 1, defs. 3, 6, 13); planes are boundaries of spaces (Bk. 11, def. 2).
[4] See also Selections, pp. 164–5.

mathematics, and make possible its synthetic and apodictically valid propositions; and consequently our transcendental deduction of the concepts of space and time[5] at the same time explains the possibility of a pure mathematics, a possibility which, without such a deduction, and without our assuming that "everything which our senses may be given (the outer in space, the inner in time) is only intuited by us as it appears to us, not as it is in itself," could indeed be granted, but into which we could have no insight at all.

§13

All those who cannot yet get free of the conception, as if space and time were actual qualities attaching to things in themselves, can exercise their acuity on the following paradox, and, if they have sought its solution in vain, can then, free of prejudice at least for a few moments, suppose that perhaps the demotion of space and of time to mere forms of our sensory intuition may indeed have foundation.

If two things are fully the same (in all determinations belonging to magnitude and quality) in all the parts of each that can always be cognized by itself alone, it should indeed then follow that one, in all cases and respects, can be put in the place of the other, without this exchange causing the least recognizable difference. In fact this is how things stand with plane figures in geometry; yet various spherical figures,[6] notwithstanding this sort of complete inner agreement, nonetheless reveal such a difference in outer relation that one cannot in any case be put in the place of the other; e.g., two spherical triangles from each of the hemispheres, which have an arc of the equator for a common base, can be fully equal with respect to their sides as well as their angles, so that nothing will be found in either, when it is fully described by [4:286] itself, that is not also in the description of the other, and still one cannot be put in the place of the other (that is, in the opposite hemisphere); and here is then after all an *inner* difference between the triangles that no understanding can specify as inner, and that reveals itself only through the outer relation in space. But I will cite more familiar instances that can be taken from ordinary life.

[5] For another mention of a deduction relating to space and time, see Selections, p. 173.
[6] A spherical figure is one inscribed in the surface of a sphere.

What indeed can be more similar to, and in all parts more equal to, my hand or my ear than its image in the mirror? And yet I cannot put such a hand as is seen in the mirror in the place of its original; for if the one was a right hand, then the other in the mirror is a left, and the image of the right ear is a left one, which can never take the place of the former. Now there are no inner differences here that any understanding could merely think; and yet the differences are inner as far as the senses teach, for the left hand cannot, after all, be enclosed within the same boundaries as the right (they cannot be made congruent), despite all reciprocal equality and similarity; one hand's glove cannot be used on the other. What then is the solution? These objects are surely not representations of things as they are in themselves, and as the pure understanding would cognize them, rather, they are sensory intuitions, i.e., appearances, whose possibility rests on the relation of certain things, unknown in themselves, to something else, namely our sensibility. Now, space is the form of outer intuition of this sensibility, and the inner determination of any space is possible only through the determination of the outer relation to the whole space of which the space is a part (the relation to outer sense); that is, the part is possible only through the whole, which never occurs with things in themselves as objects of the understanding alone, but does occur with mere appearances. We can therefore make the difference between similar and equal but nonetheless incongruent things (e.g., oppositely spiralled snails) intelligible through no concept alone, but only through the relation to right-hand and left-hand, which refers immediately to intuition.

[4:287]

Note I

Pure mathematics, and especially pure geometry, can have objective reality only under the single condition that it refers merely to objects of the senses, with regard to which objects, however, the principle remains fixed, that our sensory representation is by no means a representation of things in themselves, but only of the way in which they appear to us. From this it follows, not at all that the propositions of geometry are determinations of a mere figment of our poetic phantasy,[7] and therefore

---

[7] The word "phantasy" refers to the faculty of imagination.

38

could not with certainty be referred to actual objects, but rather, that they are valid necessarily for space and consequently for everything that may be found in space, because space is nothing other than the form of all outer appearances, under which alone objects of the senses can be given to us. Sensibility, whose form lies at the foundation of geometry, is that upon which the possibility of outer appearances rests; these, therefore, can never contain anything other than what geometry prescribes to them. It would be completely different if the senses had to represent objects as they are in themselves. For then it absolutely would not follow from the representation of space, a representation that serves *a priori*, with all the various properties of space, as foundation for the geometer, that all of this, together with what is deduced from it, must be exactly so in nature. The space of the geometer would be taken for mere fabrication and would be credited with no objective validity, because it is simply not to be seen how things would have to agree necessarily with the image that we form of them by ourselves and in advance. If, however, this image – or, better, this formal intuition – is the essential property of our sensibility by means of which alone objects are given to us, and if this sensibility represents not things in themselves but only their appearances, then it is very easy to comprehend, and at the same time to prove incontrovertibly: that all outer objects of our sensible world must necessarily agree, in complete exactitude, with the propositions of geometry, because sensibility itself, through its form of outer intuition (space), with which the geometer deals, first makes those objects possible, as mere appearances. It will forever remain a remarkable phenomenon in the history of philosophy that there was a time when even mathematicians who were at the same time philosophers began to doubt, not, indeed, the correctness of their geometrical [4:288] propositions insofar as they related merely to space, but the objective validity and application to nature of this concept itself and all its geometrical determinations, since they were concerned that a line in nature might indeed be composed of physical points, consequently that true space in objects might be composed of simple parts, notwithstanding that the space which the geometer holds in thought can by no means be composed of such things. They did not realize that this space in thought itself makes possible physical space, i.e., the extension of matter; that this space is by no means a property of things in themselves, but only a form of our power of sensory representation; that all objects in space are mere appearances, i.e., not things in themselves but representations of our sensory intuition; and that, since space as the geometer thinks it is precisely the form of sensory intuition which we find in ourselves *a priori* and which contains the ground of the possibility of all outer appearances (with respect to their form), these appearances must of necessity and with the greatest precision harmonize with the propositions of the geometer, which he extracts not from any fabricated concept, but from the subjective foundation of all outer appearances, namely sensibility itself. In this and no other way can the geometer be secured, regarding the indubitable objective reality of his propositions, against all the chicaneries of a shallow metaphysics, however strange this way must seem to such a metaphysics because it does not go back to the sources of its concepts.

Note II

Everything that is to be given to us as object must be given to us in intuition. But all our intuition happens only by means of the senses; the understanding intuits nothing, but only reflects. Because the senses, in accordance with what has just been proven, never and in no single instance enable us to cognize things in themselves, but only their appearances, and as these are mere representations of sensibility, "consequently all bodies together with the space in which they are found must be taken for nothing but mere representations in us, and exist nowhere else than merely in our thoughts." Now is this not manifest idealism?[8]

[4:289]   Idealism consists in the claim that there are none other than thinking beings; the other things that we believe we perceive in intuition are only representations in thinking beings, to which in fact no object existing outside these beings corresponds. I say in opposition: There are things given to us as objects of our senses existing outside us, yet we know[f] nothing of them as they may be in themselves, but are acquainted[g] only with their appearances, i.e., with the representations that they produce in us because they affect our senses. Accordingly, I by all means avow

---

[f] *wissen*   [g] *kennen*

[8] The charge that Kant was a traditional sort of idealist appears in the Garve–Feder review, to which he explicitly responds on pp.127–34.

that there are bodies outside us, i.e., things which, though completely unknown[h] to us as to what they may be in themselves, we know[i] through the representations which their influence on our sensibility provides for us, and to which we give the name of a body – which word therefore merely means the appearance of this object that is unknown to us but is nonetheless real. Can this be called idealism? It is the very opposite of it.

That one could, without detracting from the actual existence of outer things, say of a great many of their predicates: they belong not to these things in themselves, but only to their appearances and have no existence of their own outside our representation, is something that was generally accepted and acknowledged long before *Locke's* time, though more commonly thereafter. To these predicates belong warmth, color, taste, etc. That I, however, even beyond these, include (for weighty reasons) also among mere appearances the remaining qualities of bodies, which are called *primarias*: extension, place, and more generally space along with everything that depends on it (impenetrability or materiality, shape, etc.), is something against which not the least ground of uncertainty can be raised; and as little as someone can be called an idealist because he wants to admit colors as properties that attach not to the object in itself, but only to the sense of vision as modifications, just as little can my system be called idealist simply because I find that even more of, *nay, all of the properties that make up the intuition of a body* belong merely to its appearance: for the existence of the thing that appears is not thereby nullified, as with real idealism, but it is only shown that through the senses we cannot cognize it at all as it is in itself.

I would very much like to know how then my claims must be framed so as not to contain any idealism. Without doubt I would have to say: that the representation of space not only is perfectly in accordance with the relation that our sensibility has to objects, for I have said that, but [4:290] that it is even fully similar to the object; an assertion with which I can connect no meaning, as little as with the assertion that the sensation of red is similar to the property of cinnabar that excites this sensation in me.

---

[h] *unbekannt*   [i] *kennen*

Note III

From this an easily foreseen but empty objection can now be quite easily rejected: "namely that through the ideality of space and time the whole sensible world would be transformed into sheer illusion."[9] After all philosophical insight into the nature of sensory cognition had previously been perverted by making sensibility into merely a confused kind of representation, through which we might still cognize things as they are but without having the ability to bring everything in this representation of ours to clear consciousness, we showed on the contrary that sensibility consists not in this logical difference of clarity or obscurity, but in the genetic difference of the origin of the cognition itself, since sensory cognition does not at all represent things as they are but only in the way in which they affect our senses, and therefore that through the senses mere appearances, not the things themselves, are given to the understanding for reflection; from this necessary correction an objection arises, springing from an inexcusable and almost deliberate misinterpretation, as if my system transformed all the things of the sensible world into sheer illusion.

If an appearance is given to us, we are still completely free as to how we want to judge things from it. The former, namely the appearance, was based on the senses, but the judgment on the understanding, and the only question is whether there is truth in the determination of the object or not. The difference between truth and dream, however, is not decided through the quality of the representations that are referred to objects, for they are the same in both, but through their connection according to the rules that determine the combination of representations in the concept of an object, and how far they can or cannot stand together in one experience. And then it is not the fault of the appearances at all, if our cognition takes illusion for truth, i.e., if [4:291] intuition, through which an object is given to us, is taken for the concept of the object, or even for its existence, which only the understanding can think. The course of the planets is represented to us by the senses as now progressive, now retrogressive, and herein is neither falsehood nor truth, because as long as one grants that this is as yet only appearance, one still does not judge at all the objective quality of their

[9] This charge represents the tenor of the Garve–Feder review.

motion. Since, however, if the understanding has not taken good care to prevent this subjective mode of representation from being taken for objective, a false judgment can easily arise, one therefore says: they appear to go backwards; but the illusion is not ascribed to the senses, but to the understanding, whose lot alone it is to render an objective judgment from the appearance.

In this manner, if we do not reflect at all on the origin of our representations, and we connect our intuitions of the senses, whatever they may contain, in space and time according to rules for the combination of all cognition in one experience, then either deceptive illusion or truth can arise, according to whether we are heedless or careful; that concerns only the use of sensory representations in the understanding, and not their origin. In the same way, if I take all the representations of the senses together with their form, namely space and time, for nothing but appearances, and these last two for a mere form of sensibility that is by no means to be found outside it in the objects, and I make use of these same representations only in relation to possible experience: then in the fact that I take them for mere appearances is contained not the least illusion or temptation toward error; for they nonetheless can be connected together correctly in experience according to rules of truth. In this manner all the propositions of geometry hold good for space as well as for all objects of the senses, and hence for all possible experience, whether I regard space as a mere form of sensibility or as something inhering in things themselves; though only in the first case can I comprehend how it may be possible to know those propositions *a priori* for all objects of outer intuition; otherwise, with respect to all merely possible experience, everything remains just as if I had never undertaken this departure from the common opinion.

But if I venture to go beyond all possible experience with my concepts of space and time – which is inevitable if I pass them off for qualities that attach to things in themselves (for what should then prevent me [4:292] from still permitting them to hold good for the very same things, even if my senses might now be differently framed and either suited to them or not?) – then an important error can spring up which rests on an illusion, since I passed off as universally valid that which was a condition for the intuition of things (attaching merely to my subject, and surely valid for all objects of the senses, hence for all merely possible experience), because I referred it to the things in themselves and did not restrict it to conditions of experience.

Therefore, it is so greatly mistaken that my doctrine of the ideality of space and time makes the whole sensible world a mere illusion, that, on the contrary, my doctrine is the only means for securing the application to actual objects of one of the most important bodies of cognition – namely, that which mathematics expounds *a priori* – and for preventing it from being taken for nothing but mere illusion, since without this observation it would be quite impossible to make out whether the intuitions of space and time, which we do not derive from experience but which nevertheless lie *a priori* in our representations, were not mere self-produced fantasies, to which no object at all corresponds, at least not adequately, and therefore geometry itself a mere illusion, whereas we have been able to demonstrate the incontestable validity of geometry with respect to all objects of the sensible world for the very reason that the latter are mere appearances.

Secondly, it is so greatly mistaken that these principles of mine, because they make sensory representations into appearances, are supposed, in place of the truth of experience, to transform sensory representations into mere illusion, that, on the contrary, my principles are the only means of avoiding the transcendental illusion by which metaphysics has always been deceived and thereby tempted into the childish endeavor of chasing after soap bubbles, because appearances, which after all are mere representations, were taken for things in themselves; from which followed all those remarkable enactments of the antinomy of reason, which I will mention later on, and which is removed through this single observation: that appearance, as long as it is used in experience, brings forth truth, but as soon as it passes beyond the boundaries of experience and becomes transcendent, brings forth nothing but sheer illusion.

Since I therefore grant their reality to the things that we represent to ourselves through the senses, and limit our sensory intuition of these [4:293] things only to the extent that in no instance whatsoever, not even in the pure intuitions of space and time, does it represent anything more than mere appearances of these things, and never their quality in themselves, this is therefore no thorough-going illusion ascribed by me to nature, and my protestation against all imputation of idealism is so conclusive and clear that it would even seem superfluous if there were not unauthorized judges who, being glad to have an ancient name for every deviation from their false though common opinion, and never judging the spirit of philosophical nomenclatures but merely clinging to the letter, were ready to put their own folly in the place of well-determined concepts, and thereby to twist and deform them. For the fact that I have myself given to this theory of mine the name of transcendental idealism cannot justify anyone in confusing it with the empirical idealism of *Descartes* (although this idealism was only a problem, whose insolubility left everyone free, in *Descartes'* opinion, to deny the existence of the corporeal world, since the problem could never be answered satisfactorily) or with the mystical and fanatical[10] idealism of *Berkeley* (against which, along with other similar fantasies, our *Critique*, on the contrary, contains the proper antidote).[11] For what I called idealism did not concern the existence of things (the doubting of which, however, properly constitutes idealism according to the received meaning), for it never came into my mind to doubt that, but only the sensory representation of things, to which space and time above all belong; and about these last, hence in general about all *appearances*, I have only shown: that they are not things (but mere modes of representation), nor are they determinations that belong to things in themselves. The word transcendental, however, which with me never means a relation of our cognition to things, but only to the *faculty of cognition*, was intended to prevent this misinterpretation. But before it prompts still more of the same, I gladly withdraw this name, and I will have it called critical idealism. But if it is an in fact reprehensible idealism to transform actual things (not appearances) into mere representations,[12] with what name shall we christen that idealism which,

---

[10] The German word *schwärmerisch*, and the related *Schwärmerei*, can also be translated as "enthusiastical" and "enthusiam," in the sense of religious enthusiasm; the word has the connotation of someone's being guided by imagination and feeling, perhaps to a pathological extreme.

[11] René Descartes (1596–1650) raised a skeptical challenge concerning the existence of bodies in the First of his six *Meditations* (original Latin edition, Amsterdam, 1641), but he in fact claimed to remove it in the Sixth. George Berkeley, Bishop of Cloyne (1685–1753), presented his idealism, which granted existence only to immaterial beings, in the *Treatise Concerning the Principles of Human Knowledge* (Dublin, 1710) and *Three Dialogues between Hylas and Philonous* (London, 1713); his works appeared in German translation in 1781.

[12] At the very end of Berkeley's *Three Dialogues*, Philonous summarizes the immaterialist position by conjoining two phrases that he attributes respectively to "the vulgar" and to philosophers: "that those things they immediately perceive are the real things," and "that the things immediately perceived are ideas which exist only in the mind"; this is in effect to equate things with (mere) ideas or representations.

conversely, makes mere representations into things? I think it could be named *dreaming* idealism, to distinguish it from the preceding, which may be called *fanatical* idealism, both of which were to have been held [4:294] off by my formerly so-called transcendental, or better, *critical* idealism.

The Main Transcendental Question
Second Part
How is pure natural science possible?

§*14*

Nature is the *existence* of things, insofar as that existence is determined according to universal laws. If nature meant the existence of things *in themselves*, we would never be able to cognize it, either *a priori* or *a posteriori*. Not *a priori*, for how are we to know what is suited to things in themselves, since this can never come about through the analysis of our concepts (analytical propositions), since I do not want to know what may be contained in my concept of a thing (for that belongs to its logical being), but what would be added to this concept in the actuality of a thing and through which the thing itself would be determined in its existence apart from my concept. My understanding, and the conditions under which alone it can connect the determinations of things in their existence, prescribes no rule to the things themselves; these do not conform to my understanding, but my understanding would have to conform to them; they would therefore have to be given to me in advance so that these determinations could be taken from them, but then they would not be cognized *a priori*.

Such cognition of the nature of things in themselves would also be impossible *a posteriori*. For if experience is supposed to teach me *laws* to which the existence of things is subject, then these laws, insofar as they relate to things in themselves, would have to apply to them *necessarily* even apart from my experience. Now experience teaches me what there is and how it is, but never that it necessarily must be so and not otherwise. Therefore it can never teach me the nature of things in themselves.

§15

[4:295] Now we are nevertheless in possession of a pure natural science, which, *a priori* and with all of the necessity required for apodictic propositions, propounds laws to which nature is subject. Here I need call to witness only that propaedeutic to the theory of nature which, under the title of universal natural science, precedes all of physics (which is founded on empirical principles). Therein we find mathematics applied to appearances, and also merely discursive principles (from concepts), which make up the philosophical part of pure cognition of nature.[1] But indeed there is also much in it that is not completely pure and independent of the sources of experience, such as the concept of *motion*, of *impenetrability* (on which the empirical concept of matter is based), of *inertia*, among still others, so that it cannot be called completely pure natural science; furthermore it refers only to the objects of the outer senses, and therefore does not provide an example of a universal natural science in the strict sense; for that would have to bring nature in general – whether pertaining to an object of the outer senses or of the inner sense (the object of physics as well as psychology) – under universal laws. But among the principles of this universal physics[2] a few are found that actually have the universality we require, such as the proposition: *that substance remains* and persists, that *everything that happens is* always previously *determined by a cause* according to constant laws, and so on. These are truly universal laws of nature, that exist fully *a priori*. There is then in fact a pure natural science, and now the question is: *How is it possible?*

---

[1] In §§2 and 7 (pp. 18–20, 32), Kant contrasts the *intuitive* judgments of mathematics with the *discursive* judgments of philosophy. In the first *Critique*, A 712–38/B 740–66, he discusses more generally his doctrine that philosophical method involves the analysis of concepts whereas mathematics procedes by "constructing" concepts in intuition. (For A 712–17/B 740–5, see pp. 178–80.)

[2] The word "physics" is here used to mean the science of nature in general, and was understood by many eighteenth-century authors to include the study of living things and of the mind (psychology).

§16

The word *nature* assumes yet another meaning, namely one that determines the *object*, whereas in the above meaning it only signified the *conformity to law* of the determinations of the existence of things in general. Nature considered *materialiter*[3] is the *sum total of all objects of experience*. We are concerned here only with this, since otherwise things, which could never become objects of an experience if they had to be cognized according to their nature, would force us to concepts whose meaning could never be given *in concreto* (in any example of a possible experience), and we would therefore have to make for ourselves mere concepts of the nature of those things, the reality of which concepts, i.e., whether they actually relate to objects or are mere beings of thought, could not be decided at all. Cognition of that which cannot be [4:296] an object of experience would be hyperphysical, and here we are not concerned with such things at all, but rather with that cognition of nature, the reality of which can be confirmed through experience, even though such cognition is possible *a priori* and precedes all experience.

§17

The *formal* in nature in this narrower meaning is therefore the conformity to law of all objects of experience, and, insofar as this conformity is cognized *a priori*, the *necessary* conformity to law of those objects. But it has just been shown: that the laws of nature can never be cognized *a priori* in objects insofar as these objects are considered, not in relation to possible experience, but as things in themselves. We are here, however, concerned not with things in themselves (the properties of which we leave undetermined), but only with things as objects of a possible experience, and the sum total of such objects is properly what we here call nature. And now I ask whether, if the discussion is of the possibility of a cognition of nature *a priori*, it would be better to frame the problem in this way: How is it possible in general to cognize *a priori*

---

[3] *Materialiter* is Latin for "materially." In Kant's usage (ultimately derived from scholastic Aristotelianism), "matter" and "material" need not refer specifically to the physical matter of which objects are composed; here he uses the term to refer to the totality of objects of experience (see also §36), by contrast with the (merely "formal") general laws governing those objects (as discussed in §§15, 17).

the necessary conformity to law *of things* as objects of experience, or: How is it possible to cognize *a priori* the necessary conformity to law *of experience* itself with regard to all of its objects?

On closer examination, whether the question is posed one way or the other, its solution will come out absolutely the same with regard to the pure cognition of nature (which is actually the point of the question). For the subjective laws under which alone a cognition of things through experience[a] is possible also hold good for those things as objects of a possible experience (but obviously not for them as things in themselves, which, however, are not at all being considered here). It is completely the same, whether I say: A judgment of perception can never be considered as valid for experience without the law, that if an event is perceived then it is always referred to something preceding from which it follows according to a universal rule; or if I express myself in this way: Everything of which experience shows that it happens must have a cause.

[4:297]   It is nonetheless more appropriate to choose the first formulation. For since we can indeed, *a priori* and previous to any objects being given, have a cognition of those conditions under which alone an experience regarding objects is possible, but never of the laws to which objects may be subject in themselves without relation to possible experience, we will therefore be able to study *a priori* the nature of things in no other way than by investigating the conditions, and the universal (though subjective) laws, under which alone such a cognition is possible as experience (as regards mere form), and determining the possibility of things as objects of experience accordingly; for were I to choose the second mode of expression and to seek the *a priori* conditions under which nature is possible as an *object* of experience, I might then easily fall into misunderstanding and fancy that I had to speak about nature as a thing in itself, and in that case I would be wandering about fruitlessly in endless endeavors to find laws for things about which nothing is given to me.

We will therefore be concerned here only with experience and with the universal conditions of its possibility which are given *a priori*, and from there we will determine nature as the whole object of all possible experience. I think I will be understood: that here I do not mean the

---

[a] *Erfahrungserkenntnis*; not translated as "empirical cognition," which translates Kant's *empirische Erkenntnis*, which he distinguished from the former (§18).

rules for the *observation* of a nature that is already given, which presuppose experience already; therefore that I do not mean, how we can learn the laws from nature (through experience), for these would then not be laws *a priori* and would provide no pure natural science; but, how the *a priori* conditions of the possibility of experience are at the same time the sources out of which all universal laws of nature must be derived.

§*18*

We must therefore first of all note: that, although all judgments of experience are empirical, i.e., have their basis in the immediate perception of the senses, nonetheless the reverse is not the case, that therefore all empirical judgments are judgments of experience; rather, beyond the empirical and in general beyond what is given in sensory intuition, special concepts must yet be added, which have their origin completely *a priori* in the pure understanding, under which every perception can first be subsumed and then, by means of the same concepts, transformed into experience.

Empirical judgments, insofar as they have objective validity, are **judg-** [4:298] **ments of experience**; those, however, that are *only subjectively valid* I call mere **judgments of perception**. The latter do not require pure concepts of the understanding, but only the logical connection of perceptions in a thinking subject. But the former always demand, beyond the representations of sensory intuition, in addition special *concepts originally generated in the understanding*, which are precisely what make the judgment of experience *objectively valid*.

All of our judgments are at first mere judgments of perception; they hold only for us, i.e., for our subject, and only afterwards do we give them a new relation, namely to an object, and intend that the judgment should also be valid at all times for us and for everyone else; for if a judgment agrees with an object, then all judgments of the same object must also agree with one another, and hence the objective validity of a judgment of experience means nothing other than its necessary universal validity. But also conversely, if we find cause to deem a judgment necessarily and universally valid (which never is based on the perception, but on the pure concept of the understanding under which the perception is subsumed), we must then also deem it objective, i.e., as expressing not merely a relation of a perception to a subject, but a property of an object; for there would be no reason why other judgments necessarily would have to agree with mine, if there were not the unity of the object – an object to which they all refer, with which they all agree, and, for that reason, also must all harmonize among themselves.

§19

Consequently, objective validity and necessary universal validity (for everyone) are interchangeable concepts, and although we do not know the object in itself, nonetheless, if we regard a judgment as universally valid and hence necessary, objective validity is understood to be included. Through this judgment we cognize the object (even if it should remain otherwise unknown as it may be in itself) by means of the universally valid and necessary connection of the given perceptions; and since this is the case for all objects of the senses, judgments of experience will not derive their objective validity from the immediate [4:299] cognition of the object (for this is impossible), but merely from the condition for the universal validity of empirical judgments, which, as has been said, never rests on empirical, or indeed sensory conditions in general, but on a pure concept of the understanding. The object always remains unknown in itself; if, however, through the concept of the understanding the connection of the representations which it provides to our sensibility is determined as universally valid, then the object is determined through this relation, and the judgment is objective.

Let us provide examples: that the room is warm, the sugar sweet, the wormwood[4] repugnant,* are merely subjectively valid judgments. I do not at all require that I should find it so at every time, or that everyone else should find it just as I do; they express only a relation of two

---

* I gladly admit that these examples do not present judgments of perception such as could ever become judgments of experience if a concept of the understanding were also added, because they refer merely to feeling – which everyone acknowledges to be merely subjective and which must therefore never be attributed to the object – and therefore can never become objective; I only wanted to give for now an example of a judgment that is merely subjectively valid and that contains in itself no basis for necessary universal validity and, thereby, for a relation to an object. An example of judgments of perception that become judgments of experience through the addition of a concept of the understanding follows in the next note.

4 Wormwood (German, *Wermut*) is a bitter-tasting herb that was used in making absinthe.

sensations to the same subject, namely myself, and this only in my present state of perception, and are therefore not expected to be valid for the object: these I call judgments of perception. The case is completely different with judgments of experience. What experience teaches me under certain circumstances, it must teach me at every time and teach everyone else as well, and its validity is not limited to the subject or its state at that time. Therefore I express all such judgments as objectively valid; as, e.g., if I say: the air is elastic, then this judgment is to begin with only a judgment of perception; I relate two sensations in my senses only to one another. If I want it to be called a judgment of experience, I then require that this connection be subject to a condition that makes it universally valid. I want therefore that I, at every time, and also everyone else, would necessarily have to connect the same perceptions under the same circumstances.

§20   [4:300]

We will therefore have to analyze experience in general, in order to see what is contained in this product of the senses and the understanding, and how the judgment of experience is itself possible. At bottom lies the intuition of which I am conscious, i.e., perception (*perceptio*), which belongs solely to the senses. But, secondly, judging (which is attributed solely to the understanding) also belongs here. Now this judging can be of two types: first, when I merely compare the perceptions and connect them in a consciousness of my state, or, second, when I connect them in a consciousness in general. The first judgment is merely a judgment of perception and has thus far only subjective validity; it is merely a connection of perceptions within my mental state, without reference to the object. Hence for experience it is not, as is commonly believed, sufficient to compare perceptions and to connect them in one consciousness by means of judging; from that there arises no universal validity and necessity of the judgment, on account of which alone it can be objectively valid and so can be experience.

A completely different judgment therefore occurs before experience can arise from perception. The given intuition must be subsumed under a concept, which determines the form of judging in general with respect to the intuition, connects the empirical consciousness of the latter in a consciousness in general, and thereby furnishes empirical judgments with universal validity; a concept of this kind is a pure *a priori* concept of the understanding, which does nothing but simply determine for an intuition the mode in general in which it can serve for judging. The concept of cause being such a concept, it therefore determines the intuition which is subsumed under it, e.g., that of air, with respect to judging in general – namely, so that the concept of air serves, with respect to expansion, in the relation of the antecedent to the consequent in a hypothetical judgment. The concept of cause is therefore a pure concept of the understanding, which is completely distinct from all possible perception, and serves only, with respect to judging in general, to determine that representation which is contained under it and so to make possible a universally valid judgment.

[4:301] Now before a judgment of experience can arise from a judgment of perception, it is first required: that the perception be subsumed under a concept of the understanding of this kind; e.g., the air belongs under the concept of cause, which determines the judgment about the air as hypothetical with respect to expansion.* This expansion is represented not as belonging merely to my perception of the air in my state of perception or in several of my states or in the state of others, but as *necessarily* belonging to it, and the judgment: the air is elastic, becomes universally valid and thereby for the first time a judgment of experience, because certain judgments occur beforehand, which subsume the intuition of the air under the concept of cause and effect, and thereby determine the perceptions not merely with respect to each other in my subject, but with respect to the form of judging in general (here, the hypothetical), and in this way make the empirical judgment universally valid.

If one analyzes all of one's synthetic judgments insofar as they are objectively valid, one finds that they never consist in mere intuitions that have, as is commonly thought, merely been connected in a judgment through comparison, but rather that they would not be possible if, even beyond the concepts drawn from intuition, a pure

---

* To have a more easily understood example, consider the following: If the sun shines on the stone, it becomes warm. This judgment is a mere judgment of perception and contains no necessity, however often I and others also have perceived this; the perceptions are only usually found so conjoined. But if I say: the sun *warms* the stone, then beyond the perception is added the understanding's concept of cause, which connects *necessarily* the concept of sunshine with that of heat, and the synthetic judgment becomes necessarily universally valid, hence objective, and changes from a perception into experience.

concept of the understanding had not been added under which these concepts had been subsumed and in this way first combined into an objectively valid judgment. Even the judgments of pure mathematics in its simplest axioms are not exempt from this condition. The principle: a straight line is the shortest line between two points, presupposes that the line has been subsumed under the concept of magnitude, which certainly is no mere intuition, but has its seat solely in the understanding and serves to determine the intuition (of the line) with respect to such judgments as may be passed on it as regards the quantity of these judgments, namely plurality (as *judicia plurativa**), since through such [4:302] judgments it is understood that in a given intuition much that is homogeneous may be contained.

§21

In order therefore to explain the possibility of experience insofar as it rests on pure *a priori* concepts of the understanding, we must first present in a complete table that which belongs to judgments in general, and to the various moments of the understanding in them; for the pure concepts of the understanding – which are nothing more than concepts of intuitions in general insofar as these intuitions are, with respect to one or another of these moments, in themselves determined to judgments and therefore determined necessarily and with universal validity – will come out exactly parallel to them. By this means the *a priori* principles of the possibility of all experience as objectively valid empirical cognition will also be determined quite exactly. For they are nothing other than propositions that subsume all perception (according to certain universal conditions of intuition) under those pure concepts of the understanding.

---

* So I would prefer those judgments to be called, which are called *particularia* in logic. For the latter expression already contains the thought that the judgment is not universal. If, however, I commence from unity (in singular judgments) and then continue on to the totality, I still cannot mix in any reference to the totality; I think only a plurality without totality, not the exception to the latter.[5] This is necessary, if the logical moments are to be placed under the pure concepts of the understanding; in logical usage things can remain as they were.

5 Kant's point is that a collection of singular judgments that covers all of the individuals in a domain neither explicitly refers to the collected totality of such individuals (as a totality), nor explicitly denies the universality of its extension (a denial that would be suggested by calling such judgments "particular"); it refers to a plurality, i.e., to more than one individual, but it leaves undetermined whether or not it covers all of the individuals in the domain.

Logical table of judgments

1.

According to quantity

Universal
Particular
Singular

2.	3.
According to quality	According to relation
Affirmative	Categorical
Negative	Hypothetical
Infinite	Disjunctive

[4:303]

4.

According to modality

Problematic
Assertoric
Apodictic

Transcendental table of concepts of the understanding

1.

According to quantity

Unity (measure)
Plurality (magnitude)
Totality (the whole)

2.	3.
According to quality	According to relation
Reality	Substance
Negation	Cause
Limitation	Community

4.

According to modality
Possibility
Existence
Necessity

Pure physiological[b] table of universal principles of natural science

I.
Axioms
of intuition

2.   3.
Anticipations   Analogies
of perception   of experience

4.
Postulates
of empirical thinking in general

§*21a*   [4:304]

In order to comprise all the preceding within one concept, it is first of all necessary to remind the reader that the discussion here is not about the genesis of experience, but about that which lies in experience. The former belongs to empirical psychology and could never be properly developed even there without the latter, which belongs to the critique of cognition and especially of the understanding.

Experience consists of intuitions, which belong to sensibility, and of judgments, which are solely the understanding's business. Those judgments that the understanding forms solely from sensory intuitions, however, are still far from being judgments of experience. For in the former case the judgment would only connect perceptions as they are given in sensory intuition; but in the latter case the judgments are supposed to say what experience in general contains, therefore not what mere perception – whose validity is merely subjective – contains. The judgment of experience must still therefore, beyond the sensory intuition and its logical connection (in accordance with which the intuition has been rendered universal through comparison in a judgment), add something that determines the synthetic judgment as necessary, and thereby as universally valid; and this can be nothing but that concept which represents the intuition as in itself determined with respect to one form of judgment rather than the others, i.e., a concept of that

---

[b] *physiologische*; used to mean "pertaining to the investigation of nature," an older meaning that is consistent with its etymology.

synthetic unity of intuitions which can be represented only through a given logical function of judgments.

§22

To sum this up: the business of the senses is to intuit; that of the understanding, to think. To think, however, is to unite representations in a consciousness. This unification either arises merely in relation to the subject and is contingent and subjective, or it occurs without condition and is necessary or objective. The unification of representations in a consciousness is judgment. Therefore, thinking is the same as judging or as relating representations to judgments in general. Judgments are therefore either merely subjective, if representations are related to one consciousness in one subject alone and are united in it, or they are objective, if they are united in a consciousness in general, i.e., [4:305] are united necessarily therein. The logical moments of all judgments are so many possible ways of uniting representations in a consciousness. If the very same moments, however, serve as concepts, they are concepts of the *necessary* unification of these representations in a consciousness, and so are principles of objectively valid judgments. This unification in a consciousness is either analytic, through identity, or synthetic, through combination and addition of various representations with one another. Experience consists in the synthetic connection of appearances (perceptions) in a consciousness, insofar as this connection is necessary. Therefore pure concepts of the understanding are those under which all perceptions must first be subsumed before they can serve in judgments of experience, in which the synthetic unity of perceptions is represented as necessary and universally valid.*

---

* But how does this proposition: that judgments of experience are supposed to contain necessity in the synthesis of perceptions, square with my proposition, urged many times above: that experience, as *a posteriori* cognition, can provide merely contingent judgments? If I say: Experience teaches me something, I always mean only the perception that is in it – e.g., that upon illumination of the stone by the sun, warmth always follows – and hence the proposition from experience is, so far, always contingent. That this warming follows necessarily from illumination by the sun is indeed contained in the judgment of experience (in virtue of the concept of cause), but I do not learn it from experience; rather, conversely, experience is first generated through this addition of a concept of the understanding (of cause) to the perception. Concerning how the perception might come by this addition, the *Critique* must be consulted, in the section on transcendental judgment, pp. 137 ff.[6]

[6] See Transcendental Doctrine of Judgment (or Analytic of Principles), ch. 1, On the Schematism of the Pure Concepts of the Understanding (A 137 ff./B 176 ff.).

§23

Judgments, insofar as they are regarded merely as the condition for the unification of given representations in a consciousness, are rules. These rules, insofar as they represent the unification as necessary, are *a priori* rules, and provided that there are none above them from which they can be derived, are principles. Now since, with respect to the possibility of all experience, if merely the form of thinking is considered in the experience, no conditions on judgments of experience are above those that bring the appearances (according to the varying form of their intuition) under pure concepts of the understanding (which make the [4:306] empirical judgment objectively valid), these conditions are therefore the *a priori* principles of possible experience.

The principles of possible experience are, at the same time, universal laws of nature that can be cognized *a priori*. And so the problem that lies in our second question, now before us: *how is pure natural science possible?* is solved. For the systematization that is required for the form of a science is here found to perfection, since beyond the aforementioned formal conditions of all judgments in general, hence of all rules in general, which logic proffers, no others are possible, and these form a logical system; but the concepts based thereon, which contain the *a priori* conditions for all synthetic and necessary judgments, for that very reason form a transcendental system; finally, the principles by means of which all appearances are subsumed under these concepts form a physiological system, i.e., a system of nature, which precedes all empirical cognition of nature, makes the latter possible, and therefore can be called the true universal and pure natural science.

§24

The first* of the physiological principles subsumes all appearances, as intuitions in space and time, under the concept of *magnitude* and is to

---

* These three subsequent sections could be difficult to understand properly, if one does not have at hand what the *Critique* says about principles as well; but they might have the advantage of making it easier to survey the general features of such principles and to attend to the main points.[7]

7 In reading the next three sections, the obscurity will be reduced by keeping in mind that Kant is discussing the Tables in §21. Here he relates the first two entries in the Physiological

that extent a principle for the application of mathematics to experience. The second does not subsume the properly empirical – namely sensation, which signifies the real in intuitions – directly under the concept of *magnitude*, as sensation is no intuition *containing* space or time, although it places the object corresponding to it in both; but there nonetheless is, between reality (sensory representation) and nothing, i.e., the complete emptiness of intuition in time, a difference that has a magnitude, for indeed between every given degree of light and darkness, every degree of warmth and the completely cold, every degree of heaviness and absolute lightness, every degree of the filling of space and completely empty space, yet smaller degrees can be thought, just as between consciousness and the fully unconscious (psychological darkness) yet smaller degrees occur; therefore no perception is possible that shows a complete absence, e.g., no psychological darkness is possible that could not be regarded as a state of consciousness that simply is outweighed by another, stronger one, and thus it is in all cases of sensation; as a result of which the understanding can anticipate even sensations, which form the proper quality of empirical representations (appearances), by means of the principle that they all collectively, hence the real in all appearance, have degrees – which is the second application of mathematics (*mathesis intensorum*) to natural science.

[4:307]

§25

With respect to the relation of appearances, and indeed exclusively with regard to their existence, the determination of this relation is not mathematical but dynamical, and it can never be objectively valid, hence fit for experience, if it is not subject to *a priori* principles, which first make the cognition of experience possible with respect to that determination.[8]

table (Axioms and Anticipations) to the category of magnitude (respectively, extensive magnitude, and intensive magnitude or degree). In the "A" edition of the *Critique*, the corresponding propositions read: Axiom, "All appearances are, as regards their intuition, extensive magnitudes" (A 162); and Anticipation, "In all appearances the sensation, and the *real* that corresponds to it in the object (*realitas phaenomenon*), has an intensive magnitude, i.e., a degree" (A 166).

8 Here Kant first relates the third entry in the Physiological table to the categories of relation: Substance, Cause, and Community (a discussion that corresponds to that of the three Analogies of experience in the *Critique*, A 176–218/B 218–65). In the following paragraph, he relates the fourth entry to the categories of modality (a discussion that corresponds to that of the three Postulates of empirical thinking in the *Critique*, A 218–35/B 265–74, 279–87). The distinction between "mathematical" and "dynamical," mentioned here, is further elaborated in §§52c, 53.

Therefore appearances must be subsumed under the concept of substance, which, as a concept of the thing itself, underlies all determination of existence; or second, insofar as a temporal sequence, i.e., an event, is met with among the appearances, they must be subsumed under the concept of an effect in relation to a cause; or, insofar as coexistence is to be cognized objectively, i.e., through a judgment of experience, they must be subsumed under the concept of community (interaction): and so *a priori* principles underlie objectively valid, though empirical, judgments, i.e., they underlie the possibility of experience insofar as it is supposed to connect objects in nature according to existence. These principles are the actual laws of nature, which can be called dynamical.

Finally, there also belongs to judgments of experience the cognition of agreement and connection: not of the appearances among themselves in experience, but rather in their relation to experience in general, a relation that contains either their agreement with the formal conditions that the understanding cognizes, or their connection with the material [4:308] of the senses and perception, or both united in one concept, and consequently possibility, existence, and necessity according to universal laws of nature; all of which would constitute the physiological theory of method (the distinction of truth and hypotheses, and the boundaries of the reliability of the latter).

§26

Although the third table of principles, which is drawn *from the nature of the understanding itself* according to the critical method, in itself exhibits a perfection through which it raises itself far above every other that has (though vainly) ever been attempted or may be attempted in the future *from the things themselves* through the dogmatic method: namely, that in it all of the synthetic principles *a priori* are exhibited completely and according to a principle,[c] namely that of the faculty for judging in general (which constitutes the essence[d] of experience with respect to the understanding), so that one can be certain there are no more such principles (a satisfaction that the dogmatic method can never provide) – nevertheless this is still far from being its greatest merit.

[c] *Prinzip*   [d] *Wesen*

Notice must be taken of the ground of proof that reveals the possibility of this *a priori* cognition and at the same time limits all such principles to a condition that must never be neglected if they are not to be misunderstood and to be extended in use further than the original sense which the understanding places in them will allow: namely, that they contain only the conditions of possible experience in general, insofar as it is subject to *a priori* laws. Hence I do not say: that things *in themselves* contain a magnitude, their reality a degree, their existence a connection of accidents in a substance, and so on; for that no one can prove, because such a synthetic connection out of mere concepts, in which all relation to sensory intuition on the one hand and all connection of such intuition in a possible experience on the other is lacking, is utterly impossible. Therefore the essential limitation on the concepts in these principles is: that only *as objects of experience* are all things necessarily subject *a priori* to the aforementioned conditions.

From this follows then secondly a specifically characteristic mode of proving the same thing: that the above-mentioned principles are not [4:309] referred directly to appearances and their relation, but to the possibility of experience, for which appearances constitute only the matter but not the form, i.e., they are referred to the objectively and universally valid synthetic propositions through which judgments of experience are distinguished from mere judgments of perception. This happens because the appearances, as mere intuitions *that fill a part of space and time*, are subject to the concept of magnitude, which synthetically unifies the multiplicity of intuitions *a priori* according to rules; and because the real in the appearances must have a degree, insofar as perception contains, beyond intuition, sensation as well, between which and nothing, i.e., the complete disappearance of sensation, a transition always occurs by diminution, namely, insofar as sensation itself *fills no part of space and time,* but yet the transition to sensation from empty

---

* Warmth, light, etc. are just as great (according to degree) in a small space as in a large one; just as the inner representations (pain, consciousness in general) are not smaller according to degree whether they last a short or a long time. Hence the magnitude here is just as great in a point and in an instant as in every space and time however great. Degrees are therefore magnitudes, not, however, in intuition, but in accordance with mere sensation, or indeed with the magnitude of the ground of an intuition, and can be assessed as magnitudes only through the relation of 1 to 0, i.e., through the following: that every sensation can, in a certain time, proceed to diminution through infinite intermediate degrees, or can grow from nothing to a determinate sensation through infinite moments of accretion. (*Quantitas qualitatis est gradus.*)[9]

[9] "The magnitude of quality is degree."

time or space is possible only in time, with the consequence that although sensation, as the quality of empirical intuition with respect to that by which a sensation is distinguished specifically from other sensations, can never be cognized *a priori*, it nonetheless can, in a possible experience in general, as the magnitude of perception, be distinguished intensively from every other sensation of the same kind; from which, then, the application of mathematics to nature with respect to sensory intuition, through which nature is given to us, is first made possible and is determined.

Mostly, however, the reader should attend to the mode of proving the principles that appear under the name of the analogies of experience. For because these do not concern, as do the principles of the application of mathematics to natural science in general, the generation of intuitions, but rather the connection of their existence in one experience, and [4:310] because this connection can be nothing other than the determination of existence in time according to necessary laws, under which alone the connection is objectively valid, and therefore is experience: it follows that the proof does not refer to synthetic unity in the connection *of things* in themselves, but of *perceptions*, and indeed of these not with respect to their content, but to the determination of time and to the relation of existence in time according to universal laws. These universal laws contain therefore the necessity of determining existence in time in general (hence *a priori* according to a rule of the understanding) if the empirical determination in relative time is to be objectively valid, and therefore to be experience. For the reader who is stuck in the long habit of taking experience to be a mere empirical combining of perceptions – and who therefore does not at all think that experience goes much further than these reach, that is, who does not think that experience gives to empirical judgments universal validity and that to do so it requires a pure unity of the understanding that precedes *a priori* – I cannot adduce more here, these being prolegomena, except only to recommend: to heed well this distinction of experience from a mere aggregate of perceptions and to judge the mode of proof from this standpoint.

§27

Here is now the place to dispose thoroughly of the Humean doubt. He rightly affirmed: that we in no way have insight through reason into the possibility of causality, i.e., into the possibility of relating the existence of one thing to the existence of some other thing that would necessarily be posited through the first one. I add to this that we have just as little insight into the concept of subsistence, i.e., the concept of the necessity that a subject, which itself cannot be a predicate of any other thing, should underlie the existence of things – nay, that we cannot make any concept of the possibility of any such thing (although we can produce examples of the use of this concept in experience); and I also add that this very incomprehensiblity affects the community of things as well, since we have no insight whatsoever into how, from the state of one thing, a consequence could be drawn about the state of another thing outside it (and vice versa), and into how substances, each of which has its own separate existence, should depend on one another and should indeed do so necessarily. Nonetheless, I am very far from taking these [4:311] concepts to be merely borrowed from experience, and from taking the necessity represented in them to be falsely ascribed and to be a mere illusion through which long habit deludes us; rather, I have sufficiently shown that they and the principles taken from them stand firm *a priori* prior to all experience, and have their undoubted objective correctness, though of course only with respect to experience.

§28

Although I therefore do not have the least concept of such a connection of things in themselves, how they could exist as substances or work as causes or be in community with others (as parts of a real whole), and though I can still less think such properties of appearances as appearances (for these concepts do not contain what lies in appearances, but what the understanding alone must think), we nonetheless do have a concept of such a connection of representations in our understanding, and indeed in judging in general, namely: that representations belong in one kind of judgments as subject in relation to predicate, in another as ground in relation to consequence, and in a third as parts that together make up a whole possible experience. Further, we cognize *a priori*: that, without regarding the representation of an object as determined with respect to one or another of these moments, we could not have any cognition at all that was valid for the object; and if we were to concern ourselves with the object in itself, then no unique characteristic would be possible by which I could cognize that it had been determined with respect to one or another of the above-mentioned moments, i.e., that it belonged under the concept of substance, or that of cause, or (in relation to other substances) under the concept of community; for I have no concept of the possibililty of such a connection of existence. The question is not, however, how things in themselves, but how the cognition of things in experience is determined with respect to said moments of judgments in general, i.e., how things as objects of experience can and should be subsumed under those concepts of the understanding. And then it is clear that I have complete insight into not only the possibility but also the necessity of subsuming all appearances under these concepts, i.e., of using them as principles of the possibility of experience.

§29 [4:312]

For having a try at *Hume's* problematic concept (this, his *crux metaphysicorum*), namely the concept of cause, first there is given to me *a priori*, by means of logic: the form of a conditioned judgment in general, that is, the use of a given cognition as ground and another as consequent. It is, however, possible that in perception a rule of relation will be found, which says this: that a certain appearance is constantly followed by another (though not the reverse); and this is a case for me to use hypothetical judgment and, e.g., to say: If a body is illuminated by the sun for long enough, then it becomes warm. Here there is of course not yet a necessity of connection, hence not yet the concept of cause. But I continue on, and say: if the above proposition, which is merely a subjective connection of perceptions, is to be a proposition of experience, then it must be regarded as necessarily and universally valid. But a proposition of this sort would be: The sun through its light is the cause of the warmth. The above-mentioned empirical rule is now regarded as a law, and indeed not as valid merely of appearances, but as valid of them on behalf of a possible experience, which requires universally and therefore necessarily valid rules. I therefore have quite good insight into the concept of cause, as a concept that necessarily belongs to the mere form of experience, and into its possibility as a synthetic unification of perceptions in a consciousness in general; but I have no insight at all into the possibility of a thing in general as a cause, and indeed for this reason: because the concept of cause does not allude to any condition whatsoever that attaches to things but only to a condition that attaches to experience, namely, that experience can be an objectively valid cognition of appearances and their sequence in time only insofar as the antecedent cognition can be connected with the subsequent one according to the rule of hypothetical judgments.

§30

Consequently, even the pure concepts of the understanding have no meaning at all if they should depart from objects of experience and be referred to things in themselves (*noumena*).[10] They serve as it were only to spell out appearances, so that they can be read as experience; the [4:313] principles that arise from their relation to the sensible world serve our understanding for use in experience only; beyond this there are arbitrary connections without objective reality whose possibility cannot be cognized *a priori* and whose relation to objects cannot, through any example, be confirmed or even made intelligible, since all examples can be taken only from some possible experience or other and hence the objects of these concepts can be found nowhere else but in a possible experience.

Therefore this complete solution of the Humean problem, though coming out contrary to the conjecture of the originator, rescues the *a priori* origin of the pure concepts of the understanding and the validity of the universal laws of nature as laws of the understanding, but in such a way that it restricts their use to experience only, because their possibility is founded solely in the relation of the understanding to experience: not, however, such that these concepts and laws are derived from experience, but such that experience is derived from them, a completely reversed type of connection that never occurred to *Hume*.

From this now flows the following result of all the foregoing investigations: "All synthetic *a priori* principles[e] are nothing more than principles[f] of possible experience," and can never be related to things in themselves, but only to appearances as objects of experience. Therefore

---

[e] *Grundsätze*   [f] *Prinzipien*

[10] *Noumena* is a latinized Greek word (singular: *noumenon*) meaning "intelligible object," which Kant uses to characterize "intelligible beings" or "beings of the understanding." In §32 he contrasts *noumena* with *phaenomena*, which he speaks of as "sensible beings" or "appearances."

both pure mathematics and pure natural science can never refer to anything more than mere appearances, and they can only represent either that which makes experience in general possible, or that which, being derived from these principles,[g] must always be able to be represented in some possible experience or other.

§31

And so for once one has something determinate, and to which one can adhere in all metaphysical undertakings, which have up to now boldly enough, but always blindly, run over everything without distinction. It never occurred to dogmatic thinkers that the goal of their efforts might have been set up so close, nor even to those who, obstinate in their so-called sound common sense, went forth to insights with concepts and principles of the pure understanding that were indeed legitimate and natural, but were determined for use merely in experience, and for which they neither recognized nor could recognize any determinate boundaries, because they neither had reflected on nor were able to [4:314] reflect on the nature and even the possibility of such a pure understanding.

Many a naturalist of pure reason (by which I mean he who trusts himself, without any science, to decide in matters of metaphysics) would like to pretend that already long ago, through the prophetic spirit of his sound common sense, he had not merely suspected, but had known and understood, that which is here presented with so much preparation, or, if he prefers, with long-winded pedantic pomp: "namely that with all of our reason we can never get beyond the field of experiences." But since, if someone gradually questions him on his rational principles, he must indeed admit that among them there are many that he has not drawn from experience, which are therefore independent of it and are valid *a priori* – how and on what grounds will he then hold within limits the dogmatist (and himself), who makes use of these concepts and principles beyond all possible experience for the very reason that they are cognized independently of experience. And even he, this adept of sound common sense, is not so steadfast that, despite all of his presumed and cheaply gained wisdom, he will not stumble unawares out beyond the objects of

---

[g] *Prinzipien*

experience into the field of chimeras. Ordinarily, he is deeply enough entangled therein, although he cloaks his ill-founded claims through a popular style, since he gives everything out as mere probability, reasonable conjecture, or analogy.

§32

Already from the earliest days of philosophy, apart from the sensible beings[h] or appearances (*phaenomena*) that constitute the sensible world, investigators of pure reason have thought of special intelligible beings[i] (*noumena*), which are supposed to form an intelligible world;[j] and they have granted reality to intelligible beings alone, because they took appearance and illusion to be one and the same thing (something that may well be excused in an as yet uncultivated age).[11]

In fact, if we view the objects of the senses as mere appearances, as is fitting, then we thereby admit at the very same time that a thing in itself underlies them, although we are not acquainted with this thing as it may be constituted in itself, but only with its appearance, i.e., with the way in which our senses are affected by this unknown something. Therefore the understanding, just by the fact that it accepts appearances, also admits to the existence of things in themselves, and to that extent we can say that the representation of such beings as underlie the appearances, hence of mere intelligible beings, is not merely permitted but is unavoidable.

Our critical deduction in no way excludes things of such kind (*noumena*), but rather restricts the principles of aesthetic[12] in such a way that they are not supposed to extend to all things, whereby everything would be transformed into mere appearance, but are to be valid only for objects of a possible experience. Hence intelligible beings are thereby allowed only with the enforcement of this rule, which brooks no exception whatsoever: that we do not know and cannot know anything determinate about these intelligible beings at all, because our pure concepts of the understanding as well as our pure intuitions refer to

[4:315]

---

[h] *Sinnenwesen*   [i] *Verstandeswesen*   [j] *Verstandeswelt*

[11] The early philosophy mentioned here must include Plato's, as in the *Republic*, Bks. VI, VII.

[12] "Aesthetic" would here be taken as meaning quite generally things pertaining to, and limited to, the senses by comparison with the intellect, as the word is used in labelling the "Transcendental Aesthetic" in the *Critique*.

68

nothing but objects of possible experience, hence to mere beings of sense, and as soon as one deviates from these things not the least meaning remains for those concepts.

§33

There is in fact something insidious in our pure concepts of the understanding, as regards enticement toward a transcendent use; for so I call that use which goes out beyond all possible experience. It is not only that our concepts of substance, of force, of action, of reality, etc., are wholly independent of experience, and also contain no sensory appearance whatsoever and so in fact seem to refer to things in themselves (*noumena*); but also, which strengthens this supposition yet further, that they contain in themselves a necessity of determination which experience never equals. The concept of cause contains a rule, according to which from one state of affairs another follows with necessity; experience, however, can show us only that from one state of a thing another state often, or, at best, commonly, follows, and it can therefore furnish neither strict universality nor necessity (and so forth).

Consequently, the concepts of the understanding appear to have much more meaning and content than they would if their entire vocation were exhausted by mere use in experience, and so the understanding unwittingly builds onto the house of experience a much [4:316] roomier wing, which it crowds with beings of thought, without once noticing that it has taken its otherwise legitimate concepts far beyond the boundaries of their use.

§34

Two important, nay completely unavoidable, though utterly dry investigations were therefore needed, which were carried out in the *Critique*, pp. 137 ff. and 235 ff.[13] Through the first of these it was shown that the senses do not supply pure concepts of the understanding *in concreto*, but only the schema for their use, and that the object appropriate to this schema is found only in experience (as the product of the understanding

---

[13] On the Schematism of the Pure Concepts of the Understanding (A 137 ff./B 176 ff.); On the Basis of the Distinction of All Objects in General into *Phaenomena* and *Noumena* (A 235 ff./B 294 ff.).

from materials of sensibility). In the second investigation (*Critique*, p. 235) it is shown: that notwithstanding the independence from experience of our pure concepts of the understanding and principles, and indeed even their apparently larger sphere of use, all the same, through them absolutely nothing can be thought outside the field of experience, because they can do nothing but merely determine the logical form of judgment with respect to given intuitions; but since beyond the field of sensibility there is no intuition at all, these pure concepts are completely lacking in meaning, in that there are no means through which they could be exhibited *in concreto*, and so all such *noumena*, together with their collective aggregate – an intelligible* world – are nothing but representations of a problem, whose object is in itself perfectly possible, but whose solution, given the nature of our understanding, is completely impossible, since our understanding is no faculty of intuition but only of the connection of given intuitions in an [4:317] experience; and experience therefore has to contain all the objects for our concepts, and apart from it all concepts will be without meaning since no intuition can be put under them.

§35

The imagination can perhaps be excused if it daydreams^m every now and then, i.e., if it does not cautiously hold itself inside the limits of experience; for it will at least be enlivened and strengthened through such free flight, and it will always be easier to moderate its boldness than to remedy its dullness. That the understanding, however, which ought *to think*, should, instead of that, *daydream* – for this it can never be forgiven; for all assistance in setting bounds, where needed, to the fanatical dreams^n of the imagination depends on it alone.

The understanding begins all this very innocently and chastely. First,

---

* Not (as is commonly said) an *intellectual*^k world. For the *cognitions* through the understanding are *intellectual*, and the same sort of cognitions also refer to our sensible world; but *intelligible*^l means *objects* insofar as they can be represented *only through the understanding*, and none of our sensory intuitions can refer to them. Since, however, to each object there nonetheless must correspond some possible intuition or other, we would therefore have to think of an understanding that intuits things immediately; of this sort of understanding, however, we have not the least concept, hence also not of the *intelligible beings* to which it is supposed to refer.

^k *intellektuel*   ^l *intelligibel*
^m *schwärmt*   ^n *Schwärmerei*

it puts in order the elementary cognitions that belong to it before all experience but that must nonetheless always have their application in experience. Gradually, it removes these constraints, and what should hinder it from doing this, since the understanding has quite freely taken its principles from within itself? And now reference is made first to newly invented forces in nature, soon thereafter to beings outside nature, in a word, to a world for the furnishing of which building materials cannot fail us, because they are abundantly supplied through fertile invention, and though they are not, indeed, confirmed by experience, they are also never refuted by it. That is the reason why young thinkers so love metaphysics of the truly dogmatic sort, and often sacrifice their time and their otherwise useful talent to it.

It can, however, help nothing at all to want to curb these fruitless endeavors of pure reason by all sorts of admonitions about the difficulty of resolving such deeply obscure questions, by complaints over the limits of our reason, and by reducing assertions to mere conjectures. For if the *impossibility* of these endeavors is not to be clearly demonstrated, and reason's *knowledge of itself*° does not become true science, in which the sphere of reason's legitimate use is distinguished with geometrical certainty (so to speak) from that of its empty and fruitless use, then these futile efforts will never be fully abandoned.

§36   [4:318]

How is nature itself possible?

This question, which is the highest point that transcendental philosophy can ever reach, and up to which, as its boundary and completion, it must be taken, actually contains two questions.

First: How is nature possible in general in the *material* sense, namely, according to intuition, as the sum total of appearances; how are space, time, and that which fills them both, the object of sensation, possible in general? The answer is: by means of the constitution of our sensibility, in accordance with which our sensibility is affected in its characteristic way by objects that are in themselves unknown to it and that are wholly distinct from said appearances. This answer is, in the book itself, given

---

° *Selbsterkenntnis*

71

in the Transcendental Aesthetic,[14] but here in the *Prolegomena*, through the solution of the first main question.

Second: How is nature possible in the *formal* sense, as the sum total of the rules to which all appearances must be subject if they are to be thought as connected in an experience? The answer cannot come out otherwise than: it is possible only by means of the constitution of our understanding, in accordance with which all these representations of sensibility are necessarily referred to a consciousness, and through which, first, the characteristic mode of our thinking, namely by means of rules, is possible, and then by means of these rules experience is possible – which is to be wholly distinguished from insight into objects in themselves. This answer is, in the book itself, given in the Transcendental Logic,[15] but here in the *Prolegomena*, in the course of solving the second main question.

But how this characteristic property of our sensibility itself may be possible, or that of our understanding and of the necessary apperception that underlies it and all thinking, cannot be further solved and answered, because we always have need of them for all answering and for all thinking of objects.

There are many laws of nature that we can know only through experience, but we cannot come to know lawfulness in the connection of [4:319] appearances, i.e., nature in general, through any experience, because experience itself has need of such laws, which lie *a priori* at the basis of its possibility.

The possibility of experience in general is therefore at the same time the universal law of nature, and the principles of the former are themselves the laws of the latter. For we are not acquainted with nature except as the sum total of appearances, i.e., of the representations in us, and we cannot therefore get the laws of their connection from anywhere else except the principles of their connection in us, i.e., from the conditions of necessary unification in one consciousness, which unification constitutes the possibility of experience.

Even the main proposition that has been elaborated throughout this entire part, that universal laws of nature can be cognized *a priori*,

---

14 The Transcendental Aesthetic is the first part of the Transcendental Doctrine of Elements (see p. 141).
15 The Transcendental Logic is the second part of the Transcendental Doctrine of Elements, coordinate with the Aesthetic, though much longer (see p. 141).

already leads by itself to the proposition: that the highest legislation for nature must lie in ourselves, i.e., in our understanding, and that we must not seek the universal laws of nature from nature by means of experience, but, conversely, that we must seek nature, as regards its universal conformity to law, solely in the conditions of the possibility of experience that lie in our sensibility and understanding; for how would it otherwise be possible to become acquainted with these laws *a priori*, since they are surely not rules for analytic cognition, but are genuine synthetic amplifications of cognition? Such agreement, and indeed necessary agreement, of the principles[p] of possible experience with the laws for the possibility of nature, can come about from only two causes: either these laws are taken from nature by means of experience, or, conversely, nature is derived from the laws of the possibility of experience in general and is fully identical with the mere universal lawfulness of experience. The first one contradicts itself, for the universal laws of nature can and must be cognized *a priori* (i.e., independently of all experience) and set at the foundation of all empirical use of the understanding; therefore, only the second remains.[*]

We must, however, distinguish empirical laws of nature, which always [4:320] presuppose particular perceptions, from the pure or universal laws of nature, which, without having particular perceptions underlying them, contain merely the conditions for the necessary unification of such perceptions in an experience; with respect to the latter laws, nature and *possible* experience are thoroughly identical, and since in possible experience the lawfulness rests on the necessary connection of appearances in an experience (without which we would not be able to cognize any object of the sensible world at all), and so on the original laws of the understanding, it is, though it sounds strange at first, nonetheless certain, if I say with respect to the universal laws of nature: *the*

---

[*] Crusius[16] alone knew of a middle way: namely that a spirit who can neither err nor deceive originally implanted these natural laws in us. But, since false principles are often mixed in as well – of which this man's system itself provides not a few examples – then, with the lack of a sure criterion for distinguishing an authentic origin from a spurious one, the use of such a principle looks very precarious, since one can never know for sure what the spirit of truth or the father of lies may have put into us.

[p] *Prinzipien*

[16] Christian August Crusius (1715–75), an important opponent of the Wolffian philosophy; in *Weg zur Gewissheit und Zuverlässigkeit der menschlichen Erkenntniss* (Leipzig, 1747), he maintains that the divine understanding is the source of all truth and certainty in the human understanding, and that reflection on skepticism will bring one to see this (§§424–32).

understanding does not draw its (a priori) *laws from nature, but prescribes them to it.*

§37

We will elucidate this apparently daring proposition through an example, which is supposed to show: that laws that we discover in objects of sensory intuition, especially if these laws have been cognized as necessary, are already held by us to be such as have been placed there by the understanding, although they are otherwise in all respects like the laws of nature that we attribute to experience.

§38

If one considers the properties of the circle by which this figure instantly unifies in a universal rule so many arbitrary determinations of the space in it, one cannot refrain from ascribing a nature to this geometrical thing. Thus, in particular, two lines that intersect each other and also the circle,[17] however they happen to be drawn, nonetheless always partition each other in a regular manner such that the rectangle from the parts of any one line is equal to that from the other. Now I ask: "Does this law lie in the circle, or does it lie in the understanding?" i.e., does this figure, independent of the understanding, contain the basis for this law in itself, or does the understanding, since it has itself constructed the figure in accordance with its concepts (namely, the equality of the radii), at the same time read into it the law that chords cut one another in geometrical proportion? If one [4:321] traces the proofs of this law, one sees quickly that it could be derived only from the condition on which the understanding bases the construction of this figure, namely, the equality of the radii. If we now expand upon this concept so as to follow up still further the unity of the manifold properties of geometrical figures under common laws, and we consider the circle as a conic section, which is therefore subject to the very same fundamental conditions of construction as other conic sections, then we find that all chords that intersect within the latter (within the ellipse, the parabola, and the hyperbola) always do so such

---

[17] Kant specifies below that each line is a chord, i.e., a line segment having both end points on the circumference of the circle.

that the rectangles from their parts are not indeed equal, but always stand to one another in equal proportions. If from there we go still further, namely to the fundamental doctrines of physical astronomy, then there appears a physical law of reciprocal attraction, extending to all material nature, the rule of which is that these attractions decrease inversely with the square of the distance from each point of attraction, exactly as the spherical surfaces into which this force spreads itself increase, something that seems to reside as necessary in the nature of the things themselves and which therefore is customarily presented as cognizable *a priori*. As simple as are the sources of this law – since they rest solely on the relation of spherical surfaces with different radii – the consequence therefrom is nonetheless so excellent with respect to the variety and regularity of its agreement that not only does it follow that all possible orbits of the celestial bodies are conic sections, but also that they are so related among themselves that no other law of attraction besides the relation of the inverse square of the distances can be conceived as suitable for a system of the world.

Here therefore is nature that rests on laws that the understanding cognizes *a priori*, and indeed chiefly from universal principles of the determination of space. I ask now: do these laws of nature lie in space, and does the understanding learn them because it merely seeks to investigate the wealth of meaning that lies in this space, or do they lie in the understanding and in the way in which it determines space in accordance with the conditions of the synthetic unity toward which its concepts are collectively directed? Space is something so uniform and so indeterminate with respect to all specific properties that certainly no one will look for a stock of natural laws within it. By contrast, that which determines space into the figure of a circle, a cone, or a sphere is the understanding, insofar as it contains the basis for the unity of the [4:322] construction of these figures. The mere universal form of intuition called space is therefore certainly the substratum of all intuitions that can be determined in particular objects, and, admittedly, the condition for the possibility and variety of those intuitions lies in this space; but the unity of the objects is determined solely through the understanding, and indeed according to conditions that reside in its own nature; and so the understanding is the origin of the universal order of nature, in that it comprehends all appearances under its own laws and in this way first brings about experience *a priori* (with respect to its form), in virtue of which everything that must be cognized only through experience becomes necessarily subject to its laws. For we are not concerned with the nature of *the things in themselves*, which is independent of the conditions of both our senses and understanding, but with nature as an object of possible experience, and here the understanding, since it makes experience possible, at the same time makes it that the sensible world is either not an object of experience at all, or else is nature.

§39

Appendix to pure natural science
On the system of categories

Nothing can be more desirable to a philosopher than if he is able to derive *a priori* from a principle^q the multiplicity of concepts or basic principles^r that previously had appeared to him as disparate (in the use he had made of them *in concreto*), and so is able in this way to unite them all in one cognition. Previously, he simply believed that that which remained for him after a certain abstraction, and which, through comparison of one with another, appeared to form a distinct kind of cognitions, had been completely assembled: but this was only an *aggregate*; now he knows that only precisely so many, not more, not fewer, could constitute this kind of cognition, and he has understood the necessity of his division: this is a comprehending,^s and only now has he a *system*.

To pick out from ordinary cognition the concepts that are based on no particular experience whatsoever, and that are present nonetheless in all cognition from experience (for which they constitute as it were the mere form of the connection) requires no greater reflection or more insight than to cull from a language rules for the actual use of words in general, and so to compile the elements for a grammar (and in fact both investigations are very closely related to one another) without, for all that, even being able to give a reason why any one language should have precisely this and no other formal constitution, and still less why precisely so many, neither more nor fewer, of such formal determinations of the language can be found.

[4:323]

---

^q *Prinzip*   ^r *Grundsätze*   ^s *ein Begreifen*

76

Aristotle had compiled ten such pure elementary concepts under the name of categories.* To these, which were also called predicaments, he later saw the need to append five post-predicaments,** which are indeed already partly there in the former (like *prius, simul, motus*); but this rhapsody[20] could better pass for, and be deserving of praise as, a hint for future inquirers than as an idea worked out according to rules, and so, with the greater enlightenment of philosophy, it too could be rejected as completely useless.

During an investigation of the pure elements of human cognition (containing nothing empirical), after long reflection I succeeded first of all in reliably distinguishing and separating the pure elementary concepts of sensibility (space and time) from those of the understanding. By this means the seventh, eighth, and ninth categories were excluded from this list. The others could be of no use to me, because no principle existed by which the understanding could be fully measured and all of its functions, from which its pure concepts arise, determined exhaustively and with precision.

In order however to find such a principle, I cast about for an act of the understanding that contains all of the others and that only differentiates itself through various modifications or moments in order to bring the multiplicity of representation under the unity of thinking in general; and there I found that this act of the understanding consists in judging. Here lay before me now, already finished though not yet wholly free of defects, the work of the logicians, through which I was put in the position to present a complete table of the functions of the pure understanding, which were however undetermined with respect to [4:324] every object. Finally, I related these functions of judging to objects in general, or rather to the condition for determining judgments as objectively valid, and there arose pure concepts of the understanding, about which I could have no doubt that precisely these only, and of

---

* 1. *Substantia.* 2. *Qualitas.* 3. *Quantitas.* 4. *Relatio.* 5. *Actio.* 6. *Passio.* 7. *Quando.* 8. *Ubi.* 9. *Situs.* 10. *Habitus.*[18]

** *Oppositum, Prius, Simul, Motus, Habere.*[19]

[18] Substance, quality, quantity, relation, action, affection, time, place, position, state. (See Aristotle, *Categories*, ch. 4.)

[19] Opposition, priority, simultaneity, motion, possession.

[20] A rhapsody was a portion of an ancient Greek poem recited on a single occasion, and might carry the connotation of rote repetition of an earlier epic work; etymologically, the word means "stitched together verse."

them only so many, neither more nor fewer, can make up our entire cognition of things out of the bare understanding. As was proper, I called them *categories*, after their ancient name, whereby I reserved for myself to append in full, under the name of *predicables*, all the concepts derivable from them – whether by connecting them with one another, or with the pure form of appearance (space and time), or with its matter, provided the latter is still not determined empirically (the object of sensation in general) – just as soon as a system of transcendental philosophy should be achieved, on behalf of which I had, at the moment, been concerned only with the critique of reason itself.

The essential thing, however, in this system of categories, by which it is distinguished from that ancient rhapsody (which proceeded without any principle), and in virtue of which it alone deserves to be counted as philosophy, consists in this: that through it the true meaning of the pure concepts of the understanding and the condition of their use could be exactly determined. For here it became apparent that the pure concepts of the understanding, of themselves, are nothing but logical functions, but that as such they do not constitute the least concept of an object in itself but rather need sensory intuition as a basis; and then it became apparent that these concepts serve only to determine empirical judgments with respect to all the functions of judging (empirical judgments being otherwise undetermined and indifferent with respect to those functions), so as to procure universal validity for these judgments, and, by means of it, to make *judgments of experience* in general possible.

This sort of insight into the nature of the categories, which at the same time restricted their use merely to experience, never occurred to their first originator, or to anyone after him; but without this insight (which depends precisely on their derivation or deduction), they are completely useless and are a paltry list of names, without explanation or rule for their use. Had this sort of insight ever occurred to the ancients, then without doubt the entire study of cognition through pure reason, which under the name of metaphysics has ruined so many good minds over the centuries, would have come to us in a completely different [4:325] form and would have enlightened the human understanding, instead of, as has actually happened, exhausting it in murky and vain inquiries and making it unserviceable for true science.

This system of the categories now makes all treatment of any object of pure reason itself again systematic, and it yields an undoubted instruction or guiding thread as to how and through what points of inquiry any metaphysical contemplation must be directed if it is to be complete; for it exhausts all moments of the understanding, under which every other concept must be brought. Thus arose the table of principles, whose completeness can be assured only through the system of categories; and even in the division of concepts that are supposed to go beyond the physiological use of the understanding (*Critique*, p. 344, also p. 415),[21] there is always the same guiding thread, which, since it always must be taken through the same fixed points determined *a priori* in the human understanding, forms a closed circle every time, leaving no room for doubt that the object of a pure concept of the understanding or of reason, insofar as it is to be examined philosophically and according to *a priori* principles, can be cognized completely in this way. I have not even been able to refrain from making use of this guide with respect to one of the most abstract of ontological classifications, namely the manifold differentiation of the *concepts of something and nothing*, and accordingly from achieving a rule-governed and necessary table (*Critique*, p. 292).[*22]

---

* All sorts of nice notes can be made on a laid-out table of categories, such as: 1. that the third arises from the first and second, conjoined into one concept, 2. that in those for quantity and quality a progression simply procedes from Unity to Totality, or from something to nothing (for this purpose the categories of quality must stand thus: Reality, Limitation, full Negation), without *correlata* or *opposita*, while those of relation and modality carry the latter with them, 3. that, just as in the *logical table*, categorical judgments underlie all the others, as the category of substance underlies all concepts of real things, 4. that, just as modality in a judgment is not a separate predicate, so too the modal concepts do not add a determination to things, and so on. Considerations such as these all have their great utility. If beyond this all the *predicables* are enumerated – they can be extracted fairly completely from any good ontology (e.g., Baumgarten's)[23] – and they are ordered in classes under the categories (in which one must not neglect to add as complete an analysis as possible of all these concepts), then in this manner a solely analytical part of metaphysics will arise, which contains no synthetic propositions whatsoever, and which could precede the second (synthetic) part and might have, through its determinateness and completeness, not only utility, but also in addition, in virtue of its systematicity, a certain beauty.[24]

21 In Bk. 1, ch. 1 of the Dialectic, On the Paralogisms of Pure Reason A 344/B 402, Kant presents the doctrines of rational psychology concerning the immaterial soul in a fourfold division corresponding to the categories of Substance, Unity, and Possibility, and to the "quality" (second division of the Table) of simplicity.

22 In the *Critique*, A 292/B 348, Kant provides a fourfold division of the concept of nothing.

23 Ontology was the first major division of Baumgarten's *Metaphysica*.

24 In letters to Johann Schultz of 26 August 1783, and 17 February 1784 (*PC*, pp. 108–9, 111–13), Kant discusses the relations of the first and second to the third categories (as listed under the various headings in the Transcendental table of concepts of the understanding), and he mentions the possibility of someone such as Schultz using the categories as the basis for an *ars characteristica combinatoria*, a project associated with Leibniz.

[4:326]   This very system, just as every true system founded on a universal principle, also exhibits its usefulness (which cannot be praised enough) in that it expels all the extraneous concepts that might otherwise creep in among these pure concepts of the understanding, and it determines the place for every cognition. Those concepts, which I had, under the name of *concepts of reflection*, also put into a table under the guidance of the categories, mingle with the pure concepts of the understanding in ontology without privilege and legitimate claims, although the latter are concepts of connection and thereby of the object itself, but the former are only concepts of the mere comparison of already given concepts, and therefore have an entirely different nature and use; through my law-governed division (*Critique*, p. 260)[25] the pure concepts are extricated from this amalgam. But the usefulness of this separated table of categories shines forth yet more brightly if, as will happen shortly now, we set apart from the categories the table of transcendental concepts of reason, which are of a completely different nature and origin than the concepts of the understanding (hence their table must have a different form), a separation that, necessary as it is, has never occurred in any other system of metaphysics, as a result of which these ideas of reason and concepts of the understanding run confusedly together as if they belonged to one family, like siblings, an intermingling that could never be avoided in the absence of a separate system of categories.

[25] In the appendix to the Transcendental Analytic, On the Amphiboly of the Concepts of Reflection (A 260–68/B 316–28), Kant provides a fourfold division of concepts pertaining to judgment itself (identity/difference, agreement/opposition, inner/outer, and determinable/determinate or matter/form), which he relates to the cognition of phenomena and noumena.

How is metaphysics in general possible?

§40

Pure mathematics and pure natural science would not have needed, *for the purpose of their own security* and certainty, a deduction of the sort that we have hitherto accomplished for them both; for the first is supported by its own evidence, and the second, though arising from pure sources of the understanding, is nonetheless supported from experience and thoroughgoing confirmation by it – experience being a witness that natural science cannot fully renounce and dispense with, because, as philosophy,[1] despite all its certainty it can never rival mathematics. Neither science had need of the aforementioned investigation for itself, but for another science, namely metaphysics.

Apart from concepts of nature, which always find application in experience, metaphysics is further concerned with pure concepts of reason that are never given in any possible experience whatsoever, hence with concepts whose objective reality (that they are not mere fantasies), and assertions whose truth or falsity, cannot be confirmed or exposed by any experience; and this part of metaphysics is moreover precisely that which forms its essential end, toward which all the rest is only a means – and so this science needs such a deduction *for its own*

---

[1] The word "philosophy" is here used broadly (as was normal in Kant's time), to include natural science or "natural philosophy" as one of its branches (other branches included ethics, logic, and metaphysics). Earlier, Kant has drawn attention to the intuitive basis of mathematics, by contrast with the discursive basis of philosophy (§§1, 2, 7; see also Selections, pp. 178–80).

sake. The third question, now put before us, therefore concerns, as it were, the core and the characteristic feature of metaphysics, namely, the preoccupation of reason simply with itself, and that acquaintance with objects which is presumed to arise immediately from reason's brooding over its own concepts without its either needing mediation from experience for such an acquaintance, or being able to achieve such an acquaintance through experience at all.*

[4:328] Without a solution to this question reason will never be satisfied with itself. The use in experience to which reason limits the pure understanding does not entirely fulfill reason's own vocation. Each individual experience is only a part of the whole sphere of the domain of experience, but the *absolute totality of all possible experience* is not itself an experience, and yet is still a necessary problem for reason, for the mere representation of which reason needs concepts entirely different from the pure concepts of the understanding, whose use is only *immanent,* i.e., refers to experience insofar as such experience can be given, whereas the concepts of reason extend to the completeness, i.e., the collective unity of the whole of possible experience, and in that way exceed any given experience and become *transcendent.*

Hence, just as the understanding needs the *categories* for experience, reason contains in itself the basis for *ideas,* by which I mean necessary concepts whose object nevertheless *cannot* be given in any experience. The latter are just as intrinsic to the nature of reason as are the former to the nature of the understanding; and if the ideas carry with them an illusion that can easily mislead, this illusion is unavoidable, although it can very well be prevented "from leading us astray."

Since all illusion consists in taking the subjective basis for a judgment to be objective, pure reason's knowledge of itself in its transcendent (overreaching) use will be the only prevention against the errors into which reason falls if it misconstrues its vocation and, in a transcendent manner, refers to the object in itself that which concerns only its own subject and the guidance of that subject in every use that is immanent.

---

* If it can be said that a science is *actual* at least in the thought of all humankind from the moment it has been determined that the problems which lead to it are set before everyone by the nature of human reason, and therefore that many (if faulty) attempts at those problems are always inevitable, it will also have to be said: Metaphysics is subjectively actual (and necessarily so); and then we will rightly ask: How is it (objectively) possible?

§41

The distinction of *ideas*, i.e., of pure concepts of reason, from categories, or pure concepts of the understanding, as cognitions of completely different type, origin, and use, is so important a piece of the foundation of a science which is to contain a system of all these cognitions *a priori* that, without such a separation, metaphysics is utterly impossible, or at [4:329] best is a disorderly and bungling endeavor to patch together a house of cards, without knowledge of the materials with which one is preoccupied and of their suitability for one or another end. If the *Critique of Pure Reason* had done nothing but first point out this distinction, it would thereby have already contributed more to elucidating our conception of, and to guiding inquiry in, the field of metaphysics, than have all the fruitless efforts undertaken previously to satisfy the transcendent problems of pure reason, without it ever being imagined that one may have been situated in a completely different field from that of the understanding, and, for that reason, was listing the concepts of the understanding together with those of reason as if they were of the same kind.

§42

All the pure cognitions of the understanding are such that their concepts can be given in experience and their principles confirmed through experience; by contrast, the transcendent cognitions of reason neither allow what relates to their *ideas* to be given in experience, nor their *theses* ever to be confirmed or refuted through experience; hence, only pure reason itself can detect the error that perhaps creeps into them, but this is very hard to do, because this selfsame reason by nature becomes dialectical through its ideas, and this unavoidable illusion cannot be kept in check through any objective and dogmatic investigation of things, but only through a subjective investigation of reason itself, as a source of ideas.

§43

In the *Critique* I always gave my greatest attention not only to how I could distinguish carefully the types of cognition, but also to how I could derive all the concepts belonging to each type from their common source, so that I might not only, by learning their origin, be able to determine their use with certainty, but also might have the inestimable advantage (never yet imagined) of cognizing *a priori*, hence according to principles, the completeness of the enumeration, classification, and [4:330] specification of the concepts. Failing this, everything in metaphysics is nothing but rhapsody, in which one never knows whether what one has is enough, or whether and where something may still be lacking. This advantage is, of course, available only in pure philosophy, but it constitutes the essence of that philosophy.

Since I had found the origin of the categories in the four logical functions of all judgments of the understanding, it was completely natural to look for the origin of the ideas in the three functions of syllogisms[a] (i.e., inferences of reason); for once such pure concepts of reason (transcendental ideas) have been granted, then, if they are not to be taken for innate, they could indeed be found nowhere else except in this same act of reason, which, insofar as it relates merely to form, constitutes the logical in syllogisms, but, insofar as it represents the judgments of the understanding as determined with respect to one or another *a priori* form, constitutes the transcendental concepts of pure reason.

The formal distinction of syllogisms necessitates their division into categorical, hypothetical, and disjunctive. Therefore the concepts of reason based thereupon contain first, the idea of the complete subject (the substantial), second, the idea of the complete series of conditions, and third, the determination of all concepts in the idea of a complete sum total of the possible.[*] The first idea was psychological, the second cosmological, the third theological; and since all three give rise to a dialectic, but each in its own way, all this provided the basis for dividing the entire dialectic of pure reason into the paralogism, the antinomy,

---

[*] In disjunctive judgments we consider *all possibility* as divided with respect to a certain concept. The ontological principle of the thoroughgoing determination of a thing in general (out of all possible opposing predicates, each thing is attributed one or the other), which is at the same time the principle of all disjunctive judgments, founds itself upon the sum total of all possibility, in which the possibility of each thing in general is taken to be determinable. The following helps provide a small elucidation of the above proposition: That the act of reason in disjunctive syllogisms is the same in form with that by which reason achieves the idea of a sum total of all reality, which contains in itself the positive members of all opposing predicates.

[a] *Vernunftschlüsse* (The subsequent parenthetical expression has been added to show the literal meaning of this word.)

and finally the ideal of pure reason – through which derivation it is rendered completely certain that all claims of pure reason are represented here in full, and not one can be missing, because full measure is thereby taken of the faculty of reason itself, as that alone through which they arise.

§44

In this examination it is in general further noteworthy: that the ideas of reason are not, like the categories, helpful to us in some way in using the understanding with respect to experience, but are completely dispensable with respect to such use, nay, are contrary to and obstructive of the maxims for the cognition of nature through reason, although they are still quite necessary in another respect, yet to be determined.[2] In explaining the appearances of the soul, we can be completely indifferent to whether it is a simple substance or not; for we are unable through any possible experience to make the concept of a simple being sensorily intelligible, hence intelligible *in concreto*; and this concept is therefore completely empty with respect to all hoped-for insight into the cause of the appearances, and cannot serve as a principle of explanation of that which supplies inner or outer experience. Just as little can the cosmological ideas of the beginning of the world or the eternity of the world (*a parte ante*)[3] help us to explain any event in the world itself. Finally, in accordance with a correct maxim of natural philosophy, we must refrain from all explanations of the organization of nature drawn from the will of a supreme being, because this is no longer natural philosophy but an admission that we have come to the end of it. These ideas therefore have a completely different determination of their use from that of the categories, through which (and through the principles built upon them) experience itself first became possible. Nevertheless

---

[2] Examples of "maxims of reason" or "maxims of speculative reason" are given in the *Critique* in the Regulative Use of the Ideas of Pure Reason, at A 666–668/B 694–696, and include "principles" of homogeneity or aggregation, of variety or division into species and of affinity or continuity of forms (also, A 658/B 686). Kant says that the ideas of reason are regulative with respect to the use of the understanding in experience, and he gives the term "maxims" to the so-called principles that guide such use. In mentioning a further respect in which it is necessary to use the ideas of reason, we may suppose that Kant is speaking of their use in practical or moral reasoning.

[3] "up until now," literally, "on the side of the previous."

our laborious analytic of the understanding[4] would have been entirely superfluous, if our aim had been directed toward nothing other than mere cognition of nature insofar as such cognition can be given in experience; for reason conducts its affairs in both mathematics and natural science quite safely and quite well, even without any such subtle deduction; hence our critique of the understanding joins with the ideas of pure reason for a purpose that lies beyond the use of the under- standing in experience, though we have said above that the use of the understanding in this regard is wholly impossible and without object or meaning. There must nonetheless be agreement between what belongs to the nature of reason and what belongs to the nature of the under- standing, and the former must contribute to the perfection of the latter and cannot possibly confuse it.

[4:332] The solution to this question is as follows: Pure reason does not, among its ideas, have particular objects that might lie beyond the field of experience and toward which it is directed, but it merely demands completeness in the use of the understanding in the connection of experience. This completeness, however, can only be a completeness of principles, but not of intuitions and objects. Nonetheless, in order to represent these principles determinately, reason conceives of them as the cognition of an object, the cognition of which is completely determined with respect to these rules – though the object is only an idea – so as to bring cognition through the understanding as close as possible to the completeness that this idea signifies.

§45

Preliminary remark to the Dialectic of Pure Reason

We have shown above (§§33, 34): that the purity of the categories from all admixture with sensory determinations can mislead reason to extend their use entirely beyond all experience, to things in themselves; and yet, because the categories are themselves unable to find any intuition that could provide them with meaning and sense *in concreto*, they cannot in and of themselves provide any determinate concept of anything at all, though they can indeed, as mere logical functions, represent a thing in

---

[4] Kant refers to the Transcendental Analytic in the *Critique*, which included the Deduction (see the Table of contents in the Selections).

general. Now hyperbolical objects of this kind are what are called *noumena* or pure beings of the understanding (better: beings of thought)[b] – such as, e.g., *substance*, but which is thought *without persistence* in time, or a *cause*, which would however *not* act *in time*, and so on – because such predicates are attributed to these objects as serve only to make the lawfulness of experience possible, and yet they are nonetheless deprived of all the conditions of intuition under which alone experience is possible, as a result of which the above concepts again lose all meaning.

There is, however, no danger that the understanding will of itself wantonly stray beyond its boundaries into the field of mere beings of thought, without being urged by alien laws. But if reason, which can never be fully satisfied with any use of the rules of the understanding in experience because such use is always still conditioned, requires completion of this chain of conditions, then the understanding is driven out of its circle, in order partly to represent the objects of experience in a series stretching so far that no experience can comprise the likes of it, partly (in order to complete the series) even to look for *noumena* entirely [4:333] outside said experience to which reason can attach the chain and in that way, independent at last of the conditions of experience, can nonetheless make its hold complete. These are the transcendental ideas, which, although in accordance with the true but hidden end of the natural determination of our reason, they may be aimed, not at concepts that are overreaching, but merely at the unbounded expansion of the use of concepts in experience, may nonetheless, through an unavoidable illusion, elicit from the understanding a *transcendent* use, which, though deceitful, nonetheless cannot be constrained by any intention to stay within the bounds of experience, but only through scientific instruction, and with difficulty.

§46

1. Psychological ideas (Critique, pp. 341 ff.)[5]

It has been observed long ago that in all substances the true subject – namely that which remains after all accidents (as predicates) have been

---

[b] *Gedankenwesen*, contrasted with the just previous *Verstandeswesen*.
[5] A 341–405, Of the Paralogisms of Pure Reason; largely replaced by B 399–432.

removed – and hence the *substantial* itself, is unknown to us; and various complaints have been made about these limits to our insight. It may well be noted here, that human understanding is not to be blamed because it does not know the substantial in things, i.e., cannot determine it of itself, but on the contrary because it wants to cognize it (a mere idea) determinately, like an object that is given. Pure reason demands that for each predicate of a thing we should seek its appropriate subject, but for this subject, which is in turn necessarily only a predicate, that we should seek its subject again, and so forth to infinity (or as far as we get). But from this it follows that we should take nothing that we can attain for a final subject, and that the substantial itself could never be thought by our ever-so-deeply penetrating understanding, even if the whole of nature were laid bare before it; for the specific nature of our understanding consists in thinking everything discursively, i.e., through concepts, hence through mere predicates, among which the absolute subject must therefore always be absent. Consequently, all of the real properties by which we cognize bodies are mere accidents for which we [4:334] lack a subject, even impenetrability, which must always be conceived only as the effect of a force.

Now it does appear as if we have something substantial in the consciousness of ourselves (i.e., in the thinking subject), and indeed have it in immediate intuition; for all the predicates of the inner sense are referred to the *I* as subject, and this *I* cannot again be thought as the predicate of some other subject. It therefore appears that in this case completeness in referring the given concepts to a subject as predicates is not a mere idea, but that the object, namely the *absolute subject* itself, is given in experience. But this expectation is disappointed. For the I is not a concept* at all, but only a designation of the object of inner sense insofar as we do not further cognize it through any predicate; hence although it cannot itself be the predicate of any other thing, just as little can it be a determinate concept of an absolute subject, but as in all the other cases it can only be the referring of inner appearances to their unknown subject. Nevertheless, through a wholly natural misunder-

---

* If the representation of apperception, the *I*, were a concept through which anything might be thought, it would then be able to be used as a predicate for other things, or to contain such predicates in itself. But it is nothing more than a feeling of an existence without the least concept, and it is a representation only of that to which all thinking stands in relation (*relatione accidentis*).[6]

6 "relation of accident"

standing, this idea (which, as a regulative principle, serves perfectly well to destroy completely all materialistic explanations of the inner appearances of our soul)^c gives rise to a seemingly plausible argument for inferring the nature of our thinking being from this presumed cognition of the substantial in that being, insofar as knowledge of its nature falls completely outside the sum total of experience.

§47

This thinking self (the soul), as the ultimate subject of thinking, which cannot itself be represented as the predicate of another thing, may now indeed be called substance: but this concept nonetheless remains completely empty and without any consequences, if persistence (as that which renders the concept of substances fertile within experience) cannot be proven of it.

Persistence, however, can never be proven from the concept of a sub- [4:335] stance as a thing in itself, but only for the purposes of experience. This has been sufficiently established in the First Analogy of Experience (*Critique*, p. 182);^{7} and anyone who will not grant this proof can test for themselves whether they succeed in proving, from the concept of a subject that does not exist as the predicate of another thing, that the existence of that subject is persistent throughout, and that it can neither come into being nor pass away, either in itself or through any natural cause. Synthetic *a priori* propositions of this type can never be proven in themselves, but only in relation to things as objects of a possible experience.

§48

If, therefore, we want to infer the persistence of the soul from the concept of the soul as substance, this can be valid of the soul only for the purpose of possible experience, and not of the soul as a thing in itself and beyond all possible experience. But life is the subjective condition of all our possible experience: consequently, only the persistence of the soul during life can be inferred, for the death of a human being is the end of all experience as far as the soul as an object of experience is concerned (provided that the opposite has not been

^{c} The original has an asterisk here, with no corresponding note.
^{7} A 182–9/B 224–32.

proven, which is the very matter in question). Therefore the persistence of the soul can be proven only during the life of a human being (which proof will be granted us), but not after death (as is actually important to us) – and indeed then only from the universal ground that the concept of substance, insofar as it is to be considered as connected necessarily with the concept of persistence, can be so connected only in accordance with a principle of possible experience, and hence only for the purpose of the latter.[*]

§49

That our outer perceptions do not merely correspond to something real[d] outside us, but must so correspond, also can never be proven as a connection of things in themselves, but can well be proven for the purpose of experience. This is as much as to say: it can very well be proven that there is something outside us of an empirical kind, and hence as appearance in space; for we are not concerned with objects other than those which belong to a possible experience, just because such objects cannot be given to us in any experience and therefore are nothing for us. Outside me empirically is that which is intuited in space; and because this space, together with all the appearances it contains, belongs to those representations whose connection according to laws of experience proves their objective truth, just as the connection of the

---

[*] It is in fact quite remarkable that metaphysicians have always slid so tranquilly by the principle of the persistence of substances, without ever attempting to prove it; doubtless because they found themselves completely forsaken by all grounds of proof as soon as they commenced with the concept of substance. Common sense, being well aware that without this assumption no unification of perceptions in an experience would be possible, makes up for this defect with a postulate; for it could never extract this principle from experience itself, partly because experience cannot follow the materials (substances) through all their alterations and dissolutions far enough to be able to find matter always undiminished, partly because the principle contains *necessity*, which is always the sign of an *a priori* principle. But the metaphysicians applied this principle confidently to the concept of the soul as a *substance* and inferred its necessary continuation after the death of a human being (principally because the simplicity of this substance, which had been inferred from the indivisibility of consciousness, saved it from destruction through dissolution). Had they found the true source of this principle, which however would have required far deeper investigations than they ever wanted to start, then they would have seen: that this law of the persistence of substances is granted only for the purpose of experience and therefore can hold good only for things insofar as they are to be cognized in experience and connected with other things, but never for things irrespective of all possible experience, hence not for the soul after death.

[d] *Wirkliches*

appearances of the inner sense proves the reality[e] of my soul (as an object of inner sense), it follows that I am, by means of outer appearances, just as conscious of the reality of bodies as outer appearances in space, as I am, by means of inner experience, conscious of the existence of my soul in time – which soul I cognize only as an object of inner sense through the appearances constituting an inner state, and whose being as it is in itself, which underlies these appearances, is unknown to me. Cartesian idealism therefore distinguishes only outer experience from dream, and lawfulness as a criterion of the truth of the [4:337] former, from the disorder and false illusion of the latter. In both cases it presupposes space and time as conditions for the existence of objects and merely asks whether the objects of the outer senses are actually to be found in the space in which we put them while awake, in the way that the object of inner sense, the soul, actually is in time, i.e., whether experience carries with itself sure criteria to distinguish it from imagination. Here the doubt can be easily removed, and we always remove it in ordinary life by investigating the connection of appearances in both space and time according to universal laws of experience, and if the representation of outer things consistently agrees therewith, we cannot doubt that those things should not constitute truthful experience. Because appearances are considered as appearances only in accordance with their connection within experience, material idealism can therefore be very easily removed; and it is just as secure an experience that bodies exist outside us (in space) as that I myself exist in accordance with the representation of inner sense (in time) – for the concept: *outside us*, means only existence in space. Since, however, the I in the proposition *I am* does not mean merely the object of inner intuition (in time) but also the subject of consciousness, just as body does not mean merely outer intuition (in space) but also the thing *in itself* that underlies this appearance, accordingly the question of whether bodies (as appearances of outer sense) exist *outside my thought* as bodies in nature can without hesitation be answered negatively; but here matters do not stand otherwise for the question of whether I myself *as an appearance of inner sense* (the soul according to empirical psychology) exist in time outside my power of representation, for this question must also be answered negatively. In this way everything is, when reduced to its true meaning,

[e] *Wirklichkeit*

91

conclusive and certain. Formal idealism (elsewhere called transcendental idealism by me) actually destroys[f] material or Cartesian idealism. For if space is nothing but a form of my sensibility, then it is, as a representation in me, just as real as I am myself, and the question now concerns only the empirical truth of the appearances in this space. If this is not the case, but rather space and the appearances in it are something existing outside us, then all the criteria of experience can never, outside our perception, prove the reality of these objects outside us.

[4:338]

§50

II. Cosmological ideas (Critique, pp. 405 ff.)[8]

This product of pure reason in its transcendent use is its most remarkable phenomenon, and it works the most strongly of all to awaken philosophy from its dogmatic slumber, and to prompt it toward the difficult business of the critique of reason itself.

I call this idea cosmological because it always finds its object only in the sensible world, and because it needs no other world than that whose object[g] is an object[h] for the senses, and hence, thus far, is immanent and not transcendent, and therefore, up to this point, is not yet an idea; by contrast, to think of the soul as a simple substance is already as much as to think of it as an object (the simple), the likes of which cannot be represented at all by the senses. Notwithstanding all that, the cosmological idea expands the connection of the conditioned with its condition (be it mathematical or dynamic) so greatly that experience can never match it, and therefore it is, with respect to this point, always an idea whose object can never be adequately given in any experience whatever.

§51

In the first place, the usefulness of a system of categories is here revealed so clearly and unmistakably that even if there were no further grounds of proof of that system, this alone would sufficiently establish their indispensability in the system of pure reason. There are no more than four such transcendental ideas, as many as there are classes of categories;

---

[f] *aufhebt*   [g] *Gegenstand*   [h] *Objekt*

[8] A 405–567/B 432–595, The Antinomy of Pure Reason (see pp. 176–7).

in each of them, however, they refer only to the absolute completeness of the series of conditions for a given conditioned. In accordance with these cosmological ideas there are also only four different kinds of dialectical assertions of pure reason, which show themselves to be dialectical because for each such assertion a contradictory one stands in opposition in accordance with equally plausible principles of pure reason, a conflict that cannot be avoided by any metaphysical art of the most subtle distinctions, but that requires the philosopher to return to the first sources of pure reason itself. This antinomy, which is surely [4:339] not contrived arbitrarily, but is grounded in the nature of human reason, and so is unavoidable and never ending, contains the following four theses together with their antitheses.

I.
Thesis

The world has, as to time and space,
a beginning (a boundary).

Antithesis

The world is, as to time and space,
infinite.

2.	3.
Thesis	*Thesis*
Everything in the world is constituted out of the *simple.*	There exist in the world causes through *freedom.*
Antithesis	*Antithesis*
There is nothing simple, but everything is *composite.*	There is no freedom, but everything is *nature.*

4.
Thesis

In the series of causes in the world there is a
necessary being.

Antithesis

There is nothing necessary in this series, but in it
everything is contingent.

§52

Here now is the strangest phenomenon of human reason, no example of which can otherwise be drawn from any other use of reason. If (as normally happens) we think of the appearances of the sensible world as things in themselves, if we take the principles of their connection to be principles that are universally valid for things in themselves and not [4:340] merely for experience (as is just as common, nay, is unavoidable without our *Critique*): then an unexpected conflict comes to light, which can never be settled in the usual dogmatic manner, since both thesis and antithesis can be established through equally evident, clear, and incontestable proofs – for I will vouch for the correctness of all these proofs – and therefore reason is divided against itself, a situation that makes the skeptic rejoice, but must make the critical philosopher anxious and reflective.

§52b

One can tinker around with metaphysics in sundry ways without even suspecting that one might be venturing into untruth. For if we simply do not contradict ourselves – something that is indeed entirely possible with synthetic, though completely fabricated, propositions – then we can never be refuted by experience in all such cases in which the concepts we connect are mere ideas, which can by no means be given (in their entire content) in experience. For how will we decide through experience: Whether the world has existed from eternity, or has a beginning? Whether matter is infinitely divisible, or is constituted out of simple parts? Concepts such as these cannot be given in any experience (even the greatest possible), and so the falsity of the affirmative or negative thesis cannot be discovered through that touchstone.

The single possible case in which reason would reveal (against its will) its secret dialectic (which it falsely passes off as dogmatics) would be that in which it based an assertion on a universally acknowledged principle, and, with the greatest propriety in the mode of inference, derived the direct opposite from another equally accredited principle. Now this case is here actual, and indeed is so with respect to four natural ideas of reason, from which there arise – each with proper consistency and from universally acknowledged principles – four assertions on one side and just as many counterassertions on the other side, thereby revealing the dialectical illusion of pure reason in the use of these principles, which otherwise would have remained forever hidden.

Here is, therefore, a decisive test, which necessarily must disclose to us a fault that lies hidden in the presuppositions of reason.* Of two mutually [4:341] contradictory propositions both cannot be false except if the concept underlying them both is itself contradictory; e.g., the two propositions: a rectangular circle is round, and: a rectangular circle is not round, are both false. For, as regards the first, it is false that the aforementioned circle is round, since it is rectangular; but it is also false that it is not round, i.e., has angles, since it is a circle. The logical sign for the impossibility of a concept consists, then, in this: that under the presupposition of this concept, two contradictory propositions would be false simultaneously; and so, since in between these two a third proposition cannot be thought, through this concept *nothing at all* is thought.

§52c

Now underlying the first two antinomies, which I call mathematical because they concern adding together or dividing up the homogeneous, is a contradictory concept of this type; and by this means I explain how it happens that thesis and antithesis are both false together.

If I speak of objects in time and space, I am not speaking of things in themselves (since I know nothing of them), but only of things in appearance, i.e., of experience as a distinct mode of cognition of objects that is granted to human beings alone. I must not say of that which I think in space or time: that it is in itself in space and time, independent of this thought of mine; for then I would contradict myself, since space and time, together with the appearances in them, are nothing existing outside my representations, but are themselves only modes of represen- [4:342] tation, and it is patently contradictory to say of a mere mode of representation that it also exists outside our representation. The objects

---

* I therefore desire that the critical reader principally concern himself with this antinomy, because nature itself seems to have set it up to make reason suspicious in its bold claims and to force a self-examination. I promise to answer for each proof I have given of both thesis and antithesis, and thereby to establish the certainty of the inevitable antinomy of reason. If the reader is induced, through this strange phenomenon, to reexamine the presuppositions that underlie it, he will then feel constrained to investigate more deeply with me the primary foundation of all cognition through pure reason.

of the senses therefore exist only in experience; by contrast, to grant them their own existence without experience or prior to it, as subsisting for themselves, is as much as to imagine that experience exists without experience or prior to it.

Now if I ask about the magnitude of the world with respect to space and time, for all of my concepts it is equally impossible to assert that it is infinite as that it is finite. For neither of these two can be contained in experience, because it is not possible to have experience of either an *infinite* space or infinitely flowing time, or of a *bounding* of the world by an empty space or by an earlier, empty time; these are only ideas. Therefore the magnitude of the world, determined one or the other way, must lie in itself, separated from all experience. But this contradicts the concept of a sensible world, which is simply a sum total of the appearances whose existence and connection takes place only in representation, namely in experience, since this world is not a thing in itself, but is itself nothing but a mode of representation. From this it follows that, since the concept of a sensible world existing for itself is, in itself, contradictory, any solution to this problem as to its magnitude will always be false, whether one attempts to solve it affirmatively or negatively.

The same holds for the second antinomy, which concerns dividing up the appearances. For these appearances are mere representations, and the parts exist only in the represention of them, hence in the dividing, i.e., in a possible experience in which they are given, and the dividing therefore proceeds only as far as possible experience reaches. To assume that an appearance, e.g., that of a body, contains within itself, before all experience, all of the parts that possible experience can ever attain, means: to give to a mere appearance, which can exist only in experience, at the same time its own existence previous to experience, which is to say: that mere representations exist before they are encountered in the representational power, which contradicts itself and hence also contradicts every solution to this misunderstood problem, whether that solution asserts that bodies in themselves are constituted out of infinitely many parts or out of a finite number of simple parts.

[4:343]

§53

In the first (mathematical) class of antinomy, the falsity of the presupposition consisted in the following: that something self-contradictory (namely, appearance as a thing in itself) would be represented as being unifiable in a concept. But regarding the second, namely the dynamical, class of antinomy, the falsity of the presupposition consists in this: that something that is unifiable is represented as contradictory; consequently, while in the first case both of the mutually opposing assertions were false, here on the contrary both of the assertions, which are set in opposition to one another through misunderstanding alone, can be true.

Specifically, mathematical combination necessarily presupposes the homogeneity of the things combined (in the concept of magnitude), but dynamical connection does not require this at all. If it is a question of the magnitude of that which is extended, all of the parts must be homogeneous among themselves and with the whole; in contrast, in the connection of cause and effect homogeneity can indeed be found, but it is not necessary; for the concept of causality (by means of which through one thing, something completely different from it is posited) at least does not require it.

If the objects of the sensible world were taken for things in themselves, and the previously stated natural laws for laws of things in themselves, contradiction would be unavoidable. In the same way, if the subject of freedom were represented, like the other objects, as a mere appearance, contradiction could again not be avoided, for the same thing would simultaneously be affirmed and denied of the same object in the same sense. But if natural necessity is referred only to appearances and freedom only to things in themselves, then no contradiction arises if both kinds of causality are assumed or conceded equally, as difficult or impossible as it may be to make conceivable causality of the latter kind.

Within appearance, every effect is an event, or something that happens in time; the effect must, in accordance with the universal law of nature, be preceded by a determination of the causality of its cause (a state of the cause), from which the effect follows in accordance with a constant law. But this determination of the cause to causality must also be something *that occurs or takes place*; the cause must have *begun* to *act*, for otherwise a sequence in time cannot be thought between it and the [4:344] effect. Both the effect and the causality of the cause would have always existed. Therefore the *determination* of the cause *to produce an effect* must also arise among the appearances, and so it too, just like its effect, must be an event, which again must have its cause, and so on, and therefore natural necessity must be the condition in accordance with which efficient causes are determined. Should, by contrast, freedom be a property of certain causes of appearances, then that freedom must, in relation to the appearances as events, be a faculty of starting those events *from itself* (*sponte*),[9] i.e., without requiring that the causality of the cause itself would have to begin, and hence without need for any other ground to determine its beginning. But then *the cause*, as to its causality, would not have to be subject to temporal determinations of its state, i.e., would *not* have to be *appearance* at all, i.e., would have to be taken for a thing in itself, and only the *effects* would have to be taken for *appearances*.* If this sort of influence of intelligible beings on appearances can be thought without contradiction, then natural necessity will indeed attach to every connection of cause and effect in the sensible world, and yet that cause which is itself not an appearance (though it underlies appearance) will still be entitled to freedom, and therefore nature and freedom can be ascribed without contradiction to the very same thing, but in different respects, in the one case as appearance, in the other as a thing in itself.

We have in us a faculty that not only stands in connection with its subjectively determining grounds, which are the natural causes of its [4:345] actions – and thus far is the faculty of a being which itself belongs to appearances – but that also is related to objective grounds that are mere ideas, insofar as these ideas can determine this faculty, a connection that is expressed by *ought*.[j] This faculty is called *reason*, and insofar as we are considering a being (the human being) solely as regards this objectively determinable reason, this being cannot be considered as a being of the

---

* The idea of freedom has its place solely in the relation of the *intellectual*,[i] as cause, to the *appearance*, as effect. Therefore we cannot, in consideration of the unceasing activity by which matter fills its space, bestow freedom upon it, even though this activity occurs through an inner principle. We can just as little find any concept of freedom to fit a purely intelligible being, e.g., God, insofar as his action is immanent. For his action, although independent of causes determining it from outside, nevertheless is determined in his eternal reason, hence in the divine *nature*. Only if *something* should *begin* through an action, hence the effect be found in the time series, and so in the sensible world, does the question arise of whether the causality of the cause itself must also have a beginning, or whether the cause can originate an effect without its causality itself having a beginning. In the first case the concept of this causality is a concept of natural necessity, in the second of freedom. From this the reader will see that, since I have explained freedom as the faculty to begin an event by oneself, I have exactly hit that concept which is the problem of metaphysics.

[i] *des Intellektuellen* [j] *Sollen*
[9] "spontaneously"

senses; rather, the aforesaid property is the property of a thing in itself, and the possibility of that property – namely, how the *ought*, which has never yet happened, can determine the activity of this being and can be the cause of actions whose effect is an appearance in the sensible world – we cannot comprehend at all. Yet the causality of reason with respect to effects in the sensible world would nonetheless be freedom, insofar as *objective grounds*, which are themselves ideas, are taken to be determining with respect to that causality. For the action of that causality would in that case not depend on any subjective, hence also not on any temporal conditions, and would therefore also not depend on the natural law that serves to determine those conditions, because grounds of reason provide the rule for actions universally, from principles, without influence from the circumstances of time or place.

What I adduce here counts only as an example, for intelligibility, and does not belong necessarily to our question, which must be decided from mere concepts independently of properties that we find in the actual world.

I can now say without contradiction: all of the actions of a rational being, insofar as they are appearances (encountered in some experience or other), are subject to natural necessity; but the very same actions, with respect only to the rational subject and its faculty of acting in accordance with bare reason, are free. What, then, is required for natural necessity? Nothing more than the determinability of every event in the sensible world according to constant laws, and therefore a relation to a cause within appearance; whereby the underlying thing in itself and its causality remain unknown. But I say: *the law of nature remains*, whether the rational being be a cause of effects in the sensible world through reason and hence through freedom, or whether that being does not determine such effects through rational grounds. For if the first is the case, the action takes place according to maxims whose effect within appearance will always conform to constant laws; if the second is the [4:346] case, and the action does not take place according to principles of reason, it is subject to the empirical laws of sensibility, and in both cases the effects are connected according to constant laws; but we require nothing more for natural necessity, and indeed know nothing more of it. In the first case, however, reason is the cause of these natural laws and is therefore free, in the second case the effects flow according to mere natural laws of sensibility, because reason exercises no influence on them; but, because of this, reason is not itself determined by sensibility (which is impossible), and it is therefore also free in this case. Therefore freedom does not impede the natural law of appearances, any more than this law interferes with the freedom of the use of practical reason, a use that stands in connection with things in themselves as determining grounds.

In this way practical freedom – namely, that freedom in which reason has causality in accordance with objective determining grounds – is rescued, without natural necessity suffering the least harm with respect to the very same effects, as appearances. This can also help elucidate what we have had to say about transcendental freedom and its unification[k] with natural necessity (in the subject, but not taken in one and the same respect). For, as regards transcendental freedom, any beginning of an action of a being out of objective causes is always, with respect to these determining grounds, a *first beginning*, although the same action is, in the series of appearances, only a *subalternate beginning*, prior to which a state of the cause must precede which determines that cause and which is itself determined in the same way by an immediately preceding cause: so that in rational beings (or in general in any beings, provided that their causality is determined in them as things in themselves) one can conceive of a faculty for beginning a series of states spontaneously without falling into contradiction with the laws of nature. For the relation of an action to the objective grounds of reason is not a temporal relation; here, that which determines the causality does not precede the action as regards time, because such determining grounds do not represent the relation of objects to the senses (and so to causes within appearance), but rather they represent determining causes as things in themselves, which are not subject to temporal conditions. Hence the action can be regarded as a first beginning with respect to the causality of reason, but nonetheless at the same time it can be seen as a

[4:347] mere subordinated beginning with respect to the series of appearances, and can without contradiction be considered in the former respect as free, in the latter (since the action is mere appearance) as subject to natural necessity.

As regards the *fourth* antinomy, it is removed[l] in a similar manner as was the conflict of reason with itself in the third. For if only the *cause in*

---

    [k] *Vereinbarung*   [l] *aufgehoben wird*

the appearances is distinguished from the *cause of the appearances* insofar as the latter cause can be thought as a *thing in itself*, then these two propositions can very well exist side by side, as follows: that there occurs no cause of the sensible world (in accordance with similar laws of causality) whose existence is absolutely necessary, as also on the other side: that this world is nonetheless connected with a necessary being as its cause (but of a distinct kind and according to distinct laws) – the inconsistency of these two propositions resting solely on the mistake of extending what holds merely for appearances to things in themselves, and in general of mixing the two of these up into one concept.

§54

This is now the statement and solution of the whole antinomy in which reason finds itself entangled in the application of its principles to the sensible world, and of which the former (the mere statement) even by itself would already be of considerable benefit toward a knowledge^m of human reason, even if the solution of this conflict should not yet fully satisfy the reader, who has here to combat a natural illusion that has only recently been presented to him as such, after he had always taken that illusion for the truth. One consequence of all this is, then, unavoidable; namely, that since it is completely impossible to escape from this conflict of reason with itself as long as the objects of the sensible world are taken for things in themselves – and not for what they in fact are, that is, for mere appearances – the reader is obliged, for that reason, to take up once more the deduction of all our cognition *a priori* (and the examination of that deduction which I have provided), in order to come to a decision about it. For the present I do not require more; for if, through this pursuit, he has first thought himself deeply enough into the nature of pure reason, then the concepts by means of which alone the solution to this conflict [4:348] of reason is possible will already be familiar to him, a circumstance without which I cannot expect full approbation from even the most attentive reader.

---

^m *Kenntnis*

§55

III. Theological idea (Critique, pp. 571 ff.)[10]

The third transcendental idea, which provides material for the most important among all the uses of reason – a use that, if pursued merely speculatively, is, however, overreaching (transcendent) and thereby dialectical – is the ideal of pure reason. Here reason does not, as with the psychological and the cosmological idea, start from experience and become deceived by the upward rise of grounds into aspiring to, if possible, absolute completeness in their series, but instead breaks off entirely from experience and descends from bare concepts of what would constitute the absolute completeness of a thing in general – and so by means of the idea of a supremely perfect first being – to determination of the possibility, hence the reality, of all other things; in consequence, here the bare presupposition of a being that, although not in the series of experiences, is nonetheless thought on behalf of experience, for the sake of comprehensibility in the connection, ordering, and unity of that experience – i.e., the *idea* – is easier to distinguish from the concept of the understanding than in the previous cases. Here therefore the dialectical illusion, which arises from our taking the subjective conditions of our thinking for objective conditions of things themselves and our taking a hypothesis that is necessary for the satisfaction of our reason for a dogma, is easily exposed, and I therefore need mention nothing more about the presumptions of transcendental theology, since what the *Critique* says about them is clear, evident, and decisive.

§56

General note to the transcendental ideas

The objects that are given to us through experience are incomprehensible to us in many respects, and there are many questions to which [4:349] natural law carries us, which, if pursued to a certain height (yet always in conformity with those laws) cannot be solved at all; e.g., how pieces of matter attract one another. But if we completely abandon nature,

---

[10] A 571/B 599, On the Transcendental Ideal.

or transcend all experience in advancing the connection of nature and so lose ourselves in mere ideas, then we are unable to say that the object is incomprehensible to us and that the nature of things presents us with unsolvable problems; for then we are not concerned with nature or in general with objects that are given, but with mere concepts that have their origin solely in our reason, and with mere beings of thought, with respect to which all problems, which must originate from the concepts of those very beings, can be solved, since reason certainly can and must be held fully accountable for its own proceedings.* Because the psychological, cosmological, and theological ideas are nothing but pure concepts of reason, which cannot be given in any experience, the questions that reason puts before us with respect to them are not given to us through objects, but rather through mere maxims of reason for the sake of its self-satisfaction, and these questions must collectively be capable of sufficient answer – which occurs by its being shown that they are principles for bringing the use of our understanding into thoroughgoing harmony, completeness, and syn-thetic unity, and that they are, to that extent, valid only for experience, though in the *totality* of that experience. But although an absolute totality of experience is not possible, nonetheless the idea of a totality of cognition according to principles in general is what alone can provide it with a distinct kind of unity, namely that of a system, without which unity our cognition is nothing but piecework and cannot be used for the highest end (which is always the system of all ends); and I mean [4:350] here not only the practical use of reason, but also the highest end of its speculative use.

Therefore the transcendental ideas express the peculiar vocation of reason, namely to be a principle of the systematic unity of the use of

---

* Herr Platner in his *Aphorisms* therefore says with astuteness (§§728–9): "If reason is a criterion, then there cannot possibly be a concept that is incomprehensible to human reason. – Only in the actual does incomprehensibility have a place. Here the incomprehensibility arises from the inadequacy of acquired ideas."[11] – It therefore only sounds paradoxical, and is otherwise not strange to say: that in nature much is incomprehensible (e.g., the procreative faculty), but if we rise still higher and go out beyond nature, then once again all is comprehensible to us; for then we entirely leave behind the *objects* that can be given to us, and busy ourselves merely with ideas, with respect to which we can very well comprehend the law that reason prescribes to the understanding through these ideas, since that law is reason's own product.

[11] Ernst Platner (1744–1818), *Philosophische Aphorismen*, 2 vols. (Leipzig, 1776–82), vol. 1, p. 229. Kant omits the qualifier *menschliche* from Platner's first use of *Vernunft*; hence, a translation of Platner's text would begin: "If human reason . . ."

the understanding. But if one looks upon this unity of mode of cognition as if it were inhering in the object of cognition, if one takes that which really is only *regulative* to be *constitutive*, and becomes convinced that one's knowledge[n] can, by means of these ideas, be expanded far beyond all possible experience, hence can be expanded transcendently, then, since this unity after all serves only to bring experience in itself as near as possible to completeness (i.e., to have its advance constrained by nothing that cannot belong to experience), this is a mere misunderstanding in judging the true vocation of our reason and of its principles, and it is a dialectic, which partly confounds the use of reason in experience, and partly divides reason against itself.

Conclusion

On determining the boundary of pure reason

§57

After the extremely clear proofs we have given above, it would be an absurdity for us, with respect to any object, to hope to cognize more than belongs to a possible experience of it, or for us, with respect to any thing that we assume not to be an object of possible experience, to claim even the least cognition for determining it according to its nature as it is in itself; for by what means will we reach this determination, since time, space, and all the concepts of the understanding, and especially the concepts drawn from empirical intuition or *perception* in the sensible world, do not and cannot have any use other than merely to make experience possible, and if we relax this condition even for the pure concepts of the understanding, they then determine no object whatsoever, and generally have no meaning.

But, on the other hand, it would be an even greater absurdity for us not to allow any things in themselves at all, or for us to want to pass off our experience for the only possible mode of cognition of things – hence our intuition in space and time for the only possible intuition and our discursive understanding for the archetype of every possible under-

[4:351]

---

[n] *Kenntnis*

standing – and so to want to take principles of the possibility of experience for universal conditions on things in themselves.

Our principles, which limit the use of reason to possible experience alone, could consequently themselves become *transcendent* and could pass off the limits of our reason for limits on the possibility of things themselves (for which *Hume's* Dialogues[12] can serve as an example), if a painstaking critique did not both guard the boundaries of our reason even with respect to its empirical use, and set a limit to its pretensions. Skepticism originally arose from metaphysics and its unpoliced dialectic. At first this skepticism wanted, solely for the benefit of the use of reason in experience, to portray everything that surpasses this use as empty and deceitful; but gradually, as it came to be noticed that it was the very same *a priori* principles which are employed in experience that, unnoticed, led further than experience reaches – and did so, as it seemed, with the very same right – even the principles of experience began to be doubted. There was no real trouble with this, for sound common sense will always assert its rights in this domain; there did arise, however, a special confusion in science, which cannot determine how far (and why only that far and not further) reason is to be trusted, and this confusion can be remedied and all future relapses prevented only through a formal determination, derived from principles, of the boundaries for the use of our reason.

It is true: we cannot provide, beyond all possible experience, any determinate concept of what things in themselves may be. But we are nevertheless not free to hold back entirely in the face of inquiries about those things; for experience never fully satisfies reason; it directs us ever further back in answering questions and leaves us unsatisfied as regards their full elucidation, as everyone can sufficiently observe in the dialectic of pure reason, which for this very reason has a good subjective ground. Who can bear being brought, as regards the nature of our soul, both to the point of a clear consciousness of the subject and to the conviction that the appearances of that subject cannot be explained *materialistically*, without asking what then the soul really is, and, if no concept of [4:352] experience suffices thereto, without perchance adopting a concept of reason (that of a simple immaterial being) just for this purpose, although we can by no means prove the objective reality of that concept? Who

---

[12] *Dialogues Concerning Natural Religion* (London, 1779); German translation, 1781.

can satisfy themselves with mere cognition through experience in all the cosmological questions, of the duration and size of the world, of freedom or natural necessity, since, wherever we may begin, any answer given according to principles of experience always begets a new question which also requires an answer, and for that reason clearly proves the inadequacy of all physical modes of explanation for the satisfaction of reason? Finally, who cannot see, from the thoroughgoing contingency and dependency of everything that they might think or assume according to principles of experience, the impossibility of stopping with these, and who does not feel compelled, regardless of all prohibition against losing oneself in transcendent ideas, nevertheless to look for peace and satisfaction beyond all concepts that one can justify through experience, in the concept of a being the idea of which indeed cannot in itself be understood as regards possibility – though it cannot be refuted either, because it pertains to a mere being of the understanding – an idea without which, however, reason would always have to remain unsatisfied?

Boundaries (in extended things) always presuppose a space that is found outside a certain fixed location, and that encloses that location; limits require nothing of the kind, but are mere negations that affect a magnitude insofar as it does not possess absolute completeness. Our reason, however, sees around itself as it were a space for the cognition of things in themselves, although it can never have determinate concepts of those things and is limited to appearances alone.

As long as reason's cognition is homogeneous, no determinate boundaries can be thought for it. In mathematics and natural science human understanding recognizes limits but not boundaries, i.e., it indeed recognizes that something lies beyond it to which it can never reach, but not that it would itself at any point ever complete its inner progression. The expansion of insight in mathematics, and the possibility of ever new inventions, goes to infinity; so too does the discovery of new properties in nature (new forces and laws), through continued experience, and the unification of that experience by reason. But limits [4:353] here are nonetheless unmistakable, for mathematics refers only to *appearances*, and that which cannot be an object of sensory intuition, like the concepts of metaphysics and morals, lies outside the sphere of mathematics, and mathematics can never lead to it; but mathematics has no need whatsoever for such concepts. There is therefore no continuous progress and advancement toward those other sciences, as it were no point or line of contact. Natural science will never reveal to us the inside of things, i.e., that which is not appearance but nonetheless can serve as the highest ground of explanation for the appearances; but it does not need this for its physical explanations; nay, if such were offered to it from elsewhere (e.g., the influence of immaterial beings), natural science should indeed reject it and ought by no means bring it into the progression of its explanations, but should always base its explanations only on that which can belong to experience as an object of the senses and which can be brought into connection with our actual perceptions in accordance with laws of experience.

But metaphysics, in the dialectical endeavors of pure reason (which are not initiated arbitrarily or wantonly, but toward which the nature of reason itself drives), leads us to the boundaries; and the transcendental ideas, just because they cannot be avoided and yet will never be realized, serve not only actually to show us the boundaries of reason's pure use, but also to show us the way to determine such boundaries; and that is the purpose and benefit of this natural predisposition of our reason, which bore metaphysics as its favorite child, whose procreation (as with any other in the world) is to be ascribed not to chance accident but to an original seed that is wisely organized toward great ends. For metaphysics, perhaps more than any other science, is, as regards its fundamentals, placed in us by nature itself, and cannot at all be seen as the product of an arbitrary choice, or as an accidental extension from the progression of experiences (it wholly separates itself from those experiences).

Reason, through all of its concepts and laws of the understanding, which it finds to be adequate for empirical use, and so adequate within the sensible world, nonetheless does not thereby find satisfaction for itself; for, as a result of questions that keep recurring to infinity, it is denied all hope of completely answering those questions. The transcendental ideas, which have such completion as their aim, are such problems for reason. Now reason clearly sees: that the sensible world [4:354] could not contain this completion, any more than could therefore all of the concepts that serve solely for understanding that world: space and time, and everything that we have put forward under the name of the pure concepts of the understanding. The sensible world is nothing but a chain of appearances connected in accordance with universal laws, which therefore has no existence for itself; it truly is not the thing in itself, and therefore it necessarily refers to that which contains the ground of those appearances, to beings that can be cognized not merely as appearances, but as things in themselves. Only in the cognition of the latter can reason hope to see satisfied for once its desire for completeness in the progression from the conditioned to its conditions.

Above (§§33, 34) we noted limits of reason with respect to all cognition of mere beings of thought; now, since the transcendental ideas nevertheless make the progression up to these limits necessary for us, and have therefore led us, as it were, up to the contiguity of the filled space (of experience) with empty space (of which we can know nothing – the *noumena*), we can also determine the boundaries of pure reason; for in all boundaries there is something positive (e.g., a surface is the boundary of corporeal space, yet is nonetheless itself a space; a line is a space, which is the boundary of a surface; a point is the boundary of a line, yet is nonetheless a locus in space), whereas limits contain mere negations. The limits announced in the cited sections are still not enough after we have found that something lies beyond them (although we will never cognize what that something may be in itself). For the question now arises: How does our reason relate to the connection of that with which we are acquainted to that with which we are not acquainted, and never will be? Here is a real connection of the known to the wholly unknown (which it will always remain), and if the unknown should not become the least bit better known – as in fact is not to be hoped – the concept of this connection must still be able to be determined and brought to clarity.

We should, then, think for ourselves an immaterial being, an intelligible world, and a highest of all beings (all noumena), because only in these things, as things in themselves, does reason find completion and satisfaction, which it can never hope to find in the derivation of the appearances from the homogeneous grounds of those appearances; and we should think such things for ourselves because the appearances actually do relate to something distinct from them (and so entirely heterogeneous), in that appearances always presuppose a thing in itself, and so they provide notice of such a thing, whether or not it can be cognized more closely.

Now since we can, however, never cognize these intelligible beings according to what they may be in themselves, i.e., determinately –

[4:355]

though we must nonetheless assume such beings in relation to the sensible world, and connect them with it through reason – we can still at least think this connection by means of such concepts as express the relation of those beings to the sensible world. For, if we think an intelligible being through nothing but pure concepts of the understanding, we actually do not thereby think anything determinate for ourselves, and so our concept is without meaning; if we think it through properties borrowed from the sensible world, it is no longer an intelligible being: it is thought as one of the phenomena and belongs to the sensible world. We will take an example from the concept of the supreme being.

The *deistic* concept is a wholly pure concept of reason, which however represents only a thing that contains every reality, without being able to determine a single one of those realities, because for that an example would have to be borrowed from the sensible world, in which case I would always have to do only with an object of the senses, and not with something completely heterogeneous which cannot be an object of the senses at all. For I would, for instance, attribute understanding to it; but I have no concept of any understanding whatsoever except of one like my own, that is, one such that intuitions must be given to it through the senses, and that busies itself with bringing those intuitions under rules for the unity of consciousness. But then the elements of my concept would always lie within appearance; I was, however, forced by the inadequacy of the appearances to go beyond them, to the concept of a being that is neither dependent on appearances nor bound up with them as conditions for its determination. If, however, I separate understanding from sensibility, in order to have a pure understanding, then nothing but the mere form of thinking, without intuition, is left; through which, by itself, I cannot cognize anything determinate, hence cannot cognize any object. To that end I would have to think to myself a different understanding, which intuits objects,[13] of which, however, I do not have the least concept, since the human understanding is discursive and can cognize only by means of universal concepts. The [4:356] same thing happens to me if I attribute a will to the supreme being: For I possess this concept only by drawing it from my inner experience,

---

[13] Kant elaborated the notion of an intuitive understanding in the second edition of the *Critique*, B135, 138–9, 145.

hence from my dependence on satisfaction through objects of whose existence we have need, and which are therefore based in sensibility – which completely contradicts the pure concept of a supreme being.

Hume's objections to deism are weak and always concern the grounds of proof but never the thesis of the deistic assertion itself. But with respect to theism, which is supposed to arise through a closer determination of our concept of a supreme being (which is merely transcendent in deism), they are very strong, and, according to how this concept has been developed, they are in certain cases (in fact, in all the usual ones) irrefutable. Hume always holds to this: that through the mere concept of a first being to which we attribute none but ontological predicates (eternity, omnipresence, omnipotence), we actually do not think anything determinate at all; rather, properties must be added that can yield a concept *in concreto*; it is not enough to say: this being is a cause, rather we need to say how its causality is constituted, e.g., by understanding and willing – and here begin Hume's attacks on the matter in question, namely on theism, whereas he had previously assaulted only the grounds of proof for deism, an assault that carries no special danger with it. His dangerous arguments collectively relate to anthropomorphism, of which he holds that it is inseparable from theism and makes theism self-contradictory, but that if it is eliminated, theism falls with it and nothing but deism remains – from which nothing can be made, which can be of no use to us, and which can in no way serve as a foundation for religion and morals. If the unavoidability of this anthropomorphism were certain, then the proofs for the existence of a supreme being could be what they will, and all could be granted, and still the concept of this being could never be determined by us without our becoming entangled in contradictions.

If we combine the prohibition to avoid all transcendent judgments of pure reason with the apparently conflicting command to proceed to concepts that lie beyond the field of immanent (empirical) use, we become aware that both can subsist together, but only directly on the *boundary* of all permitted use of reason – for this boundary belongs just [4:357] as much to the field of experience as to that of beings of thought – and we are thereby at the same time taught how those remarkable ideas serve solely for determining the boundary of human reason: that is, we are taught, on the one hand, not to extend cognition from experience without bound, so that nothing at all remains for us to cognize except merely the world, and, on the other, nevertheless not to go beyond the boundary of experience and to want to judge of things outside that boundary as things in themselves.

But we hold ourselves to this boundary if we limit our judgment merely to the relation that the world may have to a being whose concept itself lies outside all cognition that we can attain within the world. For we then do not attribute to the supreme being any of the properties *in themselves* by which we think the objects of experience, and we thereby avoid *dogmatic* anthropomorphism; but we attribute those properties, nonetheless, to the relation of this being to the world, and we allow ourselves a *symbolic* anthropomorphism, which in fact concerns only language and not the object itself.

If I say that we are compelled to look upon the world *as if* it were the work of a supreme understanding and will, I actually say nothing more than: in the way that a watch, a ship, and a regiment are related to an artisan, an architect, and a commander, the sensible world (or everything that makes up the substratum of this sum total of appearances) is related to the unknown – which I therefore do not, in this way, cognize according to what it is in itself, but only according to what it is for me, that is, with respect to the world of which I am a part.

§58

This type of cognition is cognition *according to analogy*, which surely does not mean, as the word is usually taken, an imperfect similarity between two things, but rather a perfect similarity between two relations in wholly dissimilar things.* By means of this analogy there still remains [4:358] a concept of the supreme being sufficiently determinate *for us*, though we have omitted everything that could have *determined* this concept

---

* Such is an analogy between the legal relation of human actions and the mechanical relation of moving forces: I can never do something to another without giving him a right to do the same to me under the same conditions; just as a body cannot act on another body with its motive force without thereby causing the other body to react just as much on it. Right and motive force are here completely dissimilar things, but in their relation there is nonetheless complete similarity. By means of such an analogy I can therefore provide a concept of a relation to things that are absolutely unknown to me. E.g., the promotion of the happiness of the children = a is to the love of the parents = b as the welfare of humankind = c is to the unknown in God = x, which we call love: not as if this unknown had the least similarity with any human inclination, but because we can posit the relation between God's love and the world to be similar to that which things in the world have to one another. But here the concept of the relation is a mere category, namely the concept of cause, which has nothing to do with sensibility.

unconditionally and *in itself*; for we determine the concept only with respect to the world and hence with respect to us, and we have no need of more. The attacks that *Hume* makes against those who want to determine this concept absolutely – since they borrow the materials for this determination from themselves and from the world – do not touch us; he also cannot reproach us that nothing whatsoever would remain to us, if objective anthropomorphism should be subtracted from the concept of the supreme being.

For if one only grants us, at the beginning, the *deistic* concept of a first being as a necessary hypothesis (as does Hume in his *Dialogues* in the person of Philo as opposed to Cleanthes), which is a concept in which one thinks the first being by means of ontological predicates alone, of substance, cause, etc. (*something that one must do*, since reason, being driven in the sensible world solely by conditions that are always again conditioned, cannot have any satisfaction at all without this being done, and *something that one very well can do* without falling into anthropomorphism, which transfers predicates from the sensible world onto a being wholly distinct from the world, since the predicates listed here are mere categories, which cannot indeed provide any determinate concept of that being, but which, for that very reason, do not provide a concept of it that is limited to the conditions of sensibility) – then nothing can keep us from predicating of this being a *causality through reason* with respect to the world, and thus from crossing over to theism, but without our being compelled to attribute this reason to that being in itself, as a property inhering in it. For, concerning the *first point*,[o] the only possible way to compel the use of reason in the sensible world [4:359] (with respect to all possible experience) into the most thoroughgoing harmony with itself is to assume, in turn, a supreme reason as a cause of all connections in the world; such a principle must be thoroughly advantageous to reason and can nowhere harm it in its use in nature. Regarding the *second point*,[p] however, reason is not thereby transposed as a property onto the first being in itself, but only onto *the relation* of that being to the sensible world, and therefore anthropomorphism is completely avoided. For here only the *cause* of the rational form found everywhere in the world is considered, and the supreme being, insofar as it contains the basis of this rational form of the world, is indeed

---

[o] "something that one must do ..."   [p] "something that one very well can do ..."

ascribed reason, but only by analogy, i.e., insofar as this expression signifies only the relation that the highest cause (which is unknown to us) has to the world, for the sake of determining all things with the highest degree of conformity to reason. We will thereby avoid using the property of reason in order to think God, but we will use that property in order to think the world by means of it, in the way that is necessary in order to have the greatest possible use of reason with respect to the world in accordance with a principle. We thereby admit that the supreme being, as to what it may be in itself, is for us wholly inscrutable and that it cannot at all be thought by us *in a determinate manner*; and we are thereby prevented from making any transcendent use of the concepts that we have of reason as an efficient cause (by means of willing) in order to determine the divine nature through properties that are in any case always borrowed only from human nature, and so from losing ourselves in crude or fanatical concepts, and, on the other hand, we are prevented from swamping the contemplation of the world with hyperphysical modes of explanation according to concepts of human reason that we have transposed onto God, and so from diverting this contemplation from its true vocation, according to which it is supposed to be a study of mere nature through reason, and not an audacious derivation of the appearances of nature from a supreme reason. The expression suitable to our weak concepts will be: that we think the world **as if** it derives, as regards its existence and inner determination, from a supreme reason; whereby we in part cognize the constitution belonging to it (the world) itself, without presuming to want to determine in itself the constitution of the cause of the world, and, on the other hand, we in part posit the basis of this constitution (the rational [4:360] form of the world) *in the relation* of the highest cause to the world, not finding the world by itself sufficient thereto.*

In this way the difficulties that appear to oppose theism disappear, in that one conjoins to *Hume's* principle not to drive the use of reason dogmatically beyond the field of all possible experience, another

---

* I will say: the causality of the highest cause is that, with respect to the world, which human reason is with respect to its works of art. Thereby the nature of the highest cause itself remains unknown to me: I compare only its effect (the order of the world), which is known to me, and the conformity with reason of this effect, with the effects of human reason that are known to me, and in consequence I call the highest cause a reason, without thereby ascribing to it as its property the same thing I understand by this expression in humans, or anything at all that is known to me.

principle that Hume completely overlooked, namely: not to look upon the field of possible experience as something that bounds itself in the eyes of our reason. A critique of reason indicates the true middle way between the dogmatism that Hume fought and the skepticism he wanted to establish in contrast to it – a middle way that is unlike other middle ways, which are recommended for determining themselves as it were mechanically (something from one side, and something from the other), and by which no one is set right, but rather a middle way that can be determined precisely, according to principles.

§59

At the beginning of this note I made use of the metaphor of a *boundary* in order to fix the limits of reason with respect its own appropriate use. The sensible world contains only appearances, which are still not things in themselves, which latter things (noumena) the understanding must therefore assume for the very reason that it cognizes the objects of experience as mere appearances. Both are considered together in our reason, and the question arises: how does reason proceed in setting boundaries for the understanding in both fields? Experience, which contains everything that belongs to the sensible world, does not set a boundary for itself: from every conditioned[14] it always just passes to another conditioned. That which is to set its boundary must lie completely outside it, and this is the field of pure intelligible beings. For us, however, as far as concerns the *determination* of the nature of these [4:361] intelligible beings, this is an empty space, and to that extent, if dogmatically determined concepts are intended, we cannot go beyond the field of possible experience. But since a boundary is itself something positive, which belongs as much to what is within it as to the space lying outside a given totality, reason therefore, merely by expanding up to this boundary, partakes of a real, positive cognition, provided that it does not try to go out beyond the boundary, since there it finds empty space before it, in which it can indeed think the forms to things, but no things themselves. But *setting the boundary* to the field of experience through something that is otherwise unknown to it is indeed a cognition that is still left to reason from this standpoint, by which reason is

---

[14] On this use of the term "conditioned," see Introduction, p. xxv.

neither locked inside the sensible world nor adrift outside it, but, as befits knowledge of a boundary, restricts itself solely to the relation of what lies outside the boundary to what is contained within.

Natural theology is a concept of this kind, on the boundary of human reason, since reason finds itself compelled to look out toward the idea of a supreme being (and also, in relation to the practical, to the idea of an intelligible world), not in order to determine something with respect to this mere intelligible being (and hence outside the sensible world), but only in order to guide its own use within the sensible world in accordance with principles of the greatest possible unity (theoretical as well as practical), and to make use (for this purpose) of the relation of that world to a freestanding reason as the cause of all of these connections – not, however, in order thereby merely *to fabricate* a being, but, since beyond the sensible world there must necessarily be found something that is thought only by the pure understanding, in order, in this way, *to determine* this being, though of course merely through analogy.

In this manner our previous proposition, which is the result of the entire *Critique*, remains: "that reason, through all its *a priori* principles, never teaches us about anything more than objects of possible experience alone, and of these, nothing more than what can be cognized in experience"; but this limitation does not prevent reason from carrying us up to the objective *boundary* of experience – namely, to the *relation* to something that cannot itself be an object of experience, but which must nonetheless be the highest ground of all experience – without, however, teaching us anything about this ground in itself, but only in relation to reason's own complete use in the field of possible experience, as directed [4:362] to the highest ends. This is, however, all of the benefit that can reasonably even be wished for here, and there is cause to be satisfied with it.

§60

We have thus fully exhibited metaphysics in accordance with its subjective possibility, as metaphysics is actually given *in the natural predisposition* of human reason, and with respect to that which forms the essential goal of its cultivation. But because we found that, if reason is not reined in and given limits by a discipline of reason, which is only possible through a scientific critique, this *wholly natural* use of this sort of predisposition of our reason entangles it in transcendent *dialectical* inferences, which are partly specious, partly even in conflict among themselves; and, moreover, because we found that this sophistical metaphysics is superfluous, nay, even detrimental to the advancement of the cognition of nature, it therefore still remains a problem worthy of investigation, to discover the *natural purposes* toward which this predisposition of our reason to transcendent concepts may be aimed, since everything found in nature must originally be aimed at some beneficial purpose or other.

Such an investigation is in fact precarious. I also admit that it is merely conjectural (as is everything I know to say concerning the original purposes of nature), something I may be permitted in this case only, since the question does not concern the objective validity of metaphysical judgments, but rather the natural predisposition to such judgments, and therefore lies outside the system of metaphysics, in anthropology.[15]

If I consider[q] all the transcendental ideas, which together form the real problem for natural pure reason – a problem that compels reason to forsake the mere contemplation of nature and to go beyond all possible experience, and, by this effort, to bring into existence the thing called metaphysics (whether it be knowledge or sophistry) – then I believe I perceive that this natural predisposition is aimed at making our concept so free from the fetters of experience and the limits of the mere contemplation of nature that it at the least sees a field opening before it that contains only objects for the pure understanding which cannot be reached by any sensibility: not for the purpose of busying ourselves [4:363] speculatively with these objects (for we find no ground on which we can gain footing), but so that practical principles can at least be thought as possible,[r] principles which, without finding such a space before them for their necessary expectations and hopes, cannot extend themselves to the universality that reason ineluctably requires with respect to morals.

Here I now find that the *psychological* idea, as little as I may gain insight through it into the pure nature of the human soul elevated

---

[q] Supplying *betrachte* as the verb, with Vorländer.
[r] Adding *wenigstens als möglich angenommen werden können*, following Ak 4.
[15] In Kant's time, "anthropology," the science of man, included topics on the human mind, such as were also treated in empirical psychology. Kant regularly lectured on anthropology.

beyond all concepts of experience, nonetheless at least reveals clearly enough the inadequacy of those concepts of experience, and thereby leads me away from materialism as a psychological concept that is unsuited to any explanation of nature and that, moreover, constricts reason with respect to the practical. Similarly, the *cosmological* ideas, through the evident inadequacy of all possible cognition of nature to satisfy reason in its rightful demands, serve to keep us from naturalism, which wants to put forward nature as sufficient unto itself. Finally, because all natural necessity in the sensible world is always conditioned, since it always presupposes the dependence of one thing on another, and since unconditioned necessity must be sought only in the unity of a cause distinct from the sensible world, and since the causality of that cause, in turn, if the cause were merely nature, could never make comprehensible (as its consequence) the existence of the contingent; consequently reason, by means of the *theological* idea, frees itself from fatalism – from blind natural necessity both in the connection of nature itself, without a first principle, and in the causality of this principle itself – and leads the way to the concept of a cause through freedom, and so to that of a highest intelligence. The transcendental ideas therefore serve, if not to instruct us positively, at least to negate^s the impudent assertions of *materialism, naturalism,* and *fatalism* which constrict the field of reason, and in this way they serve to provide moral ideas with space outside the field of speculation; and this would, I should think, to some extent explain the aforementioned natural predisposition.

The practical benefit that a purely speculative science may have lies outside the boundaries of this science; such benefit can therefore be seen simply as a scholium,[16] and, like all scholia, it does not form a part of the science itself. Nonetheless, this relation at least lies within the boundaries of philosophy, and especially of that philosophy which draws from the well of pure reason, where the speculative use of reason in metaphysics must necessarily have unity with the practical use of [4:364] reason in morals. Hence the unavoidable dialectic of pure reason deserves, in a metaphysics considered as natural predisposition, to be explained not only as an illusion that needs to be solved, but also (if one can) as a *natural institution* in accordance with its purpose – although

---

^s *aufzuheben*

[16] A scholium is an explanatory note contained within a treatise, which elaborates or explains something without by itself adding anything that is essential to the primary argument.

this endeavor, as supererogatory, cannot rightly be demanded of metaphysics proper.

The solution to the questions that proceed in the *Critique* from pages 647 to 668 would have to be taken for a second scholium, more closely related to the content of metaphysics.[17] For there certain principles of reason are put forward that determine the order of nature *a priori*, or rather determine the understanding *a priori*, which is supposed to search for the laws of this order by means of experience. These principles seem to be constitutive and lawgiving with respect to experience, though they spring from mere reason, which cannot, like the understanding, be regarded as a principle of possible experience. Now whether or not this agreement rests on the fact that, just as nature does not inhere in the appearances or in their source (sensibility) in themselves, but is found only in the relation of sensibility to the understanding, so too, a thoroughgoing unity in the use of this under- standing, for the sake of a unified possible experience (in a system), can belong to the understanding only in relation to reason, and so experi- ence is indirectly subject to the legislation of reason – this may be further pondered by those who want to track the nature of reason even beyond its use in metaphysics, into the universal principles for making general natural history systematic; for in the book itself I have presented this problem as important, but have not attempted its solution.[*]

[4:365]   And thus I conclude the analytic[18] solution of the main question I posed: How is metaphysics in general possible?, since I have ascended from that place where its use is actually given, at least in the consequences, to the grounds of its possibility.

---

[*]   It was my unremitting intention throughout the *Critique* not to neglect anything that could bring to completion the investigation of the nature of pure reason, however deeply hidden it might lie. Afterwards it is in each person's discretion how far they will take their investigation, if one only has been apprised of what may still be left to be done; for it can properly be expected, from one who has made it his business to survey this entire field, that afterward he leave future additions and optional divisions to others. Hereto belong both of the scholia, which, on account of their dryness, can hardly be recommended to amateurs, and therefore are laid out only for experts.

[17] A portion of the section entitled On the Regulative Use of the Ideas of Pure Reason (B 675–96).

[18] "Analytic" here refers to the analytic method; see General Question (§§4, 5), and the Introduction.

Solution to the
General Question of the Prolegomena
How is metaphysics as science possible?

Metaphysics, as a natural predisposition of reason, is actual, but it is also of itself (as the analytical solution to the third main question proved) dialectical and deceitful. The desire to derive principles from it, and to follow the natural but nonetheless false illusion in their use, can therefore never bring forth science, but only vain dialectical art, in which one school outdoes another but none can ever gain legitimate and lasting approbation.

In order that metaphysics might, as science, be able to lay claim, not merely to deceitful persuasion, but to insight and conviction, a critique of reason itself must set forth the entire stock of *a priori* concepts, their division according to the different sources (sensibility, understanding, and reason), further, a complete table of those concepts, and the analysis of all of them together with everything that can be derived from that analysis; and then, especially, such a critique must set forth the possibility of synthetic cognition *a priori* through a deduction of these concepts, it must set forth the principles of their use, and finally the boundaries of that use; and all of this in a complete system. Therefore a critique, and that alone, contains within itself the whole well-tested and verified plan, and even all the means for carrying it out, by which metaphysics as science can be achieved; by any other ways or means it is impossible. Therefore the question that arises here is not so much how this endeavor is possible, but how it is to be set in motion and good minds stirred from hitherto ill-directed and fruitless cultivation to one that will not deceive, and how an alliance of this sort could best be turned toward the common end.

[4:366]   This much is certain: whosoever has once tasted of critique forever loathes all the dogmatic chatter with which he previously had to be satisfied out of necessity, since his reason was in need of something and could not find anything better for its sustenance. Critique stands to the ordinary school metaphysics precisely as *chemistry* stands to *alchemy*, or *astronomy* to the fortune-teller's *astrology*. I'll guarantee that no one who has thought through and comprehended the principles of critique, even if only in these prolegomena, will ever again return to that old and sophistical pseudoscience; he will on the contrary look out with a certain delight upon a metaphysics that is now fully at his disposal, that needs no more preliminary discoveries, and that can for the first time provide reason with lasting satisfaction. For this is an excellence upon which metaphysics alone, among all the possible sciences, can rely with confidence, namely, that it can be completed and brought into a permanent state, since it cannot be further changed and is not susceptible to any augmentation through new discoveries – because here reason has the sources of its cognition not in objects and their intuition (through which reason cannot be taught one thing more), but in itself, and, if reason has presented the fundamental laws of its faculty fully and determinately (against all misinterpretation), nothing else remains that pure reason could cognize *a priori*, or even about which it could have cause to ask. The sure prospect of a knowledge so determinate and so final has a certain attraction to it, even if all usefulness (of which I will say more hereafter) is set aside.

All false art, all empty wisdom lasts for its time; for it finally destroys itself, and the height of its cultivation is simultaneously the moment of its decline. That this time has now come as regards metaphysics is proven by the condition into which it has fallen among all learned peoples, amidst all the zeal with which sciences of all kinds are otherwise being developed. The old organization of university studies still contains the shadow of metaphysics, a lone academy of sciences now and then, by offering prizes, moves someone or other to make an effort in it, but metaphysics is no longer reckoned among serious sciences, and each may judge for himself how a clever man, whom one wished to call a great metaphysician, would perhaps receive this encomium, which might be well meant but would be the envy of almost no one.

But although the time for the collapse of all dogmatic metaphysics is [4:367] undoubtedly here, much is still lacking in order to be able to say that, on the contrary, the time for its rebirth, through a thorough and completed critique of reason, has already appeared. All transitions from one inclination to its opposite pass through a state of indifference, and this moment is the most dangerous for an author, but nonetheless, it seems to me, the most favorable for the science. For if the partisan spirit has ceased to exist through the complete dissolution of former ties, then minds are best disposed to hear out, bit by bit, proposals for an alliance according to another plan.

If I say that I hope these *Prolegomena* will perhaps excite investigation in the field of critique, and provide the universal spirit of philosophy, which seems to want nourishment in its speculative part, a new and quite promising object of sustenance, I can already imagine beforehand that everyone who has been made unwilling and weary by the thorny paths on which I led him in the *Critique* will ask me: On what do I base this hope? I answer: *On the irresistible law of necessity.*

That the human mind would someday entirely give up metaphysical investigations is just as little to be expected, as that we would someday gladly stop all breathing so as never to take in impure air. There will therefore be metaphysics in the world at every time, and what is more, in every human being, and especially the reflective ones; metaphysics that each, in the absence of a public standard of measure, will carve out for themselves in their own manner. Now that which has been called metaphysics up to now can satisfy no inquiring mind, and yet it is also impossible to give up metaphysics completely; therefore, a critique of pure reason must finally be *attempted*, or, if one exists, it must be *examined* and put to a general test, since there are no other means to relieve this pressing need, which is something more than a mere thirst for knowledge.

Ever since I have known critique, I have been unable to keep myself from asking, upon finishing reading through a book with metaphysical content, which has entertained as well as cultivated me by the determination of its concepts and by variety and organization and by an easy presentation: *Has this author advanced metaphysics even one step?* I [4:368] ask the forgiveness of the learned men whose writings have in other respects been useful to me and have always contributed to the cultivation of my mental powers, because I confess that I have not been able to find, either in their attempts or in my own inferior ones (with self-love speaking in their favor), that the science has thereby been advanced in the least, and this for the wholly natural reason that the science did not yet exist, and also that it cannot be assembled bit by bit but rather its seed must be fully preformed beforehand in the critique. However, in order to avoid all misunderstanding, it must be recalled from the preceding that although the understanding certainly benefits very much from the analytical treatment of our concepts, the science (of metaphysics) is not advanced the least bit thereby, since these analyses of concepts are only materials, out of which the science must first be constructed. The concept of substance and accident may be analyzed and determined ever so nicely; that is quite good as preparation for some future use. But if I simply cannot prove that in all that exists the substance persists and only the accidents change, then through all this analysis the science has not been advanced in the least. Now metaphysics has not as yet been able to prove, as *a priori* valid, either this proposition or the principle of sufficient reason, still less any composite proposition, such as, for instance, one that belongs to psychology or cosmology, and, in general, no synthetic proposition whatsoever; hence, through all this analysis nothing is achieved, nothing created and advanced, and, after so much bustle and clatter, the science is still right where it was in Aristotle's time, although the preparations for it, if only the guiding thread to synthetic cognition had first been found, are incontestably much better than otherwise would have been found.

If anyone believes himself wronged in this, he can easily remove the above accusation if he will cite only a single synthetic proposition belonging to metaphysics that he offers to prove *a priori* in the dogmatic manner; for only when he accomplishes this will I grant to him that he has actually advanced the science (even if the proposition may otherwise have been sufficiently established through common experience). No challenge can be more moderate and more equitable, and in the [4:369] (infallibly certain) event of nonfulfillment, no verdict more just, than this: that up to now metaphysics as science has never existed at all.

In case the challenge is accepted, I must forbid only two things: first, the plaything of *probability*[a] and conjecture, which suits metaphysics just as poorly as it does geometry; second, decision by means of the

---

[a] *Wahrscheinlichkeit*

divining rod of so-called *sound common sense*, which does not bend for everyone, but is guided by personal qualities.

For, *as regards the first*, nothing more absurd can be found than to want to base the judgments of metaphysics, a philosophy of pure reason, on probability and conjecture. Everything that is to be cognized *a priori* is for that very reason given out as apodictically certain and therefore must also be proven as such. One might just as well want to base a geometry or an arithmetic on conjectures; for as concerns the *calculus probabilium*[1] of arithmetic, it contains not probable but completely certain judgments about the degree of possibility of certain cases under given homogeneous conditions, judgments which, in the sum total of all possible cases, must be found to conform to the rule with complete infallibility, even though this rule is not sufficiently determinate with respect to any single case. Only in empirical natural science can conjectures (by means of induction and analogy) be tolerated, and even then, the possibility at least of what I am assuming must be fully certain.

Matters are, if possible, even worse with the *appeal to sound common sense*, if the discussion concerns[b] concepts and principles, not insofar as they are supposed to be valid with respect to experience, but rather insofar as they are to be taken as valid beyond the conditions of experience. For what is *sound common sense*? It is the *ordinary understanding*,[2] insofar as it judges correctly. And what now is the ordinary understanding? It is the faculty of cognition and of the use of rules *in concreto*, as distinguished from the *speculative understanding*, which is a faculty of the cognition of rules *in abstracto*. Common sense, or ordinary understanding, will hardly be able to understand the rule: that everything which happens is determined by its cause, and it will never be able to have insight into it in such a general way. It therefore demands an example from experience, and when it hears that this rule means nothing other than what it had always thought when a windowpane was [4:370] broken or a household article had disappeared, it then understands the principle and grants it. Ordinary understanding, therefore, has a use no further than the extent to which it can see its rules confirmed in

[b] Adding *die Rede ist*.
[1] "calculus of probability"
[2] The expressions translated as "sound common sense" and "ordinary understanding" both contain the root *Verstand*; Kant's play on words cannot be directly captured in English, but some accommodation is made, a little further on in the text, by using the one to gloss the other. (Another instance of such play occurs on pp. 9–10).

experience (although these rules are actually present in it *a priori*); consequently, to have insight into these rules *a priori* and independently of experience falls to the speculative understanding, and lies completely beyond the horizon of the ordinary understanding. But metaphysics is concerned indeed solely with this latter type of cognition, and it is certainly a poor sign of sound common sense to appeal to this guarantor, who has no judgment here, and upon whom one otherwise looks down, except if one finds oneself in trouble, and without either advice or help, in one's speculation.

It is a common excuse, which these false friends of ordinary common sense (which they extol on occasion, but usually despise) are accustomed to using, that they say: There must in the end be some propositions that are immediately certain, and for which one not only need give no proof, but also for which one need not, in general, be accountable, because otherwise one would never come to the end with grounds for his judgments; but in proof of this right they can never cite anything else (other than the principle of contradiction, which is however inadequate for establishing the truth of synthetic judgments) that is not doubted and that can be ascribed directly to ordinary common sense, except for mathematical propositions: e.g., that two times two makes four, that between two points there is only one straight line, and still others. These judgments are, however, vastly different from those of metaphysics. For in mathematics, everything that I conceive through a concept as possible I can make for myself (construct) by means of my thought; to one two I add the other two bit by bit, and make for myself the number four, or I draw in thought all kinds of lines from one point to the other, and can draw only one that is similar in all its parts (equal as well as unequal).[3] But from the concept of a thing I cannot, with all my powers of thought, draw forth the concept of something else whose existence is necessarily connected with the first thing, but I must consult experience; and, although my understanding provides me *a priori* (though always only in relation to possible experience) with the concept of a connection of this
[4:371] sort (causality), I nevertheless cannot exhibit this concept in intuition

---

[3] Kant here refers to the definition of a straight line. Euclid, *Elements*, Bk. 1, def. 4, defines it as "lying evenly with the points on itself." Kant's definition is closer to that given by Wolff, as a line "of which the part is similar to the whole" (*Anfangsgründe aller mathematischen Wissenschaften*, 7th edn., Frankfurt, Leipzig and Halle, 1750–7, Pt. 1, p. 119); Wolff refers to Plato's definition, to the effect that a straight line is one in which "the middle covers the ends" (when viewed end-on). Kant taught mathematics from a textbook by Wolff (Ak 2:35).

a priori, like the concepts of mathematics, and thus set forth its possibility *a priori*; rather, this concept (together with principles of its application), if it is to be valid *a priori* – as is indeed required in metaphysics – always has need of a justification and deduction of its possibility, for otherwise one does not know the extent of its validity and whether it can be used only in experience or also outside it. Therefore in metaphysics, as a speculative science of pure reason, one can never appeal to ordinary common sense, but one can very well do so if one is forced to abandon metaphysics and to renounce all pure speculative cognition, which must always be knowledge,[c] hence to renounce metaphysics itself and its teaching (on certain matters), and if a reasonable belief is alone deemed possible for us, as well as sufficient for our needs (perhaps indeed more wholesome than knowledge itself). For then the shape of things is completely altered. Metaphysics must be science, not only as a whole but also in all its parts; otherwise it is nothing at all, since, as speculation of pure reason, it has a hold on nothing else besides universal insights. But outside metaphysics, probability and sound common sense can indeed have their beneficial and legitimate use, though following principles entirely their own, whose importance always depends on a relation to the practical.

That is what I consider myself entitled to require for the possibility of a metaphysics as science.

[c] *ein Wissen*

Appendix
On What Can Be Done in Order to Make Metaphysics As Science Actual

Since all the paths that have been taken before now have not attained this end, and will never be able to attain it without a preceding critique of pure reason, the demand that the attempt at such a critique which is now before the public be subjected to an exact and careful examination does not seem unreasonable – unless one holds it to be still more advisable rather to relinquish completely all claims to metaphysics, in [4:372] which case, if one only remains true to one's intention, there is nothing to object to in this. If the course of events is taken as it actually runs and not as it should run, then there are two kinds of judgments: a *judgment that precedes the investigation*, and in our case this is one in which the reader, from his own metaphysics, passes judgment on the *Critique of Pure Reason* (which is supposed first of all to investigate the possibility of that metaphysics); and then a different *judgment that comes after the investigation*, in which the reader is able to set aside for a while the consequences of the critical investigation, which may strongly repudiate the metaphysics he otherwise accepts, and first tests the grounds from which these consequences may have been derived. If what ordinary metaphysics presents were undeniably certain (like geometry, for instance), the first way of judging would be valid; for if the consequences of certain principles conflict with undeniable truths, then these principles are false and are to be rejected without any further investigation. But if it is not the case that metaphysics has a supply of incontestably certain (synthetic) propositions, and it perhaps is the case that a good number of them, which are as plausible as the best among

126

them, nevertheless are, in their consequences, in conflict even among themselves, and that overall there is not to be found in metaphysics any secure criterion whatsoever of the truth of properly metaphysical (synthetic) propositions: then the antecedent kind of judging cannot be allowed, but rather the investigation of the principles of the *Critique* must precede all judgment of its worth or unworth.

Specimen of a judgment about the *Critique* which precedes the investigation

This sort of judgment is to be found in the *Göttingischen gelehrten Anzeigen*, the supplement to the third part, from 19 January 1782, pages 40 ff.[1]

If an author who is well acquainted with the object of his work, who has been assiduous in putting reflection into its composition that is completely his own, falls into the hands of a reviewer who for his part is sufficiently clear-sighted to espy the moments upon which the worth or unworth of the writing actually rests, who does not hang on words but follows the subject matter, and who simply sees and tests the principles from which the author proceeded, then although the severity of the judgment may displease the author, the public is, by contrast, indif- ferent to it, for the public gains from it; and the author himself can be [4:373] content that he gets the opportunity to correct or to elucidate his essays, which have been examined early on by an expert, and, if he believes he is basically right, in this way to remove in good time a stumbling block that could eventually be detrimental to his work.

I find myself in a completely different situation with my reviewer. He appears not to see at all what really mattered in the investigation with which I have (fortunately or unfortunately) occupied myself, and, whether it was impatience with thinking through a lengthy work, or ill-temper over the threatened reform of a science in which he believed he had long since put everything in order, or, what I reluctantly surmise, the fault of a truly restricted conception, with which he would never be able to think himself beyond his school metaphysics – in short, he

---

[1] The review was written by Christian Garve (1742–98), and heavily edited for publication by J. G. Feder (1740–1821); it is reprinted in Vorländer (pp. 167–74), and a translation is included in Morrison's edition of Schultz, *Exposition* (see Further reading).

impetuously passes through a long series of propositions, with which one is able to think nothing at all without knowing their premises, he disperses his censure to and fro, the basis for which the reader sees no better than he understands the propositions against which this censure is supposed to be directed, and therefore the reviewer can neither be of use to inform the public nor can he harm me the least bit in the judgment of experts; consequently, I would have passed over this review completely, if it did not provide me occasion for a few elucidations that could, in a few instances, save the reader of these *Prolegomena* from misconception.

In order, however, that the reviewer might adopt a viewpoint from which he could, without having to trouble himself with any special investigation, most easily present the entire work in a manner disadvantageous to the author, he begins and also ends by saying: "this work is a system of transcendental^a (or, as he construes it, higher)[*] idealism."

[4:374] At the sight of this line I quickly perceived what sort of review would issue thence – just about as if someone who had never heard nor seen anything of geometry were to find a Euclid, and, being asked to pass judgment on it, were perhaps to say, after stumbling onto a good many figures by turning the pages: "the book is a systematic guide to drawing; the author makes use of a special language in order to provide obscure, unintelligible instructions, which in the end can achieve nothing more than what everybody can accomplish with a good natural eye, and so on."

Let us, however, look at what sort of idealism it is that runs through my entire work, although it does not by far constitute the soul of the system.

---

[*] On no account *higher*. High towers and the metaphysically-great men that resemble them, around both of which there is usually much wind, are not for me. My place is the fertile *bathos* of experience, and the word: transcendental – whose meaning, which I indicated so many times, was not once caught by the reviewer (so hastily had he looked at everything) – does not mean something that surpasses all possible experience, but something that indeed precedes experience (*a priori*), but that, all the same, is destined to nothing more than solely to make cognition from experience possible. If these concepts cross beyond experience, their use is then called transcendent, which is distinguished from the immanent use (i.e., use limited to experience). All misinterpretations of this kind have been sufficiently forestalled in the work itself; but the reviewer found his advantage in misinterpretations.

^a Reading *transcendentalen* for *transscendenten*, in accordance with Kant's wording in his footnote; the Göttingen review itself has the word *transscendentellen* here (Vorländer, p. 167), a spelling that Kant did not use.

128

The thesis of all genuine idealists, from the Eleatic School up to Bishop Berkeley,[2] is contained in this formula: "All cognition through the senses and experience is nothing but sheer illusion, and there is truth only in the ideas of pure understanding and reason."

The principle that governs and determines my idealism throughout is, on the contrary: "All cognition of things out of mere pure understanding or pure reason is nothing but sheer illusion, and there is truth only in experience."

But this is the direct opposite of the previous, genuine idealism; how then did I come to use this expression with a completely opposite intention, and how did the reviewer come to see genuine idealism everywhere?

The solution to this difficulty rests upon something that could have been seen very easily from the context of the work, if one had wanted to. Space and time, together with everything contained in them, are not things (or properties of things) in themselves, but belong instead merely to the appearances of such things; thus far I am of one creed with the previous idealists. But these idealists, and among them especially Berkeley, viewed space as a merely empirical representation, a representation which, just like the appearances in space together with all of the determinations of space, would be known to us only by means of experience or perception; I show, on the contrary, first: that space (and [4:375] time as well, to which Berkeley gave no attention), together with all its determinations, can be cognized by us *a priori*, since space (as well as time) inheres in us before all perception or experience as a pure form of our sensibility and makes possible all intuition from sensibility, and hence all appearances. From this it follows: that, since truth rests upon universal and necessary laws as its criteria, for *Berkeley* experience could have no criteria of truth, because its appearances (according to him) had nothing underlying them *a priori*; from which it then followed that experience is nothing but sheer illusion, whereas for us space and time (in combination with the pure concepts of the understanding) prescribe *a priori* their law to all possible experience, which at the same time

---

[2] Traditionally, the "Eleatic School" is identified with the view that "all is one," and that change and plurality are unreal (strictly, the Eleatics were Parmenides and Zeno of Elea). On Berkeley, see nn. 11, 12, p. 45 above.

provides the sure criterion for distinguishing truth from illusion in experience.*

My so-called (properly, critical) idealism is therefore of a wholly peculiar kind, namely such that it overturns ordinary idealism, and such that by means of it all cognition *a priori*, even that of geometry, first receives objective reality, which, without my proven ideality of space and time, could not have been asserted by even the most zealous of realists. With matters standing so, I have wished that I could name this concept of mine something else, in order to prevent all misunderstanding; but this concept cannot be completely changed. I may therefore be permitted in the future, as has already been stated above, to call it formal, or better, critical idealism, in order to distinguish it from the dogmatic idealism of *Berkeley* and the skeptical idealism of *Descartes*.

[4:376] I find nothing else worthy of note in the review of this book. Its author judges *en gros*[3] throughout, a mode that is cleverly chosen, since it does not betray one's own knowledge or ignorance; a single extensive judgment *en détail*,[4] if it had considered the main question (as is just), would have perhaps exposed my error, perhaps disclosed the degree of the reviewer's insight into this sort of investigation. It was also no ill-considered trick, for removing early on the desire to read the book itself from readers who are used to forming a conception of books from newspaper articles only, to recite one after another a great many propositions, which, torn from the context of their arguments and explications (especially as antipodean as these propositions are in relation to all school metaphysics), must of necessity sound nonsensical; to assault the reader's patience to the point of disgust; and then, after having introduced me to the witty proposition that constant illusion is truth, to conclude with the harsh, though paternal, reprimand: To what end, then, the conflict with accepted language, to what end, and whence, the idealistic distinction?[5] A judgment that ultimately renders

---

* Genuine idealism always has a fanatical purpose and can have no other; but my idealism is solely for grasping the possibility of our *a priori* cognition of the objects of experience, which is a problem that has not been solved before now, nay, has not even once been posed. By that means all fanatical idealism collapses, which (as was already to be seen with Plato) always inferred, out of our cognitions *a priori* (even those of geometry), another sort of intuition (namely, intellectual) than that of the senses, since it did not occur to anyone that the senses might also intuit *a priori*.

[3] "in the large"   [4] "in detail"
[5] Kant paraphrases the concluding sentences of the review (Vorländer, p. 174).

everything peculiar to my book into mere linguistic novelty (though previously the book was supposed to be metaphysically heretical), and that clearly proves that my would-be judge has not correctly understood the least bit of it, and, what's more, has not correctly understood himself.*

The reviewer, however, talks like a man who himself must be aware of important and exquisite insights, which, however, he still keeps secret; for nothing has become known to me of late regarding metaphysics that could justify such a tone. But he is doing a great wrong in withholding his discoveries from the world; for there are doubtless many others like me who, with all the fine things that have been written in this field for some time past, still could not find that the science had thereby been [4:377] advanced by a finger's breadth. In other respects, we do indeed find definitions being sharpened, lame proofs being provided with new crutches, the patchwork garment of metaphysics being given new pieces, or an altered cut – but all of that is not what the world demands. The world is tired of metaphysical assertions; what is wanted is the possibility of this science, the sources from which certainty could be derived in it, and sure criteria for distinguishing truth from the dialectical illusion of pure reason. The reviewer must possess the key to all this, otherwise he would by no means have spoken in so high a tone.

But I fall into the suspicion that such a need for science may perhaps never have come into his head; for otherwise he would have directed his review toward this point, and even an unsuccessful attempt in such an important matter would have gained his attention. If that is so, then we are good friends again. He may think himself as deeply into his metaphysics as seems good to him, no one will stop him; only he is not permitted to judge of something that lies outside metaphysics, i.e., its source located in reason. But that my suspicion is not unfounded, I

---

* The reviewer fights with his own shadow for the most part. When I oppose the truth of experience to dream, it never enters his head that the point of discussion is merely the notorious *somnio objective sumto* of the Wolffian philosophy,[6] which is merely formal, and simply is not aimed at the difference between sleeping and waking, which also cannot be found in transcendental philosophy. Besides, he calls my deduction of the categories and the table of principles of the understanding, "commonly known principles of logic and ontology, expressed in the manner of idealism."[7] The reader need only look over these *Prolegomena* to be convinced that a more deplorable, and even a more historically incorrect judgment could not be given.

[6] "dreams taken objectively"; Wolff, *Psychologia empirica*, new edn. (Frankfurt and Leipzig, 1738), §§120–37.

[7] Kant paraphrases the review (Vorländer, p. 169).

prove by the fact that he did not mention a word about the possibility of synthetic cognition *a priori*, which was the real problem, on the solution of which the fate of metaphysics wholly rests, and to which my *Critique* (just as here my *Prolegomena*) was entirely directed. The idealism upon which he chanced, and to which he held fast, was taken up into the system only as the sole means for solving this problem (although it then also received its confirmation on yet other grounds); and in that case he would have had to show either that this problem does not have the importance that I attribute to it (as also now in the *Prolegomena*), or that it could not at all be solved by my concept of appearances, or could better be solved in another way; but I find not a word of this in the review. The reviewer therefore understood nothing of my work and perhaps also nothing of the spirit and nature of metaphysics itself, unless on the contrary, which I prefer to assume, a reviewer's haste, indignant at the difficulty of working through so many impediments, cast an unfavorable shadow over the work lying before him and made it unrecognizable to him in its fundamentals.

[4:378]   There is still a great deal needed for a learned gazette, however well-chosen and carefully-selected its contributors may be, to be able to uphold its otherwise well-deserved reputation in the field of metaphysics just as elsewhere. Other sciences and areas of learning[b] have their standards. Mathematics has its standard within itself, history and theology in secular or sacred books, natural science and medicine in mathematics and experience, jurisprudence in law books, and even matters of taste in ancient paradigms. But in order to assess the thing called metaphysics, the standard must first be found (I have made an attempt to determine this standard and its use). Until it is discovered, what is to be done when works of this kind must be judged? If they are of the dogmatic kind, one may do as one likes; no one will for long play the master over the others in this without his finding someone who repays him in kind. But if they are of the critical kind, and indeed not with regard to other writings but to reason itself, so that the standard of appraisal cannot be already assumed but must first be sought: then objection and censure are not to be forbidden, but they must be founded on sociability, since the need is common to us all, and the lack

---

b *Kenntnisse*

of the required insight makes an air of judicially decisive pronouncement inadmissible.

But in order to tie this my defense simultaneously to the interest of the philosophizing community, I propose a test, which is decisive of the way in which all metaphysical investigations must be directed toward their common end. This is nothing else than what mathematicians have done before, in order to settle the superiority of their methods in a competition – that is, a challenge to my reviewer to prove any single truly metaphysical (i.e., synthetic, and cognized *a priori* from concepts) proposition he holds, and at best one of the most indispensable, as, for instance, the principle of the persistence of substance, or the necessary determination of the events in the world through their cause – but, as is fitting, to prove it on *a priori* grounds. If he can't do this (and silence is confession), then he must admit: that, since metaphysics is absolutely nothing without the apodictic certainty of propositions of this sort, the possibility or impossibility of such propositions would have to be settled first, before all else, in a critique of pure reason, and hence he is obliged [4:379] either to acknowledge that my principles of critique are correct or to prove their invalidity. Since, however, I already foresee that, as heedlessly as he has been relying on the certainty of his principles before now, still, because it comes down to a rigorous test, he will not find a single principle in the entire range of metaphysics with which he can dare come forward, I will therefore grant him the most favorable terms that can ever be expected in a competition; namely, I will take the *onus probandi* [8] from him and will have it put on me.

In particular, in these *Prolegomena* and in my *Critique*, pp. 426–61,[9] he finds eight propositions that are, pair by pair, always in conflict with one another, but each of which also necessarily belongs to metaphysics, which must either accept it or refute it (although there is not a single one of these propositions that has not at one time been accepted by some philosopher or other). He now has the freedom to pick any one of these eight propositions he likes, and to assume it without proof (which I give to him); but he is to pick only one (for wasting time will be no more useful to him than to me), and then to attack my proof of the antithesis. If, however, I can rescue it, and show in this way that the opposite of the proposition he adopted can be proven exactly as clearly,

---

[8] "burden of proof"
[9] §51, above; *Critique*, A 426–61/B 454–89, The Antinomies of Pure Reason.

in accordance with principles that every dogmatic metaphysics must of necessity acknowledge, then by this means it is settled that there is an hereditary defect in metaphysics that cannot be explained, much less removed, without ascending to its birthplace, pure reason itself, and so my *Critique* must either be accepted or a better one put in its place, and therefore it must at least be studied; which is the only thing that I now desire. If, on the contrary, I cannot rescue my proof, then a synthetic *a priori* proposition is established from dogmatic principles on my opponent's side, my indictment of ordinary metaphysics was therefore unjust, and I offer to recognize his censure of my *Critique* as legitimate (although this is far from being the likely outcome). But hereto it would be necessary, I should think, *to emerge from being incognito*, since I do not otherwise see how to prevent my being honored or assailed with [4:380] many problems from unknown and indeed unbidden opponents, instead of with one problem.[10]

Proposal for an investigation of the *Critique*, after which the judgment can follow

I am obliged to the learned public for the silence with which it has honored my *Critique* for a long time; for this demonstrates a suspension of judgment, and thus some conjecture that, in a work that abandons all the usual paths and pursues a new one in which one cannot immediately find his way, something might nonetheless perhaps be found through which an important (but now decayed) branch of human knowledge could receive new life and fertility, and, consequently, it demonstrates a cautiousness, not to break off and destroy the still fresh graft through an overly hasty judgment. A specimen of a judgment that was delayed for such reasons has only just now come before me in the *Gothaischen gelehrten Zeitung*,[11] a judgment whose well-foundedness every reader will perceive for himself (without taking into consideration my own suspect praise) from the comprehensible and unadulterated presentation of a portion of the first principles of my work.

---

[10] Garve wrote to Kant on 13 July 1783, revealing his part in writing the original review, but maintaining that Feder's revisions had distorted it, and enclosing a copy of his original, which he later published (Ak 10:328–33); on 7 August 1783, Kant responded that he now understood that responsibility for the review could not be assigned publically, and he dropped his challenge (Ak 10:336–43; *PC*, pp. 98–105).

[11] 24 August 1782, pp. 56–63.

And now I propose, since the whole of a large edifice cannot possibly be judged at once through a cursory estimation, that it be examined piece by piece from its foundation, and that in this the present *Prolegomena* be used as a general synopsis, with which the work itself could then be compared on occasion. This suggestion, if it were based on nothing more than the imagined importance that vanity customarily imparts to all one's own products, would be immodest and would deserve to be dismissed with indignation. At present, however, the endeavors of all speculative philosophy stand at the point of completely dying out, although human reason clings to them with undying affection, an affection that now seeks, though vainly, to turn itself into indifference, only because it has been constantly betrayed.

In our thinking age it is not to be expected that many meritorious men would not use every good opportunity to work together toward the common interest of an ever more enlightened reason, if only there appears some hope of thereby attaining the goal. Mathematics, natural [4:381] science, law, the arts, even morals (and so on) do not completely fill up the soul; there still remains a space in it that is marked off for mere pure and speculative reason, the emptiness of which drives us to grotesques and trivialities, or else to fanaticism, ostensibly in search of activity and entertainment, but at bottom only in search of diversion to drown out the disturbing call of reason, which, in accordance with its vocation, demands something which is for its own satisfaction, and which has not been set in motion on behalf of other purposes or in the service of inclinations. There is, therefore, as I have grounds to expect, for everyone who has simply tried to expand his concepts in this way, great attraction to contemplation that occupies itself only with this sphere of reason existing for itself, because exactly in this sphere all other areas of learning and even goals must join together and unite in a whole – and, I dare say, a greater attraction than to any other theoretical knowledge, which would not readily be taken in exchange for the former.

But I propose these *Prolegomena* as the plan and guide for the investigation, and not the work itself, because, with respect to the latter, though I am even now quite satisfied as regards the content, order, and method, and the care that was taken to ponder and test each proposition thoroughly before setting it down (for it took years for me to be fully satisfied not only with the whole, but sometimes also with only a single proposition, as regards its sources), I am not fully satisfied with my presentation in some chapters of the Doctrine of Elements, e.g., the Deduction of the concepts of the understanding or the chapter on the Paralogisms of pure reason,[12] since a certain prolixity in these chapters obstructs the clarity, and in place of them, the examination can be based on what the *Prolegomena* here say with respect to these chapters.

The Germans are praised for being able to advance things further than other peoples in matters where persistence and diligence are necessary. If this opinion is well-founded, then an opportunity presents itself here to bring to completion an endeavor whose happy outcome is hardly to be doubted and in which all thinking persons share equal interest, but which has not succeeded before now – and to confirm that favorable opinion; in particular, since the science concerned is of such a [4:382] peculiar kind that it can be brought all at once to its full completion, and into a *permanent state* such that it cannot be advanced the least bit further and can be neither augmented nor altered by later discovery (herein I do not include embellishment through enhanced clarity here and there, or through added benefits with respect to all sorts of things): an advantage that no other science has or can have, since no other science is concerned with a cognitive faculty that is so fully isolated, and so fully independent of and unmingled with other faculties. The present moment does not seem unfavorable to this expectation of mine, because at present in Germany hardly anyone knows how he could keep himself still occupied outside the so-called useful sciences and have it be, not mere sport, but endeavors through which an enduring goal is reached.

How the efforts of the learned could be united toward such an end, I must leave to others to devise the means. However, it is not my intention to demand that anyone at all simply adhere to my theses, nor even to flatter myself with the hope of something like that; rather, whether, as it happens, attacks, revisions, qualifications, or else confirmation, completion, and extension should bring it about, if only the matter is investigated from the ground up, then it can no longer now fail that a system would thereby come into being (even if it were not mine) that could become a legacy to posterity for which it would have reason to be thankful.

It would be too much to show here what sort of metaphysics could be expected to follow if one were first right about the principles of a

---

[12] See the Table of contents (pp. 141–2) for the *Critique*. The chapters named were in fact heavily revised in the "B" edition.

critique, and how it would by no means have to appear paltry and cut down to just a small figure because its false feathers had been plucked, but could in other respects appear richly and respectably outfitted; but other large benefits that such a reform would draw after it come immediately into view. The ordinary metaphysics has indeed already produced benefits, because it searched for the elementary concepts of the pure understanding in order to render them clear through analysis and determinate through explication. It was thereby a cultivation of reason, wherever reason might subsequently find it proper to direct itself. But that was all the good that it did. For it undid again this merit because it promoted self-conceit through rash assertions, sophistry through subtle evasions and glosses, and shallowness through the facility [4:383] with which it overcame the most difficult problems with a little school wisdom – a shallowness that is all the more enticing the more it has the option of, on the one hand, taking on something from the language of science, and, on the other, from popularity, and thereby is everything to everyone, but in fact is nothing at all. By contrast, through critique our judgment is allotted a standard by which knowledge can, with certainty, be distinguished from pseudo knowledge; and, as a result of being brought fully into play in metaphysics, critique establishes a mode of thinking that subsequently extends its wholesome influence to every other use of reason, and for the first time excites the true philosophical spirit. But the service that it renders to theology, by making it independent of the judgment of dogmatic speculation and in that way securing it against all attacks from such opponents, is also certainly not to be underrated. For the ordinary metaphysics, although promising to assist theology greatly, was subsequently unable to fulfill this promise, and beyond this, in calling speculative dogmatism to its aid, had done nothing other than to arm enemies against itself. Fanaticism, which cannot make headway in an enlightened age except by hiding behind a school metaphysics, under the protection of which it can at the same time venture, as it were, to rave rationally, will be driven by critical philosophy from this its final hiding place; and concerning all of this, nothing else can be as important to a teacher of metaphysics than being able to say, for once with universal concurrence, that what he propounds now is finally *science* as well, and that through it genuine benefit is rendered to the commonweal.

Selections from the Critique of Pure Reason

Contents^a

---

^a The table of contents is modified from that in the "A" edition; there was no table in "B." Page numbers are given here at right only for those selections translated in this volume. For convenience the divisions of the *Critique* are shown, even when no selection is included.

Preface to the second edition

Whether or not the cultivation of those cognitions that belong to the occupation of reason treads the sure path of a science can be assessed quickly from the results. If, after repeated preparations and provisions, this cultivation gets bogged down as soon as it arrives at its goal, or if it must often backtrack and take another path to attain this goal; or equally, if it is not possible to unite the various collaborators on the manner in which their common aim should be pursued: then one can always be convinced that such a pursuit has not yet (by far) taken the sure path of science, but is merely groping about; and the discovery of this path, if possible, is already a service to reason, even if much should have to be abandoned as futile that was contained in the goal as previously accepted (without reflection).

That *logic* has tread this sure path from the most ancient times up to [B viii] now can be seen from the fact that since *Aristotle* it has not had to take a single step backward, if the removal of a few superfluous subtleties or the clearer determination of what is presented are not to be reckoned as improvements, which anyway pertain more to the elegance than to the surety of the science. It is further noteworthy about logic that it also has not, up to now, been able to take any step forward, and therefore seems, to all appearance, to be finished and complete. For, if a few moderns have thought to extend it by sticking in some *psychological* chapters on the various cognitive powers (imagination, native wit), some *metaphysical* chapters on the origin of cognition or on the various kinds of certainty in accordance with differing objects (idealism, skepticism, etc.), and some *anthropological* chapters on prejudices (their causes and remedies), this stems from their ignorance of the peculiar nature of this science. It is not an enhancement but a disfiguration of the sciences if their boundaries are allowed to run together; the boundary of logic is, [B ix] however, exactly determined by its being a science that fully lays out and rigorously proves nothing except the formal rules of all thinking – whether the thinking be *a priori* or empirical, whatever origin or object it may have, and whether the impediments it meets in our mind be incidental or natural.

That logic has succeeded so well is an advantage it owes only to its limitedness, by which it is entitled, nay, obliged to abstract from all objects of cognition and their differentiation; and in logic, therefore, the understanding is concerned with nothing more than itself and its own form. Naturally, it would have been far more difficult for reason to pursue the sure path of science if it had to deal not merely with itself but also with objects; hence logic, as a propaedeutic, forms as it were merely the vestibule of the sciences; and if knowledge is being considered, a logic must indeed be presupposed for its assessment, but the acquisition of such knowledge must be sought in sciences genuinely and objectively so called.

Insofar as reason is supposed to be found in these sciences there must be something cognized *a priori* in them; and the cognition of reason can [B x] be related to its object in two ways, either merely in *determining* this object and its concept (which must be given from somewhere else), or else *in making* the object *actual*. The first is *theoretical*, the second *practical cognition* through reason. For both, the *pure* part – namely, that part (as much or as little as it may contain) in which reason determines its object wholly *a priori* – must be presented by itself in advance, and nothing coming from other sources must be intermixed with it; for it is poor management when one blindly pays out what comes in, without being able to distinguish afterwards, if one gets stuck, which part of the revenue could carry the expense, and from which some expense must be cut.

Mathematics and *physics* are the two theoretical bodies of cognition through reason that are supposed to determine their *objects a priori* – the first completely purely, the second at least in part purely, but then in accordance with sources of cognition other than reason.

Mathematics has tread the sure path of a science from the earliest times to which the history of human reason reaches, among the amazing Greeks. But it must not be thought that it was as easy for it to find this royal path, or rather to forge it for itself, as it was for logic, in which reason is concerned only with itself; on the contrary, I believe that for a [B xi] long time it continued to grope about (especially still among the Egyptians), and that the change is to be ascribed to a *revolution*, brought about in one attempt by the lucky thought of a single man, from which point on there was no more departing from the route that had to be taken, and the sure path of a science was laid down and marked out for all times and to infinite lengths. The history of this revolution in mode of thought – which was much more important than the discovery of the way around the famous Cape of Good Hope – and of the fortunate man who brought it about, has not been preserved for us. And yet the saga that *Diogenes Laertius*[1] hands down to us, who names the presumed inventor of the smallest elements of geometrical demonstration (which never needed any proof at all, according to common opinion), proves that the recollection of this change by which the first sign of the discovery of the new path was produced must have seemed of the utmost importance to the mathematicians, and for that reason to have been unforgettable. A light came on for the first person who gave a demonstration of the *isosceles triangle* (whether he was named *Thales* or howsoever one wants);[2] for he found that he must not investigate what [B xii] he saw in the figure, or even investigate the bare concept of the figure, and as it were learn its properties by those means, but rather that he had to produce (through construction) that which he himself, in accordance with concepts, thought into and displayed in the figure, and that, in order to know something *a priori* with security, he must attribute to the thing nothing except what follows with necessity from that which he himself has put into it in accordance with his concept.

With natural science things went much more slowly before it came upon the high road of science; for it is only about a century and a half ago that the proposal of the ingenious **Bacon** of Verulam[3] partly occasioned this discovery – and partly, since some were already on its

---

[1] Diogenes Laertius (3rd century AD?), author of the *Lives of the Philosophers*.

[2] Bk. 1, proposition 5 of Euclid's *Elements* demonstrates the equality of the two angles at the base of an isosceles triangle, a demonstration traditionally credited to Thales of Miletus. The "B" edition of Kant's text reads "equilateral triangle," which would correspond to Bk. 1, proposition 1, in which it is demonstrated that such a triangle can be constructed on any finite straight line; in a letter from 1787 Kant requested the emendation (Ak 10:489).

[3] Francis Bacon (1561–1626), British thinker whose works gave impetus to the new, empirical natural philosophy (later, "natural science").

trail, simply revived it – a discovery that also can be explained only through a rapidly occurring revolution in mode of thought. Here I will take into consideration natural science only insofar as it is founded on *empirical* principles.

When **Galileo** let balls of a weight he had chosen himself roll down an inclined plane,[4] or **Torricelli** made the air carry a weight that he had himself beforehand thought to be equal to the known weight of a column of water,[5] or, at a still later time, when **Stahl** changed metals [B xiii] into lime and back into metal again[6] by depriving them of something and restoring it,* a light came on for all students of nature. They grasped that reason has insight only into that which it produces itself in accordance with its own plan, that reason must lead the way with principles of its judgments in accordance with fixed laws, and that it must require nature to answer its questions but must not let nature keep it solely as it were in leading strings;[7] for otherwise accidental observations, not being made in accordance with a previously delineated plan, do not at all cohere in a necessary law, which reason nonetheless seeks and requires. Reason must go to nature holding in one hand its principles, through which alone consilient appearances can be taken for laws, and, in the other hand, the experiment it has devised according to those principles, so as indeed to be taught by nature; but it must go in the character not of a pupil who is made to repeat whatever the teacher wishes, but of an invested judge who requires witnesses to answer the questions he puts before them. And even physics owes so advantageous [B xiv] a revolution of its manner of thinking solely to the happy idea of seeking in nature (not imputing to it) that which reason must learn from nature – and of which reason would by itself know nothing – in accordance with what reason has itself put into nature. By this means natural science was first put onto the sure path of a science, whereas

---

* I do not here follow precisely the thread of the history of the experimental method, whose first beginnings are indeed not well known.

[4] Galileo Galilei (1564–1642), Italian mathematical natural philosopher who carried out experiments on the inclined plane, which are reported in his *Two New Sciences* (originally published in Italian, with Latin sections, in 1638).

[5] Evangelista Torricelli (1608–47), Italian mathematician who was involved in the early barometric experiments for measuring the weight of the air.

[6] Georg Ernst Stahl (1660–1734), German physician and chemist who carried out experiments on metals in accordance with the celebrated hypothesis that there is a basic chemical element named "phlogiston," which can be removed from and reunited with metals.

[7] Leading strings are used to aid children in learning to walk.

throughout so many centuries it had been nothing more than a mere groping about.

To *metaphysics* – wholly isolated speculative cognition of reason which rises completely above the teachings of experience to where reason is supposed therefore to itself be its own pupil, and which so rises through mere concepts (not, like mathematics, through the application of concepts to intuition) – fate has before now not been so kind that it has been able to take up the sure path of a science, despite the fact that metaphysics is more ancient than all of the other sciences and would remain even if they should be completely swallowed up together into the abyss of an all-destroying barbarism. For in metaphysics reason continually gets bogged down, even when it wants to gain *a priori* insight (as it claims to do) into the same laws that ordinary experience confirms. In metaphysics it has been necessary to backtrack innumerable times, because the path is found not to lead where one wants to go; and as concerns unanimity in its adherents' assertions, it is [B xv] still so far away from that, that on the contrary it is a battleground which in reality appears to be fully destined for exercising its forces in shadowboxing, and upon which no fighter has ever been able to gain even the smallest place for himself by fighting, and to base a lasting possession upon his victory. There is therefore no doubt that up to now the procedure of metaphysics has been merely to grope about, and, what is the worst, to do so among mere concepts.

What, then, is the reason that here the sure path of science has not yet been able to be found? Is such a path perhaps not possible? Whence then did nature visit upon our reason, as one of its most important concerns, the ceaseless striving to search out this path? Still more, how little do we have cause to have confidence in our reason, when, in one of the most important areas of our inquisitiveness, it not only forsakes us, but detains us with idle hopes and in the end deceives us! Or have we merely missed this path up to now; what sign can we make use of, so as to have hope that with renewed investigation we will be more fortunate than others have been before us?

I should have thought that the examples of mathematics and natural science, which have become what they are now through a suddenly [B xvi] achieved revolution, would have been remarkable enough for drawing attention to the essential part played by the alteration in mode of thought that was so advantageous for them – and for at least an attempt to emulate those sciences in metaphysics, to the extent that their analogy with it, as cognitions of reason, permits. Previously it has been assumed that all of our cognition must conform itself to objects; but under this assumption all attempts to decide something about objects *a priori* through concepts, and by which our cognition would be extended, have come to nothing. Let us now, therefore, test whether we do not make better progress on the problems of metaphysics by assuming that objects must conform themselves to our cognition – which already accords better with the desired possibility for *a priori* cognition of such objects, cognition that must establish something concerning objects before those objects are given to us. Matters stand here just as they did for the first thoughts of **Copernicus**, who, when things did not go well for explaining the celestial motions if he assumed that the entire multitude of stars rotates about the observer, sought to find whether things might not go better if he had the observer rotate, and by contrast

[B xvii] left the stars at rest. The same kind of thing can now be tried in metaphysics, with respect to the *intuition* of objects. If intuition had to conform itself to the constitution of objects, I do not see how anything could be known of that constitution *a priori*; but if the object (as object of the senses) conforms itself to the constitution of our faculty of intuition, then I can very well imagine this possibility. But since, if these intuitions are to become cognitions, I cannot stop with them, but must relate them, as representations, to something else as object, and must determine this object through them, I can, therefore, either assume that the *concepts* through which I accomplish this determination conform themselves to the object, and then I am back in the same perplexity about how I could know something about the object *a priori*; or else I assume that objects, or what is the same, that the *experience* in which alone they can be cognized (as objects that are given) conforms itself to these concepts, in which case I see immediately an easier means by which I could know something about the object *a priori*, since experience is itself a type of cognition that requires the understanding, whose rule I must presume to be in me before objects are given to me, and hence to be *a priori*, a rule that is expressed *a priori* in concepts with

[B xviii] which all objects of experience must therefore necessarily conform and be in agreement. As regards objects insofar as they can be thought through reason alone (and indeed necessarily so), but which (at least as reason thinks them) cannot at all be given in experience, the attempts to think them (for they must admit of being thought) will subsequently provide an excellent touchstone for what we are taking up as the altered method in mode of thinking, namely, that we cognize *a priori* in things only what we have ourselves put into them.*

This test succeeds as hoped, and promises metaphysics, in its first part, the sure path of a science, since metaphysics occupies itself in [B xix] particular with *a priori* concepts for which the corresponding objects conforming to those concepts can be given in experience. For with this alteration in manner of thinking, the possibility of cognition *a priori* can be explained very well, and, what is still more, adequate proofs can be provided for the laws which, *a priori*, underlie nature as the sum total of the objects of experience – both of which were impossible under the previous manner of proceeding. However, from this deduction, in the first part of metaphysics, of our faculty for cognizing *a priori*, there follows a surprising result, which is, to all appearance, quite detrimental to the entire goal that occupies the second part of metaphysics – namely, the result that we can never come beyond the boundary of possible experience with this faculty, which is nonetheless precisely the essential concern of this science. But herein lies exactly the experiment [B xx] for counter testing the truth of the result of this first evaluation of our *a priori* cognition from reason, that is, that this cognition relates only to appearances, leaving the things in themselves, by contrast, indeed actual for themselves, but uncognized by us. For that which drives us necessarily to go beyond the boundary of experience and of all appearances is the *unconditioned*, something that reason necessarily demands in the things in themselves, and which it by all rights demands for every conditioned, and therefore for the series of conditions as a completed series. If it is now found, when it is assumed that our

---

* This method, imitating that of the student of nature, consists therefore in this: to seek the elements of pure reason in that *which admits of being confirmed or rejected through experiment.* But for testing the propositions of pure reason, especially if they venture out beyond all bounds of possible experience, there is no experiment to be made with their *objects* (as in natural science): therefore the experiment is feasible only with the *concepts* and *principles* that we assume *a priori* – namely, by arranging them such that the same objects can be considered, *on the one hand*, as objects of the senses and understanding for experience, but, *on the other*, as objects that one indeed merely thinks, and so perhaps as objects for isolated reason striving to exceed the bounds of experience – and so by arranging them such that the same objects can be considered from two different sides. If it is now found that when things are considered from this bifurcated point of view the principle of pure reason is in harmony, but that with a single point of view there arises an unavoidable conflict of reason with itself, then the experiment decides in favor of the correctness of this differentiation.

cognition through experience conforms itself to objects as things in themselves, that the unconditioned *cannot at all be thought without contradiction*; and if, on the contrary, it is found, when it is assumed that our representation of things as they are given to us does not conform itself to these things as things in themselves but rather that these objects, as appearances, instead conform themselves to our mode of representation, that *the contradiction vanishes*, and that, consequently, the unconditioned has to be found, not in things insofar as we are acquainted with them (i.e., as they are given to us), but indeed in things insofar as we are not acquainted with them, as things in themselves –

[B xxi] then it is shown that what we at first assumed for testing is well-founded.* Now there still remains for us, after all advance into the field of the supersensible has been forbidden to speculative reason, to investigate whether, in reason's practical cognition, data are not to be found for determining this transcendent rational concept of the unconditioned, and, in this way, for coming out beyond the boundary of all possible experience with our cognition *a priori* (as metaphysics would like), though only with respect to the practical. And with this way of proceeding speculative reason has after all at least supplied us with room for such expansion (even if speculative reason had to leave it empty), and we are therefore still quite free, nay, we are even challenged

[B xxii] by speculative reason to fill it up, if we can, through practical data of reason.**

In this attempt to change the previous procedure of metaphysics, and,

---

* This experiment of pure reason is very similar to that of the *chemists*, which they sometimes call the test by *reduction*, but in general call the *synthetic method of proceeding*. The *analysis of the metaphysician* divides pure cognition *a priori* into two quite heterogeneous elements, namely, the cognition of things as appearances, and, second, of things in themselves. The *dialectic* conjoins the two once again into a *unity* with reason's necessary idea of the *unconditioned*, and discovers that this unity can never result except through this differentiation, which is, therefore, the true one.

** Similarly, the central laws of the motion of the celestial bodies supplied fixed certainty to that which *Copernicus* at first assumed only as a hypothesis, and at the same time gave proof of the invisible force binding together the system of the world (the *Newtonian* attraction), which would have forever remained undiscovered if the former had not ventured, in a manner that was contrary to common sense, but was nonetheless correct, to seek the observed motions not in the objects in the heavens, but rather in the observer of those objects. In this preface I am also putting forth the change in mode of thinking propounded in the *Critique* (which is analogous to the preceding hypothesis) merely as a hypothesis – although in the treatise itself it is proven, not hypothetically, but apodictically, from the nature of our representations of space and time and from the elementary concepts of the understanding – in order merely to draw notice to the first attempt at such a change, which is always hypothetical.

following the example of the geometer and the student of nature, to do it by our undertaking a complete revolution in metaphysics, consists the business of this critique of pure speculative reason. It is a treatise of the method, not a system of the science itself; but it nonetheless sets down the complete outline of this science, both as regards its boundaries, and [B xxiii] in the entire internal structure of its parts. For it is peculiar to pure speculative reason that it can and must both take the measure of its own ability according to the different ways it chooses to think objects, and also enumerate completely the various ways for posing problems to itself (and so set down a complete sketch for a system of metaphysics) – since, as regards the former, in cognition *a priori* nothing can be attributed to objects except what the thinking subject takes from itself, and, concerning the latter, pure speculative reason is, as regards the principles of cognition, a completely separate and self-subsistent unity, in which, as in an organized body, any one part exists for the sake of all the others, and they exist for the sake of the one, and in which no principle can be taken with certainty in *any one* relation, without also having been examined in *thoroughgoing* relation to the entire use of pure reason. But for that very reason metaphysics has the rare good fortune, allotted to no other science of reason concerned with objects (for *logic* is concerned only with the form of thinking in general), that, if it is set onto the sure path of science through this critique, it can fully comprehend the entire field of the cognitions that belong to it, and can therefore complete its work [B xxiv] and consign it over for the use of posterity as capital stock that can never be augmented, since metaphysics is concerned solely with principles, and with limitations on their use that can be determined through these principles themselves. Metaphysics is, therefore, as fundamental science, also obligated to this completeness, and it must be able to be said of metaphysics: *nil actum reputans, si quid superesset agendum.*[8]

But, it will be asked, what sort of treasure is this that we intend to bequeath to posterity through a metaphysics such as is purified through critique, and also brought thereby into a condition of permanence? Upon a superficial survey of this work, one will believe one has perceived that its benefit is indeed merely *negative*, namely, so that we never venture beyond the boundary of experience with speculative reason; and that is, in fact, its primary benefit. This benefit, however, immediately becomes

---

[8] "thinking nothing has been accomplished if anything should remain to be done."

positive, when it is perceived that the principles with which speculative reason ventures out beyond its boundaries have as their inevitable consequence not in fact the *expansion*, but rather, if they are examined more closely, the *contraction* of our use of reason, in that they actually threaten to expand the boundaries of sensibility (to which these princi-
[B xxv] ples really belong) to include everything, and so to push aside completely the pure (practical) use of reason. A critique that limits speculative reason is, therefore, to that extent indeed *negative*, but, because it thereby simultaneously removes an obstacle that limits the practical use of reason or even threatens to destroy it, it is in fact of *positive* and very important benefit, as soon as one becomes convinced that there is an absolutely necessary practical use of pure reason (the moral use), in which it unavoidably extends itself beyond the boundaries of sensibility, for which it indeed needs no help from speculative reason, but for which it nonetheless must be secured against the counter effect of speculative reason, so as not to fall into contradiction with itself. To deny *positive* benefit to this service of the *Critique* would be as much as to say that the police provide no positive benefit because their chief occupation is merely to check the violence that citizens have to fear from other citizens so that each can go about their business peacefully and securely. It is proven in the analytic part of the *Critique* that space and time are only forms of sensory intuition and therefore only conditions of the existence of things as appearances; that, furthermore, we have no concepts of the understanding, and hence no elements whatsoever for the cognition of
[B xxvi] things, except insofar as these concepts can be given a corresponding intuition; and that, in consequence, we cannot have cognition of any object as a thing in itself, but only insofar as it is an object of sensory intuition, i.e., as appearance; from which then admittedly follows the limitation of all possible speculative cognition through reason to mere objects of *experience*. Nevertheless, it must be kept in mind that hereunto it is indeed always reserved that we must be able, if not *to cognize*, then still at least *to think* these very same objects as things in themselves.* For

---

* In order *to cognize* an object it is required that I can prove its possibility (whether from its actuality, through the testimony of experience, or *a priori* through reason). But I can *think* whatever I wish, if I merely do not contradict myself (i.e., if my concept is merely a possible thought), even if I cannot vouch for whether, within the ambit of all possibilities, an object corresponds to it or not. But in order to attribute objective validity (real possibility, for the previous possibility was merely logical) to such a concept, something more is required. But this addition need not be sought in the sources of theoretical cognition; it can also lie in the practical.

otherwise, the absurd proposition would follow that there would be appearance without there being something that now appears. Now if we [B xxvii] want to assume that the distinction (necessitated by our *Critique*) of things as objects of experience from the very same things as things in themselves had not been made at all, then the principle of causality, and hence the mechanism of nature in the determination of that causality, would have to be valid absolutely for all things in general as efficient causes. I would, therefore, not be able to say of one and the same being, e.g., the human soul, that its will is free and that it nonetheless is also subject to natural necessity, i.e., is not free, without falling into a manifest contradiction, since in both propositions I have taken the soul in *one and the same meaning*, namely, as a thing in general (as a thing in itself) – and without a preceding critique I could not have taken it otherwise. If, however, the *Critique* is not mistaken, then, since it instructs one to take the object in *two different meanings*, that is, as appearance, or as thing in itself, and if the deduction of its concepts of the understanding is correct, and so the principle of causality refers only to things taken in the first sense, namely, insofar as they are objects of experience, but the very same things are not, under the second meaning, subject to that principle: then the very same will is thought in [B xxviii] appearance (in visible actions) as conforming to natural law, and to that extent as *not free*, and yet, on the other hand, is thought as belonging to a thing in itself, which is not subject to that law, and hence is thought as being *free*, without a contradiction thereby occurring. Now, although I cannot *cognize* my soul, considered in the latter respect, through speculative reason (and still less through empirical observation), and hence also cannot *cognize* freedom as the property of a being to which I attribute effects in the sensible world, since I would have to cognize such a being determinately, in accordance with its existence, and yet not in time (something that is impossible, since I cannot bring any intuition under my concept), I can nonetheless *think* freedom; that is, the representation of freedom at least does not contain a contradiction, if our critical distinction of the two kinds of representation (sensory and intellectual), and the limitation of the pure concepts of the understanding derived from it, and hence also the limitation of the principles that flow from those concepts, are granted. Supposing, now, that morals necessarily presupposes freedom (in the strongest sense) as a property of our will – in that it produces original practical principles, inherent in

our reason, as *a priori data* for morals, principles that would be
[B xxix] absolutely impossible without presupposing freedom – but that speculative reason has proven that this freedom does not even allow of being
thought; then that presupposition (that is, the moral presupposition)
necessarily must give way to the presupposition whose opposite contains
a manifest contradiction, and consequently *freedom*, and with it, morality
(for its opposite does not contain any contradiction if freedom is not
presupposed), must make room for the *mechanism of nature*. But since,
for morals, I do not need anything more than that freedom merely does
not contradict itself, and hence that it indeed at least permits of being
thought without there being need for further insight into it, and that it
therefore does not in any way obstruct the mechanism of nature
regarding the very same action (taken in another respect), then, the
doctrine of morality retains its place and the doctrine of nature keeps its
as well, something that would not have taken place if the *Critique* had
not previously instructed us about our unavoidable ignorance with
respect to things in themselves, and had not restricted everything that
we can *cognize* theoretically to mere appearances. This same exposition
of the positive benefit of the critical principles of pure reason can be
produced with respect to the concept of *God* and the *simple nature* of
our *soul*, which, however, I pass over for brevity's sake. I can therefore
[B xxx] not so much as even *assume God, freedom*, and *immortality* on behalf of
the necessary, practical use of my reason, if I do not at the same time
deprive speculative reason of its pretension to transcendent insights,
since, in order to achieve such insights, it must make use of principles
which, because they in fact extend only to objects of possible experience, always change their object into appearance if they are indeed
applied to something that cannot be an object of experience, and which
therefore pronounce all *practical* **expansion** of pure reason to be
impossible. I therefore had to cast out *knowledge* in order to make room
for *belief*; the dogmatism of metaphysics, i.e., the preconception that it
makes progress without a critique of pure reason, is the true source of
all the unbelief (always extremely dogmatic) which conflicts with
morality. – – If, therefore, with a systematic metaphysics drawn up
according to the *Critique of Pure Reason* it cannot be very difficult to
leave a bequest for posterity, still, this gift is not to be deemed
inconsequential, whether one considers in general merely the cultivation
of reason along the sure path of a science by comparison with reason's

baseless groping and frivolous roaming about in the absence of critique, [B xxxi]
or one also considers the better use of time for inquisitive young people,
who, with the ordinary dogmatism, receive so early and so great an
encouragement to engage with ease in false subtlety – or even to seek
the invention of new thoughts and opinions – concerning things about
which they understand nothing and in which they will never (anymore
than anyone else) have insight into anything, and are therefore encouraged to neglect the learning of sciences that are better founded; but
mostly, this gift is not to be deemed inconsequential if one takes into
account the inestimable advantage of ending, in the *Socratic* manner
(that is, through the clearest proof of the ignorance of the opponents) all
opposition to morality and religion for all future time. For there has
always been one or another metaphysics in the world, and metaphysics
will be there to be found in the future as well, and also a dialectic of
pure reason with it, since this dialectic is natural to pure reason. It is
therefore the first and most important concern of philosophy to deprive
metaphysics of all detrimental influence once and for all, by blocking the
source of the errors.

With this important change in the field of the sciences, and the *loss*
that speculative reason must suffer of its previously fancied possession,
everything nonetheless remains in the same fortunate condition as it has
ever been regarding the universal concerns of humankind and the [B xxxii]
benefit that the world has hitherto derived from the doctrines of pure
reason, and the loss hits only the *monopoly of the schools* but in no way
affects the *interest of humankind*. I ask the most stubborn of dogmatics
whether the proof of the persistence of the soul after death from the
simplicity of substance, or that of the freedom of the will in opposition
to universal mechanism through the subtle, though impotent, distinctions between subjective and objective practical necessity, or that of the
existence of God from the concept of a most-real being (the concept of
the contingency of the mutable and of the necessity of a first mover),
have ever, after going out from the schools, reached the public itself and
been able to influence its conviction in the least? Now if this has not
happened, and also can never be expected to happen, because common
sense is unsuited to such subtle speculation; and if, on the contrary, as
concerns the first matter, the natural human predisposition (found in
everyone) never to be able to be satisfied by what is temporal (as
inadequate for the foundations of the complete vocation of humankind)

has to have given rise by itself to the hope of a *future life*, and if, with [Bxxxiii] respect to the second matter, the mere clear presentation of duties as opposed to all the claims of inclination has to have given rise by itself to the consciousness of *freedom*, and finally, if, regarding the third matter, the magnificent order, beauty, and foresight that shows forth everywhere in nature has to have given rise by itself to the belief in a great and wise *Author of the world* (insofar as these convictions, ever more widely held by the public, rest on rational grounds): then not only does this possession indeed remain undisturbed, but it gains much more in respect, because the schools are now taught not to lay claim to any higher or more extensive insight into a point that touches upon the universal concerns of humankind, than that insight to which the great multitude (who are for us worthy of the highest respect) can also very easily attain, and therefore to restrict themselves solely to the cultivation of these universally comprehensible grounds for proof, which are sufficient with respect to morality. The change therefore concerns only the arrogant claims of the schools, who in these matters (as indeed rightly so in many other areas) would very much like to be regarded as the sole knowers and preservers of such truths, permitting the public only their use, but reserving the key to such truths to themselves (*quod mecum nescit, solus vult scire videri*).[9] But provision is nonetheless made [B xxxiv] for a more reasonable aspiration for speculative philosophy. That philosophy remains always the exclusive depository of a science that is beneficial to the public without its knowledge, namely, the critique of reason; for this critique can never become popular, and indeed has no need to be so, because as little as the people want to comprehend finely spun arguments for useful truths, just as little do the subtle objections against such truths ever come into their minds; by contrast, since the school, as well as anyone who ascends to speculation, inevitably falls into both of these, critique is obligated, through a thorough investigation of the rights of speculative reason, to prevent once and for all the scandal, which, sooner or later, must rise up, even to the people, out of the controversies in which metaphysicians (and ultimately even ecclesiastics too, as metaphysicians) inevitably ensnarl themselves without critique, controversies that subsequently even corrupt their own doctrines. Now only through critique can *materialism, fatalism, atheism,*

[9] "what he doesn't know together with me, he alone wishes to seem to know"

freethinking *unbelief, fanaticism,* and *superstition* (which can become universally harmful), and lastly *idealism* and *skepticism* (which are more dangerous for the schools, and can scarcely pass over into the public) be cut off at the very root. If indeed governments think it proper to meddle [B xxxv] with the affairs of the learned, it would be far more conformable to their wisdom in providing for sciences as well as for humankind to countenance the freedom of such critique, through which alone the cultivation of reason can be put on firm footing, than to support the ridiculous despotism of the schools, who raise a loud cry about public danger if their cobwebs are rent, but of whom the public has never taken notice, and whose loss it therefore can never feel.

The *Critique* is not opposed to the *dogmatic procedure* of reason in its pure cognition, as science (for science must always be dogmatic, i.e., it must always be rigorously proven from secure principles *a priori*), but to *dogmatism,* i.e., to the pretension of making progress in pure cognition from concepts (philosophical cognition) using only principles such as reason has long made use of, without inquiring into the manner and the right by which reason has arrived at those principles. Dogmatism therefore is the dogmatic procedure of pure reason, *without a preceding critique of reason's own ability.* Consequently, this opposition should not, under the self-assumed name of popularity, speak in favor of babbling superficiality, nor indeed of skepticism, which makes short work of [B xxxvi] metaphysics; on the contrary, the *Critique* is the necessary preliminary preparation for the advancement of a well-founded metaphysics as science, which necessarily must be worked out dogmatically and, in accordance with the most exacting requirements, systematically, and so scholastically (not popularly), for this requirement on it is irremissible, since it obligates itself to carry out its business wholly *a priori*, hence to the complete satisfaction of speculative reason. Therefore in the execution of the plan prescribed by the *Critique*, i.e., in the future system of metaphysics, we must hereafter follow the rigorous method of the famous *Wolff*, the greatest among all the dogmatic philosophers, who first gave the example (and through this example was the author of the as yet unextinguished spirit of thoroughness in Germany) of how, through the law-governed establishment of principles, the clear determination of concepts, the well-tested rigor of proof, and the avoidance of bold leaps in inferences, the sure path of science might be taken, who even was, for that very reason, especially qualified to advance a science like metaphysics into this condition, had it occurred to him to prepare the field ahead of time through a critique of the organ, namely of pure [B xxxvii] reason itself – a failing that is to be attributed not so much to him as instead to the dogmatic mentality of his age, and concerning this the philosophers of his time as well as of all previous times have nothing to blame each other for. Whosoever rejects his method and so indeed also the procedure of the *Critique of Pure Reason* can have nothing else in mind except to cast off completely the fetters of *science*, and to transform work into play, certainty into opinion, and philosophy into philodoxy.

. . .

Introduction

VII. Idea and division of a special science, under the name of a Critique of [A 10/B 24]
*Pure Reason*ᵃ

From all of this now follows the idea of a special science, which can be
called the *critique of pure reason*. For reason is the faculty that supplies [A 11]
the *principles* of *a priori* cognition. Hence, pure reason is what contains
the principles for unconditionally cognizing something *a priori*. An
organon of pure reason would be a collection of those principles
according to which all pure cognition *a priori* can be acquired and [B 25]
actually brought about. The complete execution of such an organon
would yield a system of pure reason. But since this system is greatly
desired, and since it is still undecided whether, and in what instances,
an expansion of our cognition is in general possible here, we can look
upon a science of the mere appraisal of pure reason, its sources and
boundaries, as the *propaedeutic* to the system of pure reason. Such a
science should not be called a *doctrine*, but only a *critique* of pure reason,
and its benefit, with respect to speculation, would actually be only
negative, serving not for the expansion but only for the purification of
our reason, and for keeping reason free of error, which is already a very
great gain. I call all cognition *transcendental* that is in general concerned
not so much with objects as with the mode of our cognition of objects,
insofar as this cognition is supposed to be possible *a priori*. A *system* of [A 12]
such concepts would be called *transcendental philosophy*. But such a

---

ᵃ This heading was added in "B," and a section heading that had followed the first paragraph was
deleted. Two sentences were deleted from that paragraph, and there were other small revisions
further along.

philosophy is, again, still too much for a starting place. For since such a science would have to contain, in full, both analytic cognition and synthetic cognition *a priori*, it is therefore, as far as our aim is concerned, of too broad a compass, in that we only need to carry analysis as far as is indispensably necessary in order to gain insight into the principles of *a*
[B 26] *priori* synthesis (which is our sole concern) in its entire extent. This investigation, which we truly cannot call a doctrine but only a transcendental critique – since it does not aim at the extension of cognition itself, but only at its correction, and is supposed to furnish the touchstone of the value or lack of value of all *a priori* cognition – is what we are now engaged with. A critique of this sort is, accordingly, a preparation for, if possible, an organon, and, if that should not be achieved, at least for a canon of all *a priori* cognition, in accordance with which the complete system of the philosophy of pure reason, whether this consists in expanding or merely in bounding its cognition, could eventually be presented, both analytically and synthetically. For it can already be concluded ahead of time that this system is possible – indeed, that such a system cannot be of very great compass, so that there is hope for completing it in full – from the fact that the subject matter here is
[A 13] not the nature of things, which is inexhaustible, but rather the understanding, which judges the nature of things, and that it is, again, the understanding only as regards its cognition *a priori*, whose repertory, since we need not in any case search for it without, cannot remain hidden from us, and is, in all expectation, small enough to be completely surveyed, assessed as to its value or lack of value, and accurately
[B 27] appraised. Still less should one expect here a critique of books and systems of pure reason, but of the faculty of pure reason itself. On the basis of this critique alone does one have a sure touchstone for assessing the philosophical import of old and new works in this field; otherwise, one unauthorized reporter and judge appraises the baseless assertions of another by means of his own, equally baseless, assertions.

. . .

The Transcendental Doctrine of Elements

First Part

The Transcendental Aesthetic

§1

In whatever manner and through whatever means a cognition may relate to objects, *intuition* is that by which it relates to objects immediately, and that toward which, as a means, all thought aims. But intuition takes place only insofar as the object is given to us; this in turn, however, is made possible (for us human beings at least) only through the object's affecting the mind in a specific manner. The capacity (receptivity) to obtain representations through the way in which we are affected by objects is called **sensibility**. By means of sensibility, therefore, objects are *given* to us, and it alone provides us with *intuitions*; but through the understanding objects are **thought**, and from it there arise *concepts*. All thinking, however, whether it do so directly (*directe*), or indirectly (*indirecte*), by means of certain characters, must ultimately relate to intuitions, and hence, for us, to sensibility, for no object can be given to us in any other way.

The effect of an object upon the capacity for representation, insofar as we are affected by that object, is *sensation*. The intuition that is related to the object through sensation is called *empirical*. The indeterminate object of an empirical intuition is called *appearance*.

Within appearance, that which corresponds to sensation I call the *matter* of appearance, but that which makes it that the multiplicity of appearance can be ordered in specific relations I call the *form* of appearance. Since that in which alone sensations can be ordered and arranged in a specific form cannot itself again be sensation, it follows that although the matter of all appearance is given to us only *a posteriori*, the form of appearance must, for all sensations taken together, lie ready in the mind *a priori*, and hence must be able to be considered apart from all sensation.

I call all representations *pure* (in the transcendental sense) in which nothing is found belonging to sensation. Accordingly, the pure form of sensory intuitions in general, in which all the multiplicity of appearances is intuited in specific relations, will be found in the mind *a priori*. This

[B 35] pure form of sensibility will itself be called *pure intuition*. Thus, if I separate from the representation of a body that which the understanding thinks in it, such as substance, force, divisibility, etc., and also that

[A 21] which belongs to sensation, such as impenetrability, hardness, color, etc., then something still remains to me of this empirical intuition, namely, extension and shape. These belong to pure intuition, which occurs in the mind *a priori*, as a mere form of sensibility, even without an actual object of the senses or a sensation.

The science of all the *a priori* principles of sensibility I call

[B 36] *transcendental aesthetic.*[*] There must be such a science, which forms the first part of the Transcendental Doctrine of Elements, in contrast to that science which contains the principles of pure thinking, and is called transcendental logic.

[A 22] In transcendental aesthetic we will, therefore, first *isolate* sensibility, by separating off everything that the understanding thinks in addition through its concepts, so that nothing but empirical intuition is left over. Second, we will separate out from sensibility everything that belongs to

---

[*] The Germans are the only ones now using the word *aesthetic* to designate what others call the critique of taste. Underlying this is a misplaced hope, conceived by the excellent analyst Baumgarten,[1] to subsume the critical appraisal of the beautiful under rational principles and to elevate the rules for such appraisal to science. But this endeavor is futile. For the aforementioned rules, or criteria, are empirical (in accordance with their principal sources), and can therefore never serve as determinate laws *a priori* to which our judgment of taste would have to conform; on the contrary, our judgment of taste constitutes the true touchstone for the correctness of such rules or criteria. For that reason it is advisable either to give up this appellation, and to reserve it for that doctrine which is a true science (through which one would come closer to the speech and meaning of the ancients, for whom the division of cognition into *aestheta kai noeta*[2] was well renowned), or to divide this appellation with speculative philosophy, and to take aesthetic partly in a transcendental sense, and partly in a psychological sense.[a]

[a] From "or to divide" to the end of sentence were added in "B."
[1] Baumgarten, *Aesthetica* (Frankfurt, 1750).   [2] "sensible and intelligible"

sensation, so that nothing but pure intuition and the mere form of the appearances remains, which is all that sensibility can provide *a priori*. Through this investigation it will be found that there are two pure forms of sensory intuition as principles of *a priori* cognition, namely, space and time, to which we now turn our attention.

The Transcendental Aesthetic [B 37]

First Chapter

On Space

§2

Metaphysical exposition of this concept [b]

Through outer sense (a property of our mind) we represent objects as outside us, and all of them together as in space. Within that space the shape, size, and relation to one another of these objects are determinate or determinable. Inner sense, by means of which the mind intuits itself or its inner state, does not, it is true, provide any intuition of the soul itself as an object; but there is nonetheless a determinate form under [A 23] which alone the intuition of the soul's inner state is possible, such that everything that belongs to inner determinations is represented in relations of time. Time cannot be intuited as outer, anymore than space can be intuited as something in us. What, now, are space and time? Are they actual beings? Are they mere determinations or else relations of things, but nonetheless of the sort that would in themselves belong to such things if they were not being intuited;[3] or are they such that they inhere only in the form of intuition, and hence in the subjective [B 38] constitution of our mind, in the absence of which these predicates could not be ascribed to anything whatsoever? To inform ourselves in this matter, we will first give an exposition of the concept of space. By an *exposition* (*expositio*) I understand the clear (though not, indeed,

---

[b] The section number and heading were added in "B." "A" contained a numbered paragraph on geometry (following the first two numbered paragraphs below) which was deleted in "B," in which a corresponding section was added further on (not included in these selections).

[3] These questions formed part of dispute between Samuel Clarke (1675–1729), a friend and follower of Isaac Newton (1642–1727), and Leibniz; the *Correspondence* was published in English in 1717 and in French in 1720; it was well-known to Kant.

complete) presentation of what belongs to a concept; and the exposition is *metaphysical* if it contains what is exhibited by the concept as given *a priori*.

(1) Space is no empirical concept, which has been abstracted from outer experience. For, in order for sensations to be related to something outside me (i.e., to something in another position in space from that in which I am located), as also for me to be able to represent these sensations as outside and alongside one another, and hence not merely as different, but as in different places, the representation of space must already be there as a basis. Accordingly, the representation of space cannot be borrowed from the relations of outer appearance through experience, but this outer experience is itself first possible only by means of that representation.

[A 24] (2) Space is a necessary representation, *a priori*, which underlies all outer intuitions. One can never form a representation of the absence of space, though one can very well conceive that no objects are to be found

[B 39] in space. Space is therefore to be considered as the condition for the possibility of appearances, and not as a determination that is dependent on appearances; and it is a representation *a priori*, which necessarily underlies outer appearances.

(3) Space is no discursive, or, as one says, universal concept of the

[A 25] relations of things in general, but rather is a pure intuition. For, first, one can represent to oneself only one space, and if one speaks of many spaces, one understands thereby merely parts of one and the same unique space. These parts cannot precede the one all-encompassing space as though they were its constituent parts (out of which it was possible to compose it), but rather can only be thought *in it*. Space is essentially one; the multiplicity in it, and hence also the universal concept of spaces in general, is based solely on limitations. From this it follows that, with respect to spaces, an *a priori* intuition (which is not empirical) underlies all concepts of space. Hence all geometrical propositions, e.g., that in a triangle two sides taken together are larger than the third, are derived not from the universal concepts of line and triangle, but from intuition, *a priori* and with apodictic certainty.

(4) Space is represented as an infinite *given* magnitude. Now one

[B 40] must, it is true, think any concept as a representation that is contained in an infinity of different possible representations (as their common characteristic) and hence as a representation that contains those representations *under it*; but no concept, as such, can be thought as if it contained an infinity of representations *in it*. Yet space is thought in this way (for all parts of space, to infinity, exist simultaneously). Therefore the original representation of space is an *a priori intuition*, and not a *concept*.

. . .

The Transcendental Doctrine of Elements

Second Part

Transcendental Logic

Introduction: The idea of a transcendental logic

Our cognition arises from two fundamental sources in the mind, the first of which is the receiving of representations (receptivity of impressions), the second, the capacity to cognize an object by means of these representations (spontaneity of concepts); through the first an object is *given* to us, through the second this object is, in relation to this representation (as a mere determination of the mind), *thought*. Intuition and concepts therefore constitute the elements of all our cognition, in such a way that neither concepts without intuition in some way corresponding to them, nor intuition without concepts, can yield a cognition. Both are either pure or empirical. *Empirical*, if sensation (which presupposes the actual presence of the object) is contained in it; but *pure* if no sensation is intermixed with the representation. The sensation can be called the matter of sensory cognition. Hence, pure [B 75] intuition contains only the form under which something is intuited, and [A 51] a pure concept contains only the form of the thought of an object in general. Only pure intuitions or concepts alone are possible *a priori*; empirical intuitions or concepts are possible only *a posteriori*.

If the *receptivity* of our mind, its capacity for receiving representations insofar as it is affected in some way, is to be called *sensibility*; then, by comparison, the capacity for generating representations by itself, or the *spontaneity* of cognition, is the *understanding*. Our nature is such that *intuition* can never be other than *sensory*, i.e., it contains only the way in which we are affected by objects. In contrast, the faculty for *thinking* the object of sensory intuition is the *understanding*. Neither of these attributes is to be given precedence over the other. Without sensibility no object would be given to us, and without understanding no object would be thought by us. Thoughts without content are empty, intuitions without concepts are blind. Hence, it is just as necessary to make one's concepts sensible (i.e., to adjoin an object to them in intuition), as it is to make one's intuitions intelligible (i.e., to bring them under concepts). The two faculties or capacities cannot exchange their functions. The understanding can intuit nothing, the senses can think nothing. Only from their union can cognition arise. But one must not, [B 76] because of that, confuse the part played by each; rather, one has great cause to separate and to distinguish the one from the other. We [A 52] therefore distinguish the science of the rules of sensibility in general, i.e., aesthetic, from the science of the rules of the understanding in general, i.e., logic.

. . .

Transcendental Logic [B 89]

First Division: The Transcendental Analytic

First Book: The Analytic of Concepts [B 90]

By the *analytic of concepts* I do not mean the analysis of concepts, nor the ordinary procedure in philosophical investigation, of analyzing and clarifying (as regards their content) concepts that present themselves, but the as yet little attempted *analysis of the faculty of understanding* itself, so as to investigate the possibility of *a priori* concepts by seeking [A 66] that possibility in the understanding alone (as the birthplace of those concepts), and by analyzing the pure use of those concepts (in general); for this is the proper business of transcendental philosophy; the rest is [B 91] the logical treatment of concepts in philosophy in general. We will therefore pursue the pure concepts as far as their first seeds and predispositions in the human understanding, in which they lie ready until those concepts are, on the occasion of experience, finally developed, and are, by the very same understanding, exhibited in their purity, free of the empirical conditions attaching to them.

The Analytic of Concepts

First Chapter

On the Guiding Thread for the Discovery of All Pure Concepts of the Understanding

. . .

[A 67/B 92] Transcendental philosophy has the advantage, but also the obligation, of searching for its concepts in accordance with a principle; for these concepts spring forth pure and unmixed out of the understanding, which is an absolute unity, and therefore must cohere among themselves according to a concept, or an idea. Such coherence, however, supplies a rule according to which the place of each pure concept of the understanding, and the collective completeness of them all, can be determined *a priori*, all of which would otherwise depend on whim or chance.

The Transcendental Guiding Thread for the Discovery of All Pure Concepts of the Understanding

First section: On the logical use of the understanding in general

The understanding has above been explicated merely negatively: as a non-sensory faculty of cognition. Now we cannot obtain any intuition independent of sensibility. The understanding is therefore no faculty of [A 68] intuition. There is however, apart from intuition, no other kind of [B 93] cognition except through concepts. Hence the cognition of any (at least human) understanding is cognition through concepts; it is not intuitive, but discursive. All intuitions, as sensory, rest on affectings; concepts, therefore, rest on functions. But by *function* I understand the unity of the act of ordering diverse representations under a common representation. Concepts are therefore founded upon the spontaneity of thought, just as sensory intuitions are founded upon receptivity of impressions. The understanding can, however, make no other use of these concepts except to judge by means of them. Since no representation but intuition alone refers immediately to an object, a concept is never related immediately to an object, but rather to some other representation of that object (whether it be an intuition or even a concept). Judgment is therefore the mediate cognition of an object, and hence it is the representation of a representation of the object. In every judgment there is a concept that holds of many things, and which, among that multitude, also comprehends a given representation that is then related immediately to the object. Thus, e.g., in the judgment: *All bodies are divisible,*[a] the concept of the divisible refers to various other concepts; among these, however, it is here especially referred to the concept of body; and this concept is referred to certain appearances present to us. [A 69] These objects are therefore mediately represented through the concept [B 94] of divisibility. Accordingly, all judgments are functions of unity among our representations, since, in particular, instead of an immediate representation a higher representation – which comprehends this immediate one, and many others, under it – is used for the cognition of the object, and many possible cognitions are gathered into one. We can, however, reduce all acts of the understanding to judgments, so that the *understanding* in general can be represented as a *faculty for judging*. For the understanding, according to the above, is a faculty for thinking. Thinking is cognition through concepts. Concepts, however, refer, as predicates of possible judgments, to some representation or other of an as yet undetermined object. Hence, the concept of body denotes something, e.g., metal, which can be cognized through that concept. It is therefore a concept only because other representations are contained under it by means of which it can refer to objects. It is therefore the predicate of a possible judgment, e.g., that every metal is a body. Every one of the functions of the understanding can therefore be found, if the functions of the unity in judgments can be exhibited with completeness.

. . .

Third section: On the pure concepts of the understanding, or categories   [A 76/B 102]

General logic (as has already been said several times) abstracts from all content of cognition, and awaits representations to be given to it from somewhere else, wherever it may be, so that, proceeding analytically, it can first transform these representations into concepts. By contrast, transcendental logic has a multiplicity of sensibility lying before it *a priori*, which transcendental aesthetic offers to it in order to provide [A 77]

---

[a] Reading *teilbar* for *veränderlich* ("mutable"), with Ak, vol. 3.

material for the pure concepts of the understanding, without which they would be without any content, and so would be completely empty. Now space and time contain a multiplicity of pure *a priori* intuition, but they nonetheless belong to the conditions of receptivity of our mind under which alone representations of objects can be received, and which must therefore ever affect the concept of objects. But the spontaneity of our thought demands that the multiplicity first be gone through, taken up, and conjoined in a specific manner, in order to make a cognition out of it. I call this act synthesis.

[B 103]   By *synthesis* in its most general meaning, however, I understand the act of adding diverse representations to one another, and of comprehending their manifoldness in a cognition. Such a synthesis is *pure* if the multiplicity is given, not empirically, but *a priori* (as is the multiplicity in space and time). This synthesis must be given before all analysis of our representations, and no concepts can, *as regards content*, arise through analysis. But the synthesis of a multiplicity (whether it be given empirically or *a priori*) first produces a cognition, which can indeed still be raw and confused to begin with and therefore requiring analysis; but synthesis is nonetheless that which actually assembles the elements for [A 78] cognitions and unifies them into a specific content; it is therefore the first thing to which we must attend if we want to judge the first origin of our cognition.

Synthesis in general, as we will later see, is an effect of the imagination alone, a blind but indispensable function of the soul without which we would have no cognition at all, but of which we are hardly ever conscious. But, to bring this synthesis *to concepts* is a function that pertains to the understanding, and through which it for the first time furnishes us with cognition in the strict sense.

[B 104]   The *pure synthesis, considered generally*, yields the pure concept of the understanding. Under this synthesis I include that which rests on a basis of synthetic *a priori* unity: thus, our counting (as is especially noticeable with larger numbers) is a *synthesis according to concepts*, since this synthesis occurs in accordance with a common basis of unity (e.g., the decade). Under this concept the unity in the synthesis of the multiplicity is, therefore, rendered necessary.

Various representations are brought *under* a concept analytically (a matter treated in general logic). But to bring, not the representations, but the *pure synthesis* of representations *to* concepts, is taught by transcendental logic. The first thing that must be given for the sake of the cognition of all objects *a priori* is the *multiplicity* of pure intuition; [A 79] the second is the *synthesis* of this multiplicity through imagination, but it still does not yield cognition. The concepts that give *unity* to this pure synthesis, and that consist solely in the representation of this necessary synthetic unity, make the third requisite for the cognition of an occurrent object, and they rest on the understanding.

. . .

The Analytic of Concepts [A 84/B 116]

Second Chapter

On the Deduction of the Pure Concepts of the Understanding

First section: On the principles of transcendental deduction in general

Jurists, when they are discussing rights and claims, distinguish in a legal action the question of what is right (*quid juris*) from the question that concerns the matter of fact (*quid facti*), and, as they require proof of both, they call the first proof, which is supposed to establish the right or legal claim, a *deduction*. We use a number of empirical concepts without anyone's objecting, and we consider ourselves, even without a deduction, entitled to attribute to them a sense and a presumed meaning, since we always have experience at hand for demonstrating their [B 117] objective reality. There are also, however, usurpatory concepts, such as *luck* or *fate*, which, though they meet with almost universal forbearance, are nonetheless sometimes challenged with the question: *quid juris*, at which point there arises no small embarrassment concerning their deduction, because no appeal can be made to any clear legal ground, [A 85] either from experience or reason, through which the right to use them would be made evident.

However, among the various concepts that form the very diverse fabric of human cognition there are some that are destined for pure, *a priori* use (entirely independent of all experience), and the right of their use always has need of a deduction; since proofs from experience are not sufficient to establish the legitimacy of such use, one wants indeed to know how these concepts can relate to objects that they do not obtain from any experience. Hence I call the explanation of the way in which concepts can relate *a priori* to objects the *transcendental deduction* of those concepts, and I distinguish it from an *empirical* deduction, which shows how a concept is acquired through experience and reflection on experience, and which concerns therefore not the legitimacy of the possession, but the fact of how possession came about.

[B 118] Now we have indeed two sorts of concepts, completely different in kind, that nonetheless agree with one another in that both of them refer to objects entirely *a priori*: namely, the concepts of space and time, as forms of sensibility, and the categories, as concepts of the understanding. To attempt an empirical deduction of these concepts would be [A 86] completely idle labor, because the differentia of their nature consists in the very fact that they refer to their objects without having to borrow anything from experience for the representation of those objects. If therefore a deduction of these concepts is needed, it will always have to be transcendental.

Nonetheless one can, with respect to these concepts, as with all cognition, try to find in experience, if not the principle of their possibility, at least the occasioning causes of their generation; regarding which, the impressions of the senses provide the initial occasion for the whole power of cognition to open up with respect to them and to bring about experience, which contains two quite heterogeneous elements, namely, from the senses, a *matter* of cognition, and, from the inner source of pure intuition and thought, a certain *form* for ordering that matter, which two elements, upon the instigation of the matter, are first put into play, and bring forth concepts. This kind of tracing out of the initial stirrings of our power of cognition, so as to ascend from [B 119] single perceptions to universal concepts, is without doubt of great use, and we are indebted to the famous *Locke* for first having opened up this path. But a *deduction* of the pure *a priori* concepts will never be achieved by this means, for it does not lie on this path at all, since these concepts, as regards their future use, which is supposed to be wholly independent of experience, will have to produce a completely different certificate of birth than that of descent from experiences. This attempted physiological[b] derivation, which, since it concerns a

---

[b] *physiologische* (This word is used in its etymological sense, to mean "pertaining to the investigation of nature"; it does not here suggest a concern with physiological psychology or brain mechanisms.)

quaestionem facti, cannot properly be termed a deduction at all, I will [A 87] consequently call the explanation of the *possession* of pure cognition. It is therefore clear that for these concepts there can be only a transcendental deduction, and by no means an empirical one, and that, as regards pure *a priori* concepts, any such empirical deduction is nothing but wasted effort, which can occupy only someone who has not grasped the wholly peculiar nature of such cognitions.

But although it be granted that a deduction along the transcendental path is the only kind possible for pure *a priori* cognitions, it is by no means thereby made clear that this deduction is so indispensably necessary. We have above, by means of a transcendental deduction, pursued the concepts of space and time to their sources, and explained and determined their *a priori* objective validity. Nonetheless, geometry [B 120] proceeds securely through nothing but *a priori* cognitions without needing to petition philosophy for certification of the pure and legitimate descent of its fundamental concept of space. But in this science the use of the concept refers only to the outer, sensible world, of which space is the pure form of intuition; and so in this world all geometrical cognition, being grounded in *a priori* intuition, possesses immediate evidence, and objects are given via cognition itself, *a priori* (as regards form) in intuition. By contrast, with the *pure concepts of the* [A 88] *understanding* the unavoidable need arises to seek a transcendental deduction not only for these concepts themselves, but also for space; for, since these concepts speak of objects not through the predicates of intuition and sensibility, but through those of pure *a priori* thought, they relate universally to objects in the absence of all conditions of sensibility; and the need also arises because these concepts are not based on experience, and cannot exhibit any object *a priori* in intuition upon which they grounded their synthesis prior to all experience, and they therefore not only arouse suspicion concerning the objective validity and limits of their use, but also render the earlier *concept of space* equivocal, in that they are inclined to employ that concept beyond [B 121] the conditions of sensory intuition – for which reason it was also necessary to give above a transcendental deduction for the concept of space. The reader must, then, be convinced of the indispensable necessity for such a transcendental deduction before he has taken a single step in the field of pure reason, because otherwise he proceeds blindly, and, after blundering about in various ways, must come back again to the state of ignorance from which he started out. But the reader must also clearly understand ahead of time the unavoidable difficulty, so that he does not complain about the obscurity that deeply envelops the subject matter itself, or become discouraged too early

[A 89] about the clearing away of obstacles; for it comes down to this: either completely giving up all claims to insights of pure reason in relation to that most beloved of fields, namely, that which is beyond the boundaries of all possible experience, or else bringing this critical investigation to completion.

We have above easily been able to make comprehensible how the concepts of space and time, which are *a priori* cognitions, nonetheless must necessarily refer to objects, and how they would make possible a synthetic cognition of such objects independent of all experience. For since an object can appear to us (i.e., can be an object of empirical intuition) only by means of pure forms of sensibility of this sort, space

[B 122] and time are therefore pure intuitions that contain *a priori* the condition for the possibility of objects as appearances, and the synthesis in space and time has objective validity.

By contrast, the categories of the understanding by no means present to us the conditions under which objects are given in intuition, and so objects can certainly appear to us without their necessarily having to be related to functions of the understanding, and therefore without the understanding containing their conditions *a priori*. In consequence, a difficulty turns up here that we did not meet with in the field of sensibility, namely, how *subjective conditions of thought* are supposed to have *objective validity*, i.e., how they are supposed to furnish conditions

[A 90] for the possibility of all cognition of objects: for appearances can certainly be given in intuition in the absence of functions of the understanding. Let us take, e.g., the concept of cause, which signifies a specific kind of synthesis, since upon something, A, something quite different, B, is posited according to a rule. It is not *a priori* clear why appearances would have to contain anything like that (since appearances cannot be cited for a proof, because the objective validity of this concept must be able to be established *a priori*), and so it is, consequently, *a priori* dubious whether such a concept might not perhaps be completely empty and might not find any object anywhere among the appearances.

[B 123] For it is clear that objects of sensory intuition must conform to the formal conditions of sensibility that lie *a priori* in the mind, since otherwise they would not be objects for us; but it is not so easy to grasp the inference that these objects should, beyond that, conform to the conditions that the understanding requires for the synthetic unity of thought. For appearances could indeed perhaps be so constituted that the understanding did not at all find them to conform to the conditions for its unity, and everything might stand in such confusion that, e.g., nothing would present itself in the sequence of appearances that furnished a rule of synthesis, and therefore nothing would correspond to the concept of cause and effect, so that this concept would, then, be completely empty, null, and without meaning. Appearances would nonetheless present objects to our intuition, for intuition in no way [A 91] needs the functions of thought.

If one might consider extricating oneself from the difficulty of this investigation by saying: Experience presents unceasing examples of such regularity in appearances, which provide sufficient occasion for abstracting the concept of cause from those appearances and, by that means, for simultaneously verifying the objective validity of such a concept – then one has not observed that the concept of cause can by no means arise in this manner, but must either be grounded in the understanding completely *a priori*, or else be given up entirely as a mere [B 124] self-produced fantasy. For this concept requires, in all cases, that something, A, should be such that something else, B, should follow from it *necessarily and according to an absolutely universal rule*. Appearances indeed do furnish instances from which it is possible to form a rule according to which something usually happens, but never a rule according to which the consequence is *necessary*; thus there attaches to the synthesis of cause and effect a dignity that cannot at all be expressed empirically, namely, that the effect is not merely adjoined to the cause, but that it is posited *through* that cause and follows *from* it. The strict universality of this rule is by no means a property of empirical rules, which, through induction, can obtain nothing but comparative univers- [A 92] ality, i.e., wide applicability. The use of the pure concepts of the understanding would, then, be completely altered if one wanted to treat them merely as empirical products.

. . .

175

The Transcendental Dialectic

Second Book

On the Dialectical Inferences of Pure Reason

The Antinomy of Pure Reason

First Conflict of the Transcendental Ideas

[A 426/B 454]

Thesis	*Antithesis* [A 427/]
The world has a beginning in time and is, as regards space, also enclosed in boundaries.	The world has no beginning, and it has no boundaries in space, but is, with respect to time as well as space, infinite.

Proof	*Proof*
For, if one assumes that the world has no beginning in time: then up to any given point in time an eternity has transpired and therefore in the world an infinite series of successive states of things has gone by. But the infinity of a series consists, however, in the very fact that it can never be completed through successive synthesis. Therefore an infinitely flowing world-series is impossible, and so a beginning to the world is a necessary condition of its existence; which was the first thing to be proven.	Let it be posited: the world has a beginning. Since a beginning is an existent thing which is preceded by a time in which that thing does not exist, there must, then, have been a time in which the world did not exist, i.e., an empty time. Now in an empty time, however, it is not possible for there to be a beginning of anything whatever, because no part of such a time, coming before another part, has in itself any distinguishing condition of existence rather than nonexistence (whether it be assumed that this condition begin of itself, or through another cause). And so, although many series of things can begin in the world, the world itself cannot have a beginning, and is therefore infinite as regards the preceding time.
As regards the *second*, one again assumes the opposite: then the world will be an infinite, given whole of simultaneously existing things. Now the magnitude of a quantum that is not given within the specific	

176

boundaries of any intuition* cannot be [B 456] thought in any other manner except through the synthesis of parts, and the totality of such a quantum only through the completed synthesis, or through repeated addition of unity to itself.** Accordingly, in order for the world, which fills up all of space, to be thought as a whole, the successive synthesis of the parts of an infinite world would have to be considered as completed, i.e., in counting through all coexisting things an infinite time would have to be considered as having transpired; which is impossible. Accordingly, an infinite aggregate of actual things cannot be regarded as a whole that is given, and hence not as a whole that is *simultaneously* given. Consequently the world is, with respect to extension in space, *not infinite*, but is enclosed in its boundaries; which was the second thing to be proven.

. . .

Concerning the second part, if one first of all assumes the opposite, namely, that the world is, as regards space, finite and bounded, then the world finds itself in an empty space that is not bounded. There would, therefore, not only be a relation of things *in space*, but also of things *to space*. Since the world is an absolute whole, apart from which no object of intuition, and hence no correlate of the world, is to be found to which the world stands in relation, the relation of the world to empty space would, therefore, be a relation of the world to *no object*. But such a relationship, and hence also the bounding of the world through empty space, is nothing; therefore the world, as regards space, is not bounded at all, i.e., it is, with respect to extension, infinite.*** [A 429/B 457]

---

* If it is enclosed in boundaries, we can intuit an indeterminate quantum as a whole without needing to construct the totality by means of measurement, i.e., by means of successive synthesis of its parts. For the boundaries already determine completeness, in that they cut off anything more.

** The concept of the totality is in this case nothing other than the representation of the completed synthesis of its parts, because, since we cannot extract the concept from the intuition of the whole (that being impossible in this case), we can grasp this concept, at least in idea, only through the synthesis of the parts up to the completion of the infinite.

*** Space is merely the form of outer intuition (merely formal intuition), but it is not a real object that can be outwardly intuited. Prior to all things that determine it (fill or bound it), or, better, that furnish it with *empirical intuition* in accordance with its form, space is, under the name of absolute space, nothing other than the mere possibility of outer appearances, insofar as these can either exist in themselves or be added to appearances that are already given. Empirical intuition is not, therefore, composed from appearances and space (perception and empty intuition). The one is not a correlatum of synthesis for the other,[1] but they are conjoined only in one and the same empirical intuition, as its matter and form. If one wants to set one of these two items apart from the other (space apart from all appearances), then all sorts of empty determinations of outer intuition result, which are not possible perceptions at all – e.g., the motion or rest of the world in infinite empty space, which is a determination of a relation between the two that can never be perceived, and so is the predicate of a mere being of thought.

[1] Kant's point is that space should not be conceived as an empty framework into which the matter of empirical intuition can be placed through an act of synthesis.

The Transcendental Doctrine of Method

First Chapter

The Discipline of Pure Reason

First section

The discipline of pure reason in its dogmatic use

Mathematics provides the brightest example of pure reason augmenting itself successfully by itself, without any help from experience. Examples are contagious, especially to one and the same faculty, which naturally flatters itself that it will have the very same luck in other cases as has

come its way in the one case. Hence, pure reason hopes to be able to extend itself just as successfully and well-foundedly in its transcendental use as it has managed to do in its mathematical use, especially if it uses the same method in the former case as has been of such manifest benefit in the latter. It is therefore very important for us to know: whether the method for achieving apodictic certainty that one calls *mathematical* in the latter science is the same as the method by which one seeks to achieve the same kind of certainty in philosophy, and which would in that field have to be called *dogmatic*.

Philosophical cognition is *cognition through reason* from *concepts*; mathematical cognition is cognition through reason from the *construction* of concepts. *To construct* a concept means, however: to exhibit *a priori* the intuition corresponding to it. For the construction of a concept, then, a *nonempirical* intuition is required, which therefore, as intuition, is a *single* object, but which, as the construction of a concept (a universal representation), must nonetheless express (in the representation) universal validity for all possible intuitions belonging under that same concept. Thus I construct a triangle by exhibiting the object that corresponds to this concept, either through bare imagination in pure intuition, or else (in accordance with imagination) on paper in empirical intuition, but in either case fully *a priori*, without having to borrow the pattern for the object from one or another experience. This single sketched-out figure is empirical, and yet it nonetheless serves to express [A 714/B 742 the concept without prejudice to the universality of the concept, because in connection with this empirical intuition only the act of the construction of the concept is looked to, for which many determinations, e.g., of size, sides, and angles, are equivalent, and so these differences, which do not alter the concept of the triangle, are abstracted from.

Therefore philosophical cognition considers the particular only in the universal; mathematical cognition considers the universal in the particular, nay, even in a single instance, but nonetheless does so *a priori* and by means of reason, in such a way that, just as this single instance is determined under certain universal conditions of construction, so too the object of the concept (to which concept this single instance corresponds only as its schema) must be thought in a universally determined manner.

In this form, therefore, consists the essential difference between these two kinds of cognition through reason; it does not rest on the difference in their matter, or objects. Those who have presumed to distinguish philosophy from mathematics by saying that the former has only *quality* for an object and the latter only *quantity*, have taken the effect for the cause. The form of mathematical cognition is the cause of its being able to relate solely to quanta. For only the concept of magnitude admits of being constructed, i.e., of being displayed *a priori* in intuition; qualities, [A 715/B 743 however, admit of being exhibited in none other except empirical intuition. Rational cognition of qualities is possible, therefore, only by means of concepts. Thus, no one can receive an intuition corresponding to the concept of reality from anywhere except experience, and one can never obtain it *a priori* out of oneself and prior to the empirical consciousness of reality. The shape of a cone will be able to be made intuitable without any empirical assistance at all, in accordance with the concept alone, but the color of this cone will have to be given beforehand in one or another experience. I can exhibit in intuition the concept of a cause in general in no way except in an example furnished to me from experience; and so on. Besides, philosophy deals with magnitudes just as much as mathematics, e.g., it deals with totality, infinity, etc. And mathematics concerns itself with the distinction between lines and planes, as spaces of differing quality, and with the continuity of extension, as a quality of that extension. But, although in such cases philosophy and mathematics have a common object, the manner in which they treat of this object by means of reason is nonetheless completely different in philosophical as opposed to mathematical contemplation. The former restricts itself entirely to universal concepts; the latter can accomplish nothing with the mere concept, but hastens forthwith to intuition, in which it contemplates the concept *in* [A 716/B 744] *concreto*, though still not empirically, but only in an intuition that it has exhibited *a priori*, i.e., has constructed, and in which that which follows from the universal conditions of construction must also hold universally of the object of the constructed concept.

Give the concept of a triangle to a philosopher and have him find out, in his manner, how the sum of its angles may be related to the right angle. He has then nothing but the concept of a figure that is enclosed in three straight lines, and the concept of the same number of angles in that figure. Let him now contemplate this concept for as long as he wants, he will ascertain nothing new. He can analyze and clarify the concept of a straight line, or of an angle, or of the number three, but he cannot come upon any other properties, which simply are not to be found in these concepts. But let the geometer take up this question. He begins forthwith to construct a triangle. Because he knows that two right angles taken together amount to exactly as much as all the adjacent angles taken together that can be erected from a point on a straight line, he therefore extends one side of his triangle and gets two adjacent angles, which are equal to two right angles taken together. Of these two angles, he now divides the exterior one by erecting a line parallel to the opposite side of the triangle, and he sees that here an exterior adjacent angle is produced that is equal to an interior angle, and so on. In this [A 717/B 745] way, through a chain of inferences, always led by intuition, he arrives at a fully evident and (at the same time) universal solution to the question.

Index

Academy Edition, xxxix, xl

accident, relation of, 88

accidents, as the only properties we cognize in bodies, 88; as predicates, 87; and substance, xvi, 62, 87, 122

action, Aristotelian category of, 77; in appearances, 98–100, 153–4; and force, 7, 69; human, compared to mechanical force, 111; as determined by reason, 98–100

actuality, of cognition, 31; of object, 34, 152; of science, 6; of a thing, 47; see also reality

aesthetic, division of critical or transcendental philosophy, xxiii, 72, 162, 167, 170; theory of sensory cognition, 68, 162–3, 167

Albertus University, in Königsberg, xii, xiii

alchemy, 120

alterations, of bodies, 35; of substance, 90

analogy, 68, 111–13, 115, 123, 148, 150; see also experience

analytic, division of critical philosophy, xxiii, xxiv, 28, 58, 86, 152; judgments or propositions, see judgments, analytic; see also cognition; concepts; consciousness; and method

Anschauung, see intuition

anthropology, 116, 143; as school subject, xiii, xv

anthropomorphism, 110–12

antinomies of reason, xiv, 44, 84, 93–101, 133, 176–7; certainty of, 95; dynamical, 97; mathematical, 95–7

apodictic, see certainty

a posteriori, see appearances; cognition; and judgments

appearances, explanation of term, 161; and form vs matter, 35, 62, 161–2; inner, 89; and magnitude, 59–60; matter of, given a posteriori, 162; outer, 39, 91; possibility of, 35, 38, 40; space and time as forms of, 35–6; sum total of, 71–2, 96; and

things in themselves, xxxiii, 34–45, 68, 71, 91, 94, 95, 97–100, 107–8, 114, 149–50, 152–3; transcendent use of, 44; given independent of understanding, 174–5

apperception, 72, 88

a priori, see cognition; intuition; judgments; mathematics; metaphysics; mind; and natural science

Aristotle, xvi–xvii; categories of 77; metaphysics since, 122; logic since, 143

arithmetic, 18–19, 35, 123, 124, 170

astrology, 120

astronomy, 120; physical 75

atheism, 156

Bacon, Francis, 145

Baumeister, Friedrich Christian, 21

Baumgarten, Alexander, xvi, 22

Beattie, James, 8–9

Beck, Lewis White, xli

being/beings, that belong to appearances, 98; beyond all concepts justified through experience, 106; distinct from the world, 112; first, 102, 110, 112; highest, 108; human, as thing in itself, 98–9; human, taken as both free and not free, 153; immaterial, 105, 107, 108; intelligible, xix, 68, 70, 108–9, 114–15, see also God and soul; intelligible, influence on appearances, freedom and, 98; logical, 47; necessary, 93, 101; and ontology, xvi; outside nature, 71; rational, 99–100; most-real, 155; of sense, 69; sensible, 68; simple, 85, 105, see also soul; of soul in itself, 91; are space and time actual?, 163; supreme, 24, 85, 109–13, 115, see also God; cognized as things in themselves, 108; thinking, and idealism, 40; thinking, and substance, 89; our thinking, nature of, 89; of

Index

Cambridge texts in the history of philosophy

Titles published in the series thus far

Arnauld and Nicole *Logic or the Art of Thinking* (edited by Jill Vance Buroker)

Boyle *A Free Enquiry into the Vulgarly Received Notion of Nature* (edited by Edward B. Davis and Michael Hunter)

Conway *The Principles of the Most Ancient and Modern Philosophy* (edited by Allison P. Coudert and Taylor Corse)

Cudworth *A Treatise Concerning Eternal and Immutable Morality* with *A Treatise of Freewill* (edited by Sarah Hutton)

Descartes *Meditations on First Philosophy*, with selections from the *Objections and Replies* (edited with an introduction by John Cottingham)

Kant *The Metaphysics of Morals* (edited by Mary Gregor with an introduction by Roger Sullivan)

Kant *Prolegomena to Any Future Metaphysics* (edited by Gary Hatfield)

La Mettrie *Machine Man and Other Writings* (edited by Ann Thomson)

Leibniz *New Essays on Human Understanding* (edited by Peter Remnant and Jonathan Bennett)

Malebranche *Dialogues on Metaphysics and on Religion* (edited by Nicholas Jolley and David Scott)

Malebranche *The Search after Truth* (edited by Thomas M. Lennon and Paul J. Olscamp)

Mendelssohn *Philosophical Writings* (edited by Daniel O. Dahlstrom)

Nietzsche *Human, All Too Human* (translated by R. J. Hollingdale with an introduction by Richard Schacht)

Schleiermacher *On Religion: Speeches to its Cultured Despisers* (edited by Richard Crouter)